Formatting Briefs
in
Word

John M. Miano, J.D.

Table of Contents

vi

Acknowledgements

Thanks to the Profs. E. Judson Jennings, Michael Zimmer, Jennifer Brendel, and Alice Perlin; Drs. Ralph Miano and Margaret Miano; Brittany Robbins.

Chapter 1
Introduction

Formatting is an integral part of written communication. The format of a brief sets the tone and provides the physical structure to the underlying text. It is true that the strength of the text is the most important factor in the quality of a document—good formatting cannot save a poorly written document. However, bad formatting can wreck a well-written brief.

There was a time when lawyers relied heavily on professional printers to produce briefs. By using a printer, a lawyer could shift the burden of document formatting to someone skilled in the trade. Now every lawyer has access to a computer that can run the very same software that the professional printer uses. The availability of these computer tools has nearly eliminated the print shop from the brief production process. The ability of lawyers to self-format has not necessarily been a good thing. When lawyers try to format briefs, "the filed product is often disastrous."[1]

There are a number of reasons for the problem of poorly formatted briefs. First, the rules of many courts do not encourage readability in briefs. Second, text-processing software tends to be rather complicated for the user. Third, there is surprisingly little information about how to use text-processing software to create briefs. Even templates for creating briefs are difficult to find.

A simple example demonstrates the goal of this book. Figure 1.1 shows a page from a brief. The example was chosen for comparison because it is reasonably well formatted. The author clearly has taken care in the formatting and there is nothing particularlly bad about it.

Now take this brief to the next level. Figure 1.2 shows the same brief reformatted according to the principles of this book and to the same court rules. This difference in appearance is striking. The reformatted version is much easier to read. After working through the book, you should be able to format documents to the level of the one shown in Figure 1.2.

This book explains how to format briefs using Microsoft Word. The objective here is not to teach how to use Word but rather how to use Word to

---

[1] Scalia, p. 136.

FIGURE 1.1
A brief as originally
filed

ARGUMENT

I. **THE TRIAL COURT ERRED IN FINDING THAT THE AFFIDAVIT IN SUPPORT OF THE SEARCH WARRANT ESTABLISHED PROBABLE CAUSE.**

A. Standard of Review

A two step standard of review is applied when reviewing motions to suppress. *State v. Sloan*, 2007 WI App 146, ¶7, 303 Wis.2d 438, 446, 736 N.W.2d 189 (Ct. App. 2007), citing *State v. Eason*, 2001 WI 98, ¶9, 245 Wis.2d 206, 629 N.W.2d 625 (2001). The trial court's findings of historical fact are reviewed under the clearly erroneous standard. *Id.* The application of constitutional law to those facts are given *de novo* review. *Id.*

In reviewing whether probable cause exists to issue a search warrant, great deference is given to the warrant issuing magistrate. *Eason*, 2001 WI 98, ¶8, 245 Wis.2d at 446. The reviewing court is "confined to the record as it existed before the magistrate and must consider whether he or she was 'apprised of sufficient facts to excite an honest belief in a reasonable mind that the objects sought are linked with the commission of a crime, and that they will be found in the place searched.'" *Id.*, quoting *State v. Starke*, 81 Wis.2d 399, 408, 260 N.W.2d 739 (1978). The magistrate's decision will be upheld unless the facts before the

FIGURE 1.2
The brief
reformatted

1

ARGUMENT

I. The trial court erred in finding that the affidavit in support of the search warrant established probable cause.

A. Standard of Review

A two step standard of review is applied when reviewing motions to suppress. *State v. Sloan*, 2007 WI App 146, ¶7, 303 Wis.2d 438, 466, 736 N.W.2d 189 (Ct. App. 2007), citing *State v. Eason*, 2001 WI 98, 9, 245 Wis.2d 206, 629 N.W.2d 625 (2001). The trial court's findings of historical fact are review under the clearly erroneous standard. *Id.* The application of constitutional law to those facts are given *de novo* review. *Id.*

In reviewing whether probable cause exists to issue a search warrant, great deference is given to the warrant issuing magistrate. *Eason*, 2001 WI 98, ¶8, 245 Wis.2d at 446. The reviewing court is "confined to the record as it existed before the magistrate and must consider whether he or she was 'apprised of sufficient facts to excite an honest belief in a reasonable mind that the objects sought are linked with the commission of a crime, and that they will be found in the place searched.' " *Id.*, quoting *State v. Starke*, 81 Wis.2d 399, 408, 260 N.W.2d 739 (1978). The magistrate's decision will be upheld unless the facts before the magistrate at the time the warrant was issued were "clearly insufficient to support a finding of probable cause." *Id.*, quoting *State v. Higginbotham*, 162 Wis.2d 978, 989, 471 N.W.2d 24 (1991).

B. The facts before the court commissioner were clearly insufficient to support a finding of probable cause.

Whether there is probable cause to believe that evidence is located in a particular place is determined by examining the perform this specific task. Focusing on the task of writing briefs limits the scope of the book. If a feature is not likely to be used while writing briefs, it is not covered here.

This book expects that the reader already has a basic knowledge of Word. It assumes that the reader can open and save files, enter text, and do basic formatting.

The Windows and Mac versions of Word have nearly the same capabilities and work nearly the same way. The examples focus on Word 2010 for Windows. Where there are differences, the examples show how to perform the same task on Word 2011 for Mac. The differences tend to be in the mechanism for accessing the features. Likewise, nearly everything shown in this book can be accomplished on older versions of Word.

This book takes a compromise approach to creating documents. Pragmatic considerations take precedence over typographic purism. There are three major areas of compromise. First, court rules reign over all other considerations in brief writing. In a few courts the rules are designed to encourage quality formatting. Unfortunately, most court rules are designed to reign in abuse by lawyers and do not promote creating readable documents. That means compromise. Second, tradition plays a major role in how briefs are formatted. Take heading numbering as an example. In briefs, headings levels are traditionally differentiated using different styles of numbers (*i.e.*, combinations of arabic and roman numerals with italic and regular typefaces). However, I find that outline numbered (1, 1.1, 1.2, 1.2.1) headings make a document's structure much easier to understand. That is the method I use for internal documents. Even so, the weight of tradition is against outline numbering in briefs. Third, Word is a word processor; not a page layout application. No matter how hard one tries, it is not possible to create documents in Word that have the same level of quality possible with a typesetting-oriented, page layout program.

1.1. After Reading this Book

When you finish this book, you should be able to create document templates for your briefs. This book operates on a document-formatting model that is based upon templates and styles. Under that model, each set of court rules has its own brief template. In addition, there should be templates for other types of documents (*e.g.*, pleadings, letters). The template defines the page layout, boilerplate text (*e.g.*, certifications, cover page) and styles for formatting the document.

Once the template exists, page layout and formatting is easy. To create a brief, start a Word document using the appropriate template. To format the brief text, apply the appropriate style defined within the template. This method yields consistent formatting within and across documents.

The core of this process is how to create the templates—that is what this book is mostly about. Creating templates requires a bit of upfront work. Usually, the effort to create a template can be recovered in producing just one document. Once you have one good brief template, you can easily modify it to create templates for other court rules.

Unfortunately, many lawyers always work on immediate needs. Styles and templates rarely get set up in advance. This short term thinking makes formatting unnecessarily difficult and usually results in a poorly formatted work product.

The book is organized so that each chapter builds upon the previous:

◊ Chapter 2 shows how to set Word up for legal writing. Word's default settings are not optimal for writing briefs. This chapter shows configuration setings that you can change to make writing brief easier.

◊ Chapter 3 covers the basics of templates. It shows how to create, save and manage templates.

◊ Chapter 4 shows how to create, modify and delete styles.

◊ Chapter 5 describes how to determine the styles needed for writing briefs. It concludes with a basic style set for brief writing.

◊ Chapter 6 addresses the basics of typefaces. It shows how to use Word's font settings and how to pick fonts for a brief.

◊ Chapter 7 shows how to set up the page layout in a template. It covers margins, headers and footers, line numbers, and page numbering.

◊ Chapter 8 covers how to format paragraphs in Word.

◊ Chapter 9 explains how to set up various types of styles used in a brief template.

◊ Chapter 10 departs a bit from templates to show how to use the right character in various situations when writing a brief.

◊ Chapter 11 explains how to divide a brief into multiple sections with different layouts.

◊ Chapter 12 shows how to create tables of authorities and contents.

◊ Chapter 13 shows how to create three types of brief cover pages that can be inserted into a template.

◊ Chapter 14 describes the process of assigning keyboard shortcuts to styles and symbols. Shortcut make it easier to use your templates.

◊ Chapter 15 covers several topics required for preparing a brief for filing.

At the end of this process you should be able to create high quality templates for writing briefs.

1.2. Word Basics

We now present a high level, terminology review of basic Word features. This review is to ensure that you are familiar with the terms this book uses to describe Word features. It is not intended to teach Word's basic functions.

1.2.1. Pointers

Word uses two types of pointers that are given various names. The book uses the term *cursor* to refer to the pointer controlled by the mouse. There is only one cursor and Word changes its appearance, depending upon what it is hovering over. The *caret* is the blinking vertical bar that marks the insertion point for text.

1.2.2. The Word 2010 Main Window

Figure 1.3 shows the appearance of the Word 2010 main window. Its major features are:

◊ Document Window—The large white area in the center for editing the document text

◊ Ribbon—This feature, introduced in Office 2007, replaces the menus in Microsoft Office applications. It contains the controls used to edit documents

◊ Status Bar—A customizable area for displaying information about the document

◊ Navigation pane—A tabbed window that supports various ways to move about in a document.

FIGURE 1.3
The Word
2010 main
window

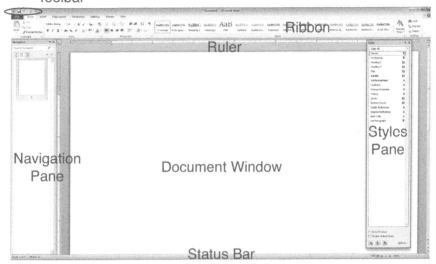

◊ Styles pane—A dockable window that applies styles to text and supports managing styles.

◊ Quick Access toolbar—A configurable set of controls for accessing frequently-used Word features.

1.2.3. The Word 2011 Main Window

The main window for Word 2011 on the Mac is very similar to its Windows counterpart (Figure 1.4). The main difference is that the Mac version retains dropdown menus that have been entirely replaced by the **Ribbon** in the Windows version. The features of the Windows and Mac version of Word are nearly identical. The difference is how you access some of those features.

1.2.4. The Ribbon

The **Ribbon** is the main point of control in Word (Figure 1.5). The **Ribbon** provides a visual display of Word functions. Because it is not possible to display all the controls at once, the **Ribbon** is divided into tabs. Only the contents of one tab at a time are visible. The set of tabs visible at any time is variable, depending upon what is being edited. When editing an element with special formatting requirements, such as a picture or a table,

FIGURE 1.4
The Word 2011
[Mac] main window

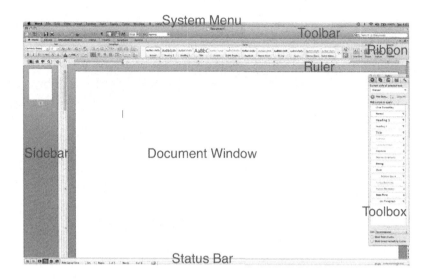

Word displays contextual ribbon tabs containing the features that apply to that element.

FIGURE 1.5
The Ribbon

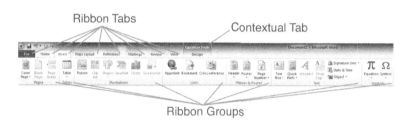

The ribbon tabs are subdivided into named ribbon groups (Figure 1.6). The name of the group is shown at the bottom of the **Ribbon** on Windows

FIGURE 1.6
An example Ribbon
Group

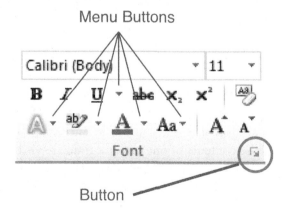

and at the top on the Mac. On Windows, ribbon groups automatically re-configure and adjust to available space when the main window is resized. On Windows, a number of ribbon groups have a small button in the lower right corner. Clicking this button displays a dialog box with additional, related settings. On the Mac, the corresponding functions are available from the system menu.

1.3. Conventions

This book uses the names of tabs, ribbon groups and controls to form a path for a command. For example, on Windows

Insert>Pages>Page Break

means to go to the **Insert** tab on the **Ribbon**, then to the **Pages** ribbon group, and click on the **Page Break** button.

On the Mac, controls can be either on the **Ribbon** or in the system menu. Therefore, the control path can reference either a menu or ribbon item. No ribbon tab has the same name as a top-level menu item, so it is easy to tell whether the **Ribbon** or the menu is being referred to. If you examine this path on the Mac

Insert>Break>Page Break

you will find there is no Insert ribbon tab but there is an **Insert** menu item. This means to go to the **Insert** dropdown menu, select the **Break** submenu and click on the **Page Break** button.

Key sequences are indicated like this

CTRL/'-e

Keys separated by a slash should be held down together. Those separated by a dash should be pressed sequentially. The previous example means to press and hold the **CTRL** key; press the ' key; release those two keys; and press the **e** key.

Many Mac keyboards have keys that serve as both hardware control keys and as the function keys **F1** through **F12** . On such keyboards, you have to press the **FN** key On such keyboards, the key sequence **Option/F9** actually requires you to use **Option/FN/F9**.

1.4. Court Rules

Court rules are the starting point for formatting briefs. The rules are inviolate. Lawyers should follow both the letter and the spirit of rules governing formatting. Often court rules are at odds with the goal of readability. With a few exceptions (notably the U.S. Supreme Court), court rules usually focus on reigning in lawyers rather than promoting readability. Ways in which court rules hinder readability include requiring:

◊ Double or 1-½ spacing rather than single-spacing.

◊ Excessively large typeface faces rather than those of normal reading size (10–12 pt.).

◊ Monospaced fonts rather than proportional fonts.

◊ The use of poor typefaces, such as Arial.

It is unfortunate that some courts have rules that appear designed to cause early blindness in judges, but that is the handicap lawyers work under. The goal is to create the best possible briefs under the rules set down by the courts.

1.4.1. What Court Rules Address in Formatting

Court rules vary in their level of detail. One trend is that appellate court rules tend to be much more specific in regard the form of papers than the rules of trial courts. Even among appellate courts, the level of specificity varies considerably.

There tends to be three general groups of formatting requirements in court rules:

1. Page layout (*e.g.*, Paper size, margins, page numbering)

2. Typeface

3. Text formatting (*e.g.*, Footnotes, block quotations)

The starting point for looking at court rules is the paper size. Court rules generally specify one or more of three paper sizes. First, most courts require briefs to be printed of 8-½″ × 11″, letter-sized paper. Second, a few courts permit briefs to be printed on 8-½″ × 14″ legal-sized paper as well. Third, the U.S. Supreme Court requires briefs to be printed on 6-⅛″ × 9-¼″ booklet sized paper. A few other courts permit briefs to be printed on booklet-sized paper. This option reflects the tradition of professionally printed briefs. Preparing booklet-sized briefs requires using a commercial printer or a sophisticated in house print shop. Booklet-sized sheets of paper are not commercially available (except through custom cutting). Instead booklet sized pages generally are created by folding and trimming industrial, sized sheets of paper.

There are several rule considerations that affect the page layout. The first of these is the question of whether the text is printed on one side of the page or both sides. With the former, each page is laid out the same. For the latter, pages are generally laid out such that even and odd numbered pages are mirrors of each other. Court rules have a wide range on this issue. Some rules require two-sided printing; other rules state a preference for two-sided printing; still others permit two-sided printing; many court rules require single-sided printing; some rules are completely silent on the question.

Another page layout issue is margins. There are three general approaches to margins in court rules. First, most courts specify minimum margins. This allows adjusting the margins for desired line lengths or for binding. Second, some rules specify margins exactly or approximately. In that case, there is no flexibility when formatting the brief. Third, the rules specify the maximum size of the text field (and possibly one or more minimum margins). The margins can be adjusted to control the position of the text. Courts that require binding (rather than stapling) are likely to require wider margins at the bound edge. When two-sided printing is used, the wider margin is likely to be specified as the inside margin. For one-sided printing, the left margin will be the wider margin.

It is implicit that pages in a brief will have numbers (a *folio*). Most court rules do not specify the location of page numbers. The page number can be placed either at the top or bottom of the page and at either the center or outside of the page. A few court rules do specify the location of the page number, removing this choice from the formatting equation.

A few court rules specify other elements of the page layout. These elements can include line numbers, page rules or the content of headers or footers. Courts with such requirements are in the minority and many rules specifically prohibit such elements.

Most court rules specify the typeface in some way. In most cases, court rules specify the type size. This is always the point size for proportional fonts. For monospaced fonts, it can either be the pitch or the point size. Typeface requirements vary widely. They range in specificity from complete silence to permitting only specific typefaces to be used.

There are four major elements within the text of a brief: the body text, block quotations, footnotes and headings. Rules generally specify the line spacing for body text. This is most frequently given using vague terms, such as *double-spacing* or *1-½ spacing*. However, some court rules give more specific line spacing in terms of leading. Even when the text is spaced wider, rules often (but not always) permit block quotations, headings and footnotes to be single-spaced. Footnotes are often permitted in a smaller font. Sometimes this traditional formatting is explicitly permitted or prohibited by the rules. Other times the rules are silent. In that case, one needs to look at briefs filed in the court to determine local custom or (best) to contact the clerk.

1.4.2. Interpreting Court Rules

Here is an example of formatting requirements in a court's rules:

U.S. Supreme Court R. 33

1. Booklet Format: (a) Except for a document expressly permitted by these Rules to be submitted on 8 ½- by 11-inch paper, see, e. g., Rules 21, 22, and 39, every document filed with the Court shall be prepared in a 6 ⅛- by 9 ¼-inch booklet format using a standard typesetting process (e. g., hot metal, photocomposition, or computer typesetting) to produce text printed in typographic (as opposed to typewriter) characters. The process used must produce a clear, black image on white paper. The text must be reproduced with a clarity that equals or exceeds the output of a laser printer.

(b) The text of every booklet-format document, including any appendix thereto, shall be typeset in a Century family (*e. g.*, Century Expanded, New Century Schoolbook, or Century Schoolbook) 12-point type with 2-point or more leading between lines. Quotations in excess of 50 words shall be indented. The typeface of footnotes shall be 10-point type with 2-point or more leading between lines. The text of the document must appear on both sides of the page.

(c) Every booklet-format document shall be produced on paper that is opaque, unglazed, and not less than 60 pounds in weight, and shall have margins of at least three-fourths of an inch on all sides. The text field, including footnotes, may not exceed 4 ⅛ by 7 ⅛ inches. The document shall be bound firmly in at least two places along the left margin (saddle stitch or perfect binding preferred) so as to permit easy opening, and no part of the text should be obscured by the binding. Spiral, plastic, metal, or string bindings may not be used. Copies of patent documents, except opinions, may be duplicated in such size as is necessary in a separate appendix.

The page layout is spread across all three sections. R. 33(1)(a) specifies the page size as booklet. R. 33(1)(b) requires brief to be printed on both sides the page. Margins are defined in R. 33(1)(c). The Court specifies both a minimum margin of ¾" and a maximum text field size of 4-⅛" × 7-⅛". Notice that this gives ½" of leeway horizontally and ⅝" vertically for adjusting the margins. A brief must add at least that much space to the margins but there is a choice of which margin to add it to. This gives flexibility to add a larger margin to the inside to support binding and to add more space where the page number is placed (top or bottom). The rules give no other layout requirements.

The typeface for the body text is specified generally as a "Century family" font. This gives a choice of a number of similar typefaces. One should look at examples to use as a guide to what the court it looking for. The Court has rigorously specified the line spacing as 12 pt. text with a least 2 pt. of leading or space between the lines. This represents single-spaced text.

The rules specify quotations and footnotes R. 33(1)(B). Quotations must be indented. Footnotes can be in a smaller (10 pt.) font size. The rules are silent on headings. With single-spaced text used elsewhere, once can infer that single-spaced headings are expected as well.

Here is a different set of formatting rules that are far less specific.

Supreme Court of the State of New Hampshire R. 16.

(1) Briefs may be prepared using a printing, duplicating or copying process capable of producing a clear letter quality black image on white paper, but shall not include ordinary carbon copies. If briefs timely filed do not conform to this rule or are not clearly legible, the clerk of the supreme court may require that new copies be substituted, but the filing shall not thereby be deemed untimely.

Each brief shall be in pamphlet form upon good quality, nonclinging paper 8 ½ by 11 inches in size, with front and back covers of durable quality. Each brief shall have a minimum margin of one inch on the binding side and shall be firmly bound at the left margin. . . .

(II) Each brief and memorandum of law shall consist of standard sized typewriter characters or size 12 font produced on one side of each leaf only. The text shall be double spaced.

R. 16(I) specifies letter-sized paper and a 1″ margin on the left side. R. 16(II) requires printing on one side of the paper only. That leaves the rest of the margins unspecified.

R. 16(II) specifies a 12 pt. font and that the text is double-spaced. The rules do not specify whether quotations, headings or footnotes are permitted to be single-spaced. In examining accepted briefs, it appears that the New Hampshire Supreme Court grants lawyers a great deal of flexibility in formatting. Perhaps the lawyers in New Hampshire have not tried to abuse the process to the point that the court has had to crack down.

1.4.3. Concluding Thoughts on Court Rules

Briefs are not a place to play games. There are many rules that are implicit. When the rules say use specific size of paper, it is implicit that they mean the text should be oriented in portrait mode where the text runs across the narrow size of the page. It is implicit that the body text font under the rules is a roman font; not a script font, bold font or italic font. The fact that some court rules explicitly require roman fonts demonstrates that some lawyers have defied common sense and actually tried this kind of abuse. One should pay particular attention where courts limit brief lengths by page counts. A court is not likely to appreciate a brief that goes to extraordinary measures to circumvent page limits. One should be able to justify to a court every formatting choice made in a submission to that court.

Chapter 2
Setting up Word
for
Legal Writing

Word is a large, complex application that is designed to appeal to a wide range of users. Meeting the needs of everyone creates a number of special challenges. For example, a standard installation must be able to handle the needs of basic users who will be unable to do customizations. Word also must be backwards compatible so that users who upgrade will not find keyboard commands they have memorized have changed or features they depend on are missing.

Briefs are a unique form of document. Many of Word's default settings that make things easier for most users are a nuisance for brief writing. This chapter shows how to make changes to Word's default configuration that can make writing briefs easier.

One of Word's configuratable features is its ability to intercept key sequences and replace them with other characters. This feature can be used to enter characters that do not appear on the keyboard. If you type

"I'm so sorry for causing this."

Word's default behavior automatically replaces the typewriter-style, straight quotation marks with typesetting quotation marks. Word displays

"I'm so sorry for causing this."

This particular substitition is usually desirable when writing briefs.

On the other hand, Word's default configuration causes text like this to be replaced with with

© 2012

While having quick access to the copyright symbol is of use to lawyers, that same substitution changes

8 U.S.C. § 1182(c)

to

8 U.S.C. § 1182©

This tends to be a major annoyance in legal writing.

Another default Word substitution is to change ordinals to use super-scripts. If you type

(7th Cir. 2005)

Word changes the text to appear like this:

(7th Cir. 2005)

This substitution creates citations that do not conform to either AWLD or Blue Book formats.

There may be some lawyers who think that such a deviation from stan-dard legal citation form might be an improvement. If so, what happens with this?

(3d Cir. 1997)

Word does not automatically convert this ordinal to use a superscript. You have to live with inconsistency or manually format to the odd-looking

(3^{d} Cir. 1997)

or be even more nonconformating by using this

(3rd Cir. 1997)

Some of Word's default settings are made for compatibility. They are the way they are simply because that is how they have always been. One of these settings controls how Word does justification. By default, Word justifies text by expanding spaces. This has the effect of creating rivers of white space that are a distinctive feature of documents formatted in Word (Figure 2.1). One can change that behavior so that Word justifies by contracting spaces to reduce the rivers in the text

FIGURE 2.1
Rivers created when WordPerfect spacing is disabled (top) and how the same text appears with it enabled (bottom)

Respondent's trial began that same day, August 14, 2006. J.A. 30 (Docket entry No. 78). The next day, respondent filed a motion for reconsideration of the order denying his motion to dismiss on speedy trial grounds. *Ibid.* (Docket entry No. 79); J.A. 194–198. The district court denied the motion. J.A. 31 (Docket entry No. 81); Pet. App. 33a–36a; see Tr. 296.

Respondent's trial began that same day, August 14, 2006. J.A. 30 (Docket entry No. 78). The next day, respondent filed a motion for reconsideration of the order denying his motion to dismiss on speedy trial grounds. *Ibid.* (Docket entry No. 79); J.A. 194–198. The district court denied the motion. J.A. 31 (Docket entry No. 81); Pet. App. 33a–36a; see Tr. 296.

The remainder of the chapter shows the specific steps how to configure Word for legal writing. This is one of the few places where the process and features are significantly different between Word 2010 for Windows and Word 2011 for Mac. Therefore, the chapter is divided into separate Windows and Mac sections. This is the only place in the book with such a division.

2.1. Configuring Word 2010 for Legal Writing

The steps in this section only apply to the Windows version of Word. If you are using the Mac, skip to the next section.

2.1.1. Displaying the Current Style

The approach of this book is to use styles for formatting text. Style formatting is much easier when you can see what style is currently in use; something Word does not do by default. It is possible to configure Word to dis-

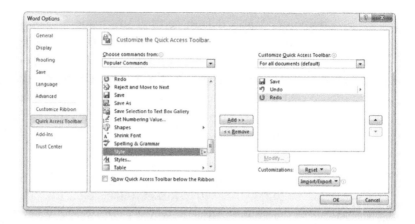

play continuously a combo box that shows the style at the current insertion point. This combo box can also be used to change the style as well.

To make this change:

1. Click the ⯆ button in **Quick Access** toolbar.

2. Select **More Commands** from the dropdown menu.

3. This displays the **Word Options** dialog box (Figure 2.2).

4. Select **Customize Quick Access Toolbar** from the listbox at the left.

5. Select **Style** from the list box below Choose commands from:.

6. Click **Add**.

7. Click **OK** to save.

The **Styles** combo box should appear in the **Quick Access** toolbar as shown in Figure 2.3.

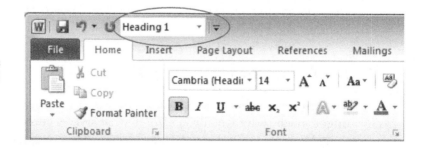

2.1.2. Word Compatibility Options

Word's compatibility options control the way the document is formatted. These options are stored in the Word document. The suggested changes reduce poor spacing when justifying text and make vertical line spacing more predictable.

To change the compatibility options:

1. Select **File>Options**.

   This displays the **Word Options** dialog box (Figure 2.4).

2. Select **Advanced** from the list box at the left.

3. Set **Compatibility options for** to **All New Documents**.

4. Click **Layout Options** to expand the list.

5. Set these options by checking the corresponding box:

Do full justification the way WordPerfect 6.x for Windows does
If this setting is not enabled, Word justifies text by inserting spaces between words. This produces odd spacing that is characteristic of Word documents. When this option is enabled, Word will justify by moving words closer together.

Don't center "exact height" lines

Enabling this setting causes Word to add the space for line spacing after the line. By default, Word centers exactly spaced lines within the line spacing. The default setting makes alining text vertically very difficult.

Don't use HTML autospacing

Enabling this setting causes Word to use both the **Before** and **After** paragraph spacing of adjacent paragraphs. If this is not set, Word inserts the largest of the two values to insert space between paragraphs.

6. Click **OK** to save.

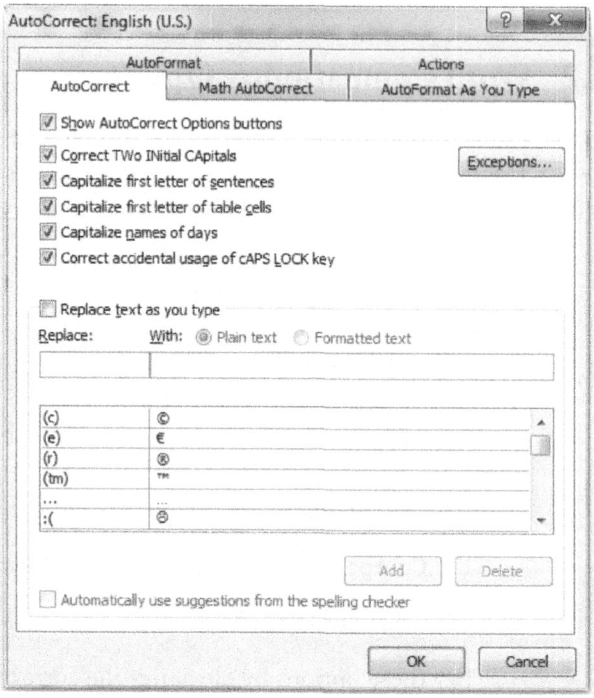

FIGURE 2.5
Changing
AutoCorrect
options [Windows]

2.1.3. AutoCorrect Settings

AutoCorrect settings controls Word's automatic substitutions. These suggested changes to Word's default settings disable substitutions that cause annoying problems with briefs, such as having "§ 1184(c)" become "§ 1184©" and "(4th Cir. 1995)" becoming "(4ᵗʰ Cir. 1995)."

Word for Windows has two tabs of AutoCorrect Settings: **AutoCorrect** and **AutoFormat As You Type**. However, both types of settings effectively behave the same. The inability to place all the controls on a single tab appears to be the reason they are divided across two tabs.

To change the AutoCorrect settings:

1. Select **File>Options** from the Ribbon to display the **Word Options** dialog box (Figure 2.4).

2. Select **Proofing** from the list box at the left.

3. Click the **AutoCorrect Options** button.

   This displays the **AutoCorrect** dialog box.

4. Select the **AutoCorrect** tab (Figure 2.5).

5. Uncheck **Replace text as you type**.

6. Click on the **AutoFormat as You Type** tab (Figure 2.6).

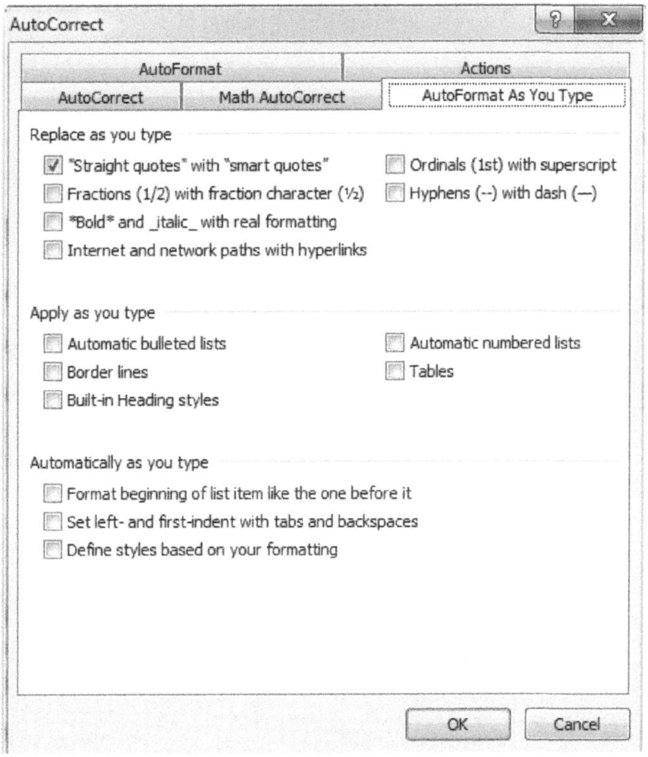

FIGURE 2.6
Changing
AutoFormat
options [Windows]

Be sure you select **AutoFormat as You Type** and not **AutoFormat**. It is easy to confuse the two because of the similar names and settings on the two tabs. The former controls how Word translates keystrokes. The latter configures the behavior of the **AutoFormat** command that applies to many of the same types of formatting to the entire document. The **AutoFormat** command is not directly accessible in Word 2010 by default.

7. Uncheck all the settings except for **"Straight quotes" with "smart quotes"**.

2.1.4. Disabling Linked Styles

Linked styles are a bizarre combination of character and paragraph styles. They can be created, used and disabled on Windows. Linked styles can be used on Mac (predefined styles or styles imported from Windows) but not created or disabled. Linked styles should be disabled on Windows.

1. Display the Styles Pane by pressing **ALT/CTRL/SHIFT/S**.

2. Check the **Disable Linked Styles** box as shown in Figure 2.7.

FIGURE 2.7
Disabling Linked Styles
[Windows Only]

2.1.5. Page Number Display

Word only displays the absolute page number in the status bar by default. This can cause the page number displayed in the current page of your document to be different from the value shown on the statute bar. For example, if you have a document with an unnumbered cover page, the status bar displays Page 10 when you are actually on Page 9.

To make Word display the actual page number:

1. Right click on the status bar to display the **Configure Status Bar** menu (Figure 2.8).

2. Check the **Formatted Page Number** box.

3. Check the **Section** box.

4. When finished, click anywhere outside the menu to hide it.

This causes the page numbers to be displayed as shown in the lower left corner of Figure 2.8.

FIGURE 2.8
How to configure
the status bar
[Windows Only]

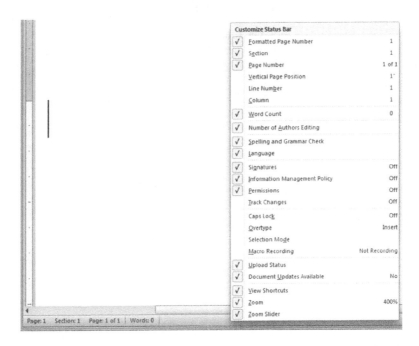

2.1.6. Embedding Fonts

The set of installed fonts varies among computers. If a document is created using a specific font, then edited on a computer that does not have that font, the system substitutes an available font. Font substitution nearly always creates formatting problems because a different font will have characters of different sizes, resulting in different text placement. This problem usually occurs when multiple people edit a document.

Word for Windows has a mechanism that can alleviate this problem. Word can embed a copy of the fonts used into the document. When the document is read on another machine that does not have the font available, it can use the embedded version.

Enabled font embedding by:

1. Select **File>Options** to display the **Word Option**s dialog box.

2. Select **Save** from the list box at the left (Figure 2.9).

3. Set **Preserve fidelity when sharing this document** to **All New Documents**.

4. Check the **Embed fonts** in the file box.

5. Click **OK** to save.

FIGURE 2.9
Enabling font
embedding
[Windows Only]

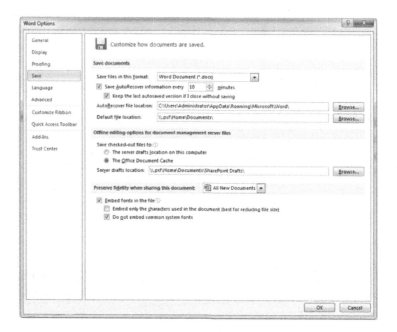

There are two common problems with embedded fonts. First, not all fonts can be embedded. The font designer can set up the font so that Word will not embed it. Fortunately, most fonts are set up so that they can be embedded. Second, font embedding only works on Windows. If someone using a Mac edits the file, they will not be able to use the embedded version of the font. The document will not appear correctly unless the font is installed on the Mac as well.

2.2. Configuring Word 2011 for Mac

The steps in this section only apply to the Mac version of Word. If you are using the Windows version, skip over this section.

2.2.1. Displaying the Current Style

This section shows how to add the **Style** combo box to the editing toolbar. This change allows you to always see the style in use at the caret.

FIGURE 2.10
Locating the Styles
combo box [Mac]

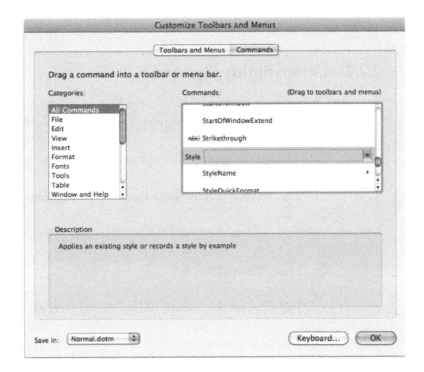

From the system menu:

1. Select **View>Toolbars>Customize Toolbars and Menu**.

    This displays the **Customize Toolbars and Menus** dialog box (Figure 2.10).

2. Select the **Commands** tab.

3. Use the mouse to drag the **Style** combo box on to the Editing toolbar.

4. Click OK to close the dialog box.

The **Style** combo box should appear in the Editing toolbar as shown in Figure 2.11 (at the far right).

FIGURE 2.11
The Styles combo box added to the Editing toolbar [Mac]

2.2.2. Compatibility Options

Compatibility options control how Word lays out text. These settings are saved within the Word document. The suggested settings below make laying out briefs simpler.

To change the compability options:

1. Select **Word>Preferences** from the system menu.

    This displays the **Word Preferences** dialog box.

2. Select **Compatibility**.

    This displays the **Compatibility** dialog box (Figure 2.12).

3. Set these options:

Do full justification the way WordPerfect 6.x for Windows does

If this setting is not enabled, Word justifies text solely by inserting spaces between words. This produces odd spacing that is characteristic of Word documents. When enabled, Word justifies by moving words closer together.

Don't center "exact height" lines

Enabling this setting causes Word to add the space for line spacing after the line. By default, Word centers exactly spaced lines within the line spacing. Enabling this option makes it easier to align text vertically.

Don't use HTML autospacing

Enabling this setting causes Word to use both the **Before** and **After** paragraph spacing of adjacent paragraphs. Otherwise, Word uses just the largest of the two values to insert space between paragraphs.

4. Click **OK** to save.

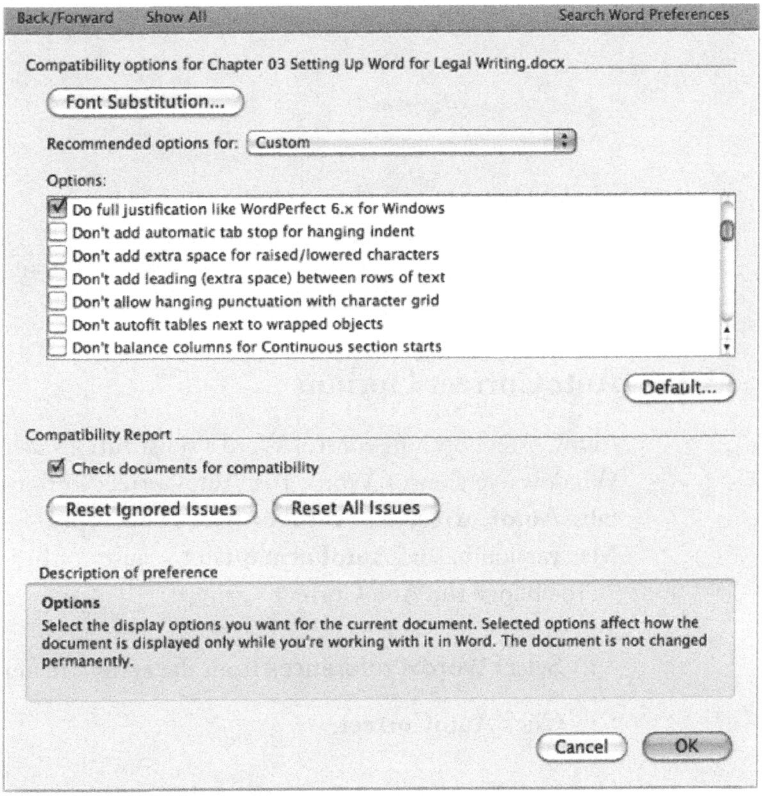

FIGURE 2.12
Setting
compatibility
options [Mac]

Figure 2.13
AutoCorrect
options [Mac]

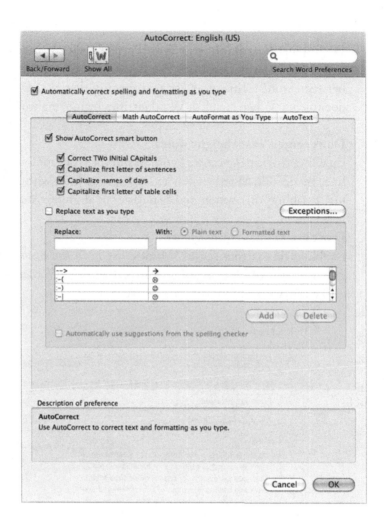

2.2.3. AutoCorrect Options

AutoCorrect options control Word's substitutions as you type. As with the Windows version of Word, the AutoCorrect options are split across two tabs: **AutoCorrest** and **AutoFormat as You Type**. Unlike on Windows, the Mac version has no **AutoFormat** tab to cause confusion.

To change the AutoCorrect settings:

1. Select **Word>Preference**s from the system menu.

2. Click **AutoCorrect**.

This displays the **AutoCorrect** dialog box.

3. Select the **AutoCorrect** tab.

4. Uncheck **Replace text as you type** (Figure 2.13).

5. Select the **AutoFormat** as you type tab.

6. Uncheck all the formatting options except for **"Straight quotes" with "smart quotes"** as shown in (Figure 2.14).

7. Click **OK** to save.

FIGURE 2.14
AutoFormat options
[Mac]

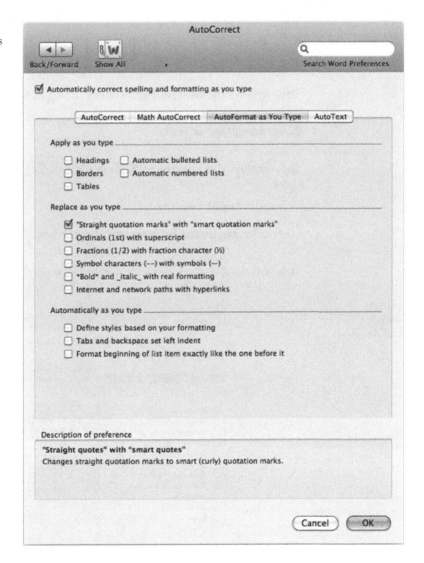

2.2.4. Using the Character Viewer

The Mac Character Viewer serves as an extension of the keyboard. It permits the typing of any character within a font. This can be useful for typing characters that do not have a keyboard equivalent.

2.2.4.1. Enabling the Character Viewer

The Character Viewer is not enabled by default. To add the Character viewer to the system menu:

1. On the system menu, select >**System Preferences**.

    This displays the **System Preferences** dialog box.

2. Select **Language & Text**.

    This displays the **Language & Text** dialog box (Figure 2.15).

3. Select the **Input Sources** tab.

4. Check the **Keyboard & Character Viewer** box.

    This will display the Character Viewer icon on the system menu.

FIGURE 2.15
Enabling the Character
Viewer [Mac Only]

2.2.4.2. Using the Character Viewer

The Character Viewer is a non-model dialog box that floats on top of other windows. To open the character viewer:

1. Click the Character View icon on the system menu (Figure 2.16).

FIGURE 2.16
How to access the
Character Viewer
from the system
menu [Mac Only].

2. Select a category of character from the list at the left of the Character Viewer (Figure 2.17)

3. Double click or drag the character to the document.

FIGURE 2.17
The Character
Viewer can insert
any character in a
font [Mac Only]

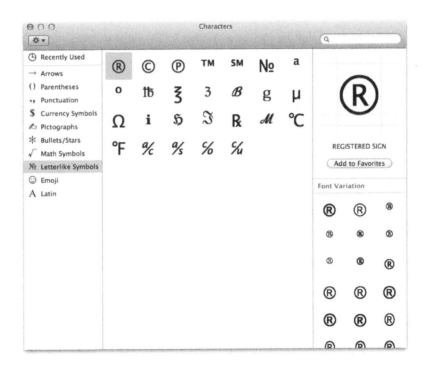

2.3. Notes on Configuring Word

The settings shown in this chapter are merely a recommendations on how to configure Word options. They represent a preference for having Word make a minimum of substitutions. Set these options any way that makes creating documents easiest for you. Keep in mind that you can define keyboard shortcuts to insert symbols, so using Word's substitution of character sequences features is not necessary for direct access to symbols that do not appear on the keyboard.

One stylistic note is in order. If you are creating briefs using a monospaced (typewriter) font, you may find that straight quotes look more appropriate than typesetting quotes.

```
The defendant stated at the accident scene,
"I'm so sorry for causing this."

The defendant stated at the accident scene,
"I'm so sorry for causing this."
```

If that be the case, uncheck **"Straight quotes" with "smart quotes"** in the AutoFormat options.

Chapter 3
Templates

The objective of this chapter is for you to learn to create and manage *templates*. A template is a special type of document that defines the initial state of other documents. Every Word document starts out as a template. When you create a document, Word copies the contents of the template into the document. A template defines the initial:

◊ Page size and orientation

◊ Margins

◊ Formatting settings

A template can also define

◊ Headers and footers

◊ Page layout elements, such as rules and line numbering

◊ Boilerplate text

◊ Document subdivisions

The default template in Word is a file called Normal.dotx. Word uses the Normal.dotx template whenever it creates a new, blank document. You can (and should) customize Normal.dotx to include your own settings that reflect how you use Word most of the time.

Lawyers create many different types of documents. A lawyer using Word should have a different template for each type of document. In the realm of briefs, you should have a template for each set of court rules you file briefs under. In addition, you should have templates for letters, pleadings and any other type of document you create. The advantages of using specialized templates is that you only have to set up the document once and that your documents will be consistently formatted.

The scope of this chapter is limited to local templates that are stored on your own system. It is also possible to set up workgroup templates that are shared among a group of people on the same network. Workgroup templates allow you to maintain consistency in document formatting within an organization. However, setting up workgroup templates (including security) is beyond the scope of this book.

Most of the remaining chapters cover the elements that go into a template and how to use them. When you finish this chapter, your templates are likely to be very simple. As you progress through the book you should add to them so that the templates become increasingly full featured.

3.1. How to Create a Template

A template is a document. Therefore a template starts with a template. The easiest way to create a template is to start with another template with a similar purpose. Once you have created one solid brief template, you can modify that template to conform to other court rules.

If you wanted to create a template to use for letters (or *nearly* any other type of document) from your firm, you could start with an existing letter template. Microsoft maintains a library of templates that is accessible directly from Word. You can preview letter templates that have already been written. Take the template that most closely matches your needs, customize it, save it and reuse it.

Unfortunately, templates for briefs are as rare as hen's teeth. At the time of this writing, there were none in Microsoft's library. They are equally unavailable through other on-line sources. Perhaps, this illustrates the lack of sophistication in Word use among lawyers.

FIGURE 3.1
Saving a template

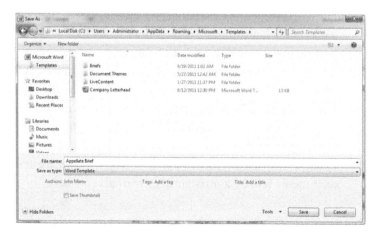

To learn how to create a template, start with some boilerplate text. Under Fed. R. App. P. 32(a), one must certify that a brief complies with typeface and length requirements. Type such a certification (or something similar) into a blank document.

Certificate of Compliance with Fed. R. App. P. 32(a)

     1. This brief complies with the type-volume limitation of Fed. R. App. P. 32(a)(7)(B) because this brief contains _____ words, excluding the parts of the brief exempted by Fed. R. App. P. 32(a)(7)(B)(iii).
     2. This brief complies with the typeface requirements of Fed. R. App. P. 32(a)(5) and the type styles requirements of Fed. R. App. P. 32(a)(6) because it is typeset in the proportionally-spaced 14 pt. _____ serif font.

/s/
_____

Robin Stern
The Conner Law Firm
_____, 2012

To create the template from the document:

1. Select **File>Save As** (from the Ribbon on Windows, from the menu on Mac.

   This displays the **Save** dialog box (Figure 3.1).

2. Set set the output type to be a Word template:

Windows	Mac
Set **Save as type** to **Word Template**.	Set **Format** to **Word Template (.dotx)**

3. [Windows Only] Click on **Templates** in the list box to the left.

   At this point, Word should be trying to save to the user template folder. Click the **New Folder** button to create new subfolder or select an existing subfolder to save the document within it.

4. Enter a name for the document.

5. Click **OK** to save.

3.2. Creating a Document from the Template

The process for creating a document from a template differs slightly between Windows and Mac. The following sections describe the process for each system separately.

3.2.1. How to Create a Document on Windows

To create a new document from a template:

1. Select **File>New** from the Ribbon.

2. This displays the **New** dialog box (Figure 3.2).

FIGURE 3.2
Create a document from a template on the New dialog box [Windows].

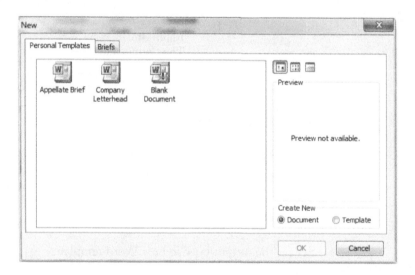

Notice that the dialog box stores the templates on tabbed pages. The **Personal Templates** tab contains the templates in the user template folder. Subfolders of the root folder have a separate tab. Subfolders of subfolders do not create tabs. Instead, the templates they contain appear in their parent's tab. If you have a set up workgroup templates directory, those templates and local templates show up together.

3. Double click on the desired template.

This creates a new word document based on the template. The new document should look just like the template before it was saved. If you

FIGURE 3.3
A new document
created from the
template.

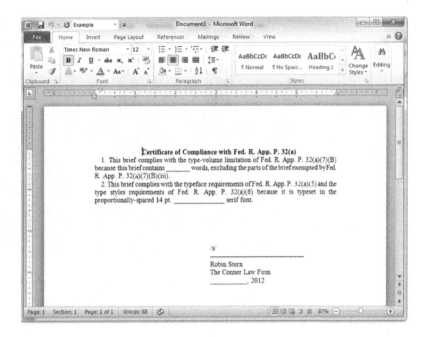

created the template using the text shown above, the new document
should appear like the one in Figure 3.3.

3.2.2. How to Create a Document on the Mac

To create a new document from a template:

1. Select **File>New** from Template from the system menu.

    This displays the **Word Document Gallery** (Figure 3.4).

2. Click **My Templates** in the list box at the right.

    Word 2011 for Mac displays subfolders created in the user template
    folder indented below **My Templates**. If you placed the desired tem-
    plate in a subfolder of the user template folder, you can select that fold-
    er to find the template more easily. In Figure 3.4, Briefs is a subfolder.

    Unlike on Windows, the template display aggregates all templates in
    subfolders. Instead of just showing the documents in the default tem-
    plate folder, selecting **My Templates** displays all the templates in that
    folder and its subfolders.

FIGURE 3.4
Create a new
document using the
Word Document
Gallery [Mac].

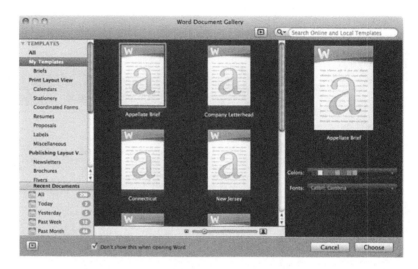

If you have a workgroup templates directory you will find an entry called **Templates** listed below **My Templates.** Select **Templates** if you wish to use a workgroup template.

Word only displays one level of template subfolders. If you create additional levels of subfolders, Word displays their contents when the parent folder is selected. In that case, Word gives no indication that the template is in a subfolder.

3. Double click on the desired folder.

This creates a new word document based on the template. The new document should look just like the template before it was saved.

3.3. Managing Templates

Conceptually, templates are managed in the same way on Windows and on the Mac. A template, like any other document, can be edited, renamed, deleted or moved to a different folder. On Windows, Windows Explorer performs this function. Finder does the same on the Mac. In order to manage templates, first you have to determine where Word stores them.

Word manages all configurable directories in the **File Locations** dialog box (Figure 3.5) as part of its options settings. On this dialog box you can set the locations for:

◊ Default folder for saving documents

◊ Default location to find pictures

◊ Location for user templates

◊ Location Workgroup templates

◊ A directory whose documents are opened when Word starts

3.3.1. How to Find the User Template Folder

The user template folder is the location where Word looks for and stores templates that you create. This folder location is configurable. The default location for user templates on Windows is

C:/Users/*Username*/AppData/Roaming/Microsoft/Templates

where *Username* is your user name. On the Mac, the default location is

~/Library/Application Support/Microsoft/Office/User Templates

On the Mac (and Unix in general) the tilde character expands to the home folder of the user.

The user template folder will be the default if you have a standalone computer that you set up. If your computer was set up by a systems administrator, it is possible that the folder could be in a different location.

There are a number of reasons why this may be changed. Your system may be configured to store data on a different disk than the one containing the operating system. It may be set up so that the data is stored to a network location that can be backed up remotely. The recommendation here is that you should not change the user template folder location unless it is absolutely necessary.

To view the user template folder:

1. Display the **File Locations** dialog box:

Windows	Mac
a. Select **File>Options** from the Ribbon to display the **Word Options** dialog box.	
b. Click on **Advanced** in the list box to the left as shown in Figure 3.5.	a. Select **Word>Preferences** on the system menu.
c. Use the scroll bar at the right to move the display until the **File Locations** button becomes visble. This button is located near the bottom of the window.	b. On the **Word Preferences** dialog box click **File Locations**.
d. Click the **File Locations** button.	

You may be able to read the folder directly off the **File Locations** dialog box. If the folder path is too long to fit the display, Word uses ellipses to shorten it to fit. Be that the case, use the following steps to get the full page.

FIGURE 3.5
Finding the File
Locations settings
[Windows]

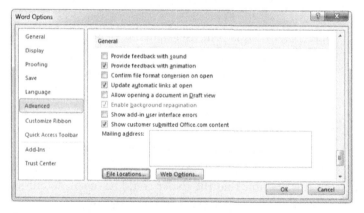

2. Select **User templates**.

3. Click the **Modify** button.

   This displays the **Modify Location** dialog box shown in Figure 3.6 (**Choose a Folder** on the Mac). Use this dialog box to determine the user template folder

4. Click **Cancel** after determining the user template folder.

FIGURE 3.6
File location
settings

3.3.2. Managing Template Files and Folders.

On Windows, use the Windows Explorer (**Window/E**, or under **Accessories** in the Windows Start menu) to manage templates. Through the Windows Explorer you can create, delete or rename subfolders in the user templates directory. You also can rename, delete, copy and move among folders template files.

A potential problem with using Windows Explorer is hidden files. In the default configuration, the AppData folder is hidden. If you cannot see a folder that is part of the path to the user template directory, you must type in the hidden part of the path into Windows Explorer.

On the Mac, use Finder to organize templates and template folders. Finder can perform the same functions as Windows Explorer.

3.4. Editing Templates

Modify templates the same way as any other document: open, edit and save. The challenge with editing templates is to be sure that you are editing the template and not a document created from the template. If you double click on a document using Windows Explorer (or Finder on the Mac), you edit the document. In contrast, if you double click on a template, Word creates a new document from that template—you will not be editing the template itself.

You have to open a template from within Word to edit it. If you have edited the template recently, the template may be in the recently edited file lists (Word: **File>Recent**, Mac: **File>Open Recent**). Otherwise, you must open the file (**File>Open**) and navigate to the folder containing the template (usually the user template folder) to open it.

3.5. Moving on from Here

Identify one or more courts to which you submit briefs. Then create a template for each one. At this point do not worry about formatting or content. All you need is some text that can be used to identify the template. If the court requires specific text, such as certifications, considering adding that to the template. Then be sure that you are able to create documents using the templates. As you work through the book, you can add to these templates. Keep the court rules available. You will need them to refine your templates.

Chapter 4
Styles

The objective of this chapter is for you to learn how to:

◊ Understand style types and structure.

◊ Use paragraph and character styles to format text.

◊ Create and modify styles.

A *style* is a named set of predefined formatting attributes that can be applied to text in a document. Formatting using styles is faster and simpler than applying formatting directly to text. The barrier to using styles is that they require an investment in time to set up. However, once a set of styles is created and saved in a template, it can be reused for any number of documents.

All major text-processing applications support styles in generally the same manner as word, including WordPerfect, WordPro, InDesign, Quark, Pages and OpenOffice. Learning to format using styles is a skill that can be transferred to many different software applications.

All of your text formatting should be done using styles. Using styles has a number of advantages over direct formatting used by Word amateurs:

◊ One click formatting—A style applies all the text formatting in one step.

◊ Consistency within documents—text formatted using styles appears the same throughout the document.

◊ Consistency among documents—text formatted with the same style, using the same template appears the same in all documents.

◊ Rapid Reformatting—changes to styles are automatically propagated throughout the document.

◊ Moving documents among text processing applications—most text processing applications recognize styles.

Here is an example of how styles are a time saver. Assume you have written a 30-page brief and have carefully formatted it. Then you take the brief to your supervisor. He tells you that he likes it except that he wants the party names in case citations underlined rather than in italics. If you formatted the text directly using the italics buttons, it could take an hour to make that change. If you used styles, reformatting the entire document would take 4 seconds.

If you format documents with these controls you are doing it wrong.

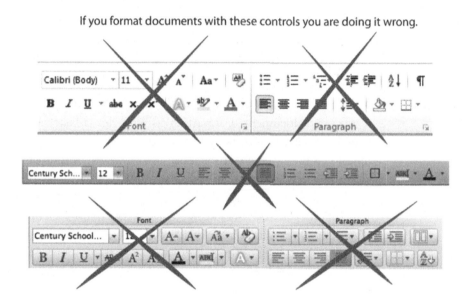

4.1. Types of Styles

There are five types of styles in Word:

1. Character—Applies formatting to a range of text

2. Paragraph—Applies formatting to a paragraph

3. Linked (Word for Windows Only—should not be used)

4. Table (Not generally used in briefs)

5. List (Not generally used in briefs)

For brief writing, you only need to concern yourself with character and paragraph styles. Character styles have a very limited range of settings. The only ones used in briefs are the typeface settings.

Paragraph styles are supersets of character styles. A paragraph style has all the attributes of a character style with a number of additions. These include paragraph settings (*e.g.*, indentation and line spacing), bullets and numbering and tab settings.

Be aware that a paragraph in Word is not the same as a paragraph according to the rules of grammar. In Word, a paragraph is a sequence of characters terminated by a **Return**. Figure 4.1 shows indented text, followed by a block quotation, and finally flush text. Grammatically this is one paragraph. However, Word treats this sequence as three distinct paragraphs.

FIGURE 4.1
A complex
paragraph

> After discussing the ways in which the CTEA "supplement[ed] the[] traditional First Amendment safeguards," *Eldred*, 537 U.S. at 220, the Court concluded:
>
> > To the extent [the petitioners'] assertions raise First Amendment concerns, copyright's built-in free speech safeguards are generally adequate to address them. We recognize that the D.C. Circuit spoke too broadly when it declared copyrights "categorically immune from challenges under the First Amendment." But when, as in this case, Congress has not altered the *traditional contours of copyright protection,* further First Amendment scrutiny is unnecessary.
>
> *Id.* at 221 (emphasis added; citation omitted). And, in a footnote to the last sentence quoted above, the Court reiterated that "it is appropriate to construe copyright's internal safeguards to accommodate First Amendment concerns." *Id.* at 221 n.24.

4.2. Order of Precedence in Formatting

A range of text can have a character style applied. The paragraph containing the text will have paragraph style as well. The ability to have both a character

46

FIGURE 4.2
Text has a
paragraph style and
can have a character
style as well.

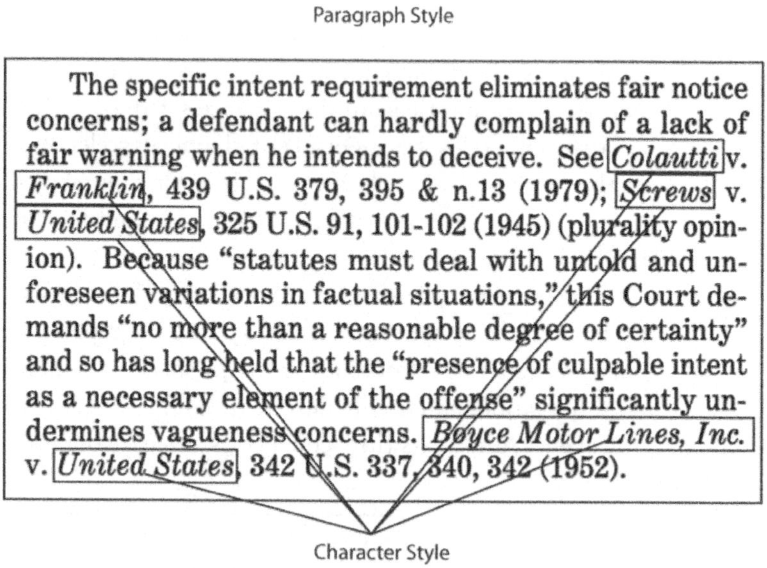

Paragraph Style

> The specific intent requirement eliminates fair notice concerns; a defendant can hardly complain of a lack of fair warning when he intends to deceive. See *Colautti* v. *Franklin*, 439 U.S. 379, 395 & n.13 (1979); *Screws* v. *United States*, 325 U.S. 91, 101-102 (1945) (plurality opinion). Because "statutes must deal with untold and unforeseen variations in factual situations," this Court demands "no more than a reasonable degree of certainty" and so has long held that the "presence of culpable intent as a necessary element of the offense" significantly undermines vagueness concerns. *Boyce Motor Lines, Inc.* v. *United States*, 342 U.S. 337, 340, 342 (1952).

Character Style

style and paragraph style applied to the same text allows text to be formatted differently from that of its underlying paragraph (Figure 4.2).

Formatting can also be applied directly to the text. This gives three possible, overlapping sources of formatting for a range of text. If there are any conflicts among these, direct formatting takes precedence over character style formatting. Character formatting takes precedence over paragraph style formatting.

4.3. Style Hierarchies

Styles are based upon other styles. The *based on* style is defined when a new style is created. The new style adopts all the attributes of the based on style. Styles then form a hierarchical tree structure.

This inheritance of attributes has two major effects. First, you do not have to define all the attributes of a new style. New styles inherit the properties of the style they are based on. Second, it allows styles to work in groups. When an attribute changes in a style, that change propagates down through all styles based on that style that have not explicitly set that attribute. For example, you can set up all your footnote styles so that they are based on one common style. Changing the font size in this one style can then propagate through all the footnote styles. This allows you to keep the font size the same throughout footnotes.

Word predefines the Normal style that serves as the ultimate ancestor of all other paragraph styles. The Normal style is used to define basic settings

FIGURE 4.3 (LEFT)
Apply styles using
the Styles pane
[Windows]

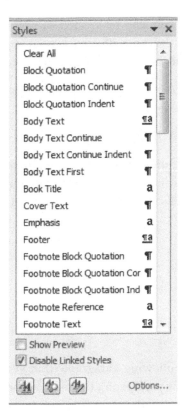

FIGURE 4.4 (RIGHT)
Apply styles using
the Styles window
[Mac].

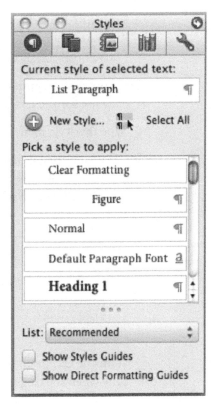

that apply throughout a document, such as the typeface, type size and line spacing. The Normal style should never be used directly within a document. Unfortunately, Word's default templates make avoiding the Normal style rather difficult.

The analog to Normal for character styles is called Default Paragraph Font. Applying this style has the effect of removing all character level formatting and reverting to the formatting of the underlying paragraph. Unlike Normal, the Default Paragraph Font style cannot be modified.

4.4. Ways to Apply Styles

There are a number of ways to apply styles in Word. These include:

◊ Select a style in the **Styles** pane [Windows] (Figure 4.3) or **Styles** window [Mac](Figure 4.4). This the best general-purpose method for applying styles.

◊ Keyboard Shortcuts—These can be created as part of the style definition. Keyboard shortcuts are the most effective way to apply styles but is not intuitive until the shortcuts are memorized (see Chapter 14).

◊ Following Paragraph—A paragraph style can define the style to automatically use for the next paragraph.

◊ Type the style name into the **Style** dropdown list (see Chapter 2).

◊ Click on a style in the **Quick Style** list on the **Home** tab (Figure 4.5). This is nearly as effective as using the Styles pane or window. The disadvantage is that the **Quick Style** list is only visible when the **Home** tab is selected.

FIGURE 4.5
The Quick Style list

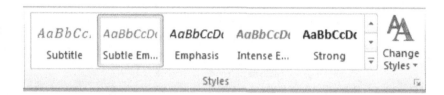

With the exception of Following Paragraph (that Word performs automatically when starting a new paragraph), the method for applying styles is very similar for all of these methods.

Applying a style takes two steps. First, select the text you want to format. For a character style, select the range of text. Simply place the caret within the paragraph for paragraph style.[1] Second, apply the desired style using one of the methods above.

It is recommended that you have the **Styles** pane [Windows] or **Styles** window [Mac] displayed at all times when you are editing text in Word. This will give you a formatting palette that is immediately available at all times. On the Mac, this window always floats. On Windows, you can drag the title bar of the **Styles** pane to make it float or dock at the left or right side.

To display the styles window:

Windows	Mac
ALT/CTRL/SHIFT/S or click the button at the lower right corner of the **Quick Style** list on the **Home** tab.	**View>Styles**

---

[1] On the Mac it is critical not to select a range of text within the paragraph when applying a paragraph style.

4.4.1. Paragraph Style Example

Most document formatting is applying character styles. Try typing the following paragraph into a blank document:

> The INA expressly authorizes removal of an alien to his country of birth, and the Act does not make that authorization contingent on the alien's acceptance by the receiving country's government.

Now format it as an heading. First, place the caret anywhere within the paragraph. Second, apply the paragraph style using any of the methods described previously. For example, select Heading 2 from the Styles pane (or Styles window).

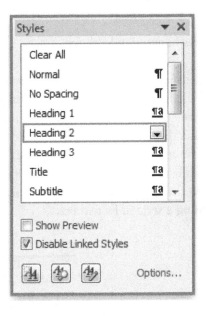

With Word's default template, the text will be reformatted like this:

> **The INA expressly authorizes removal of an alien to his country of birth, and the Act does not make that authorization contingent on the alien's acceptance by the receiving country's government.**

If you were using a template designed for briefs, the very same procedure could cause the text to appear like this:

I. The INA expressly authorizes removal of an alien to his country of birth, and the Act does not make that authorization contingent on the alien's acceptance by the receiving country's government.

Notice that the one step of applying the style:

◊ Numbers the paragraph

◊ Switches to a bold font

◊ Removes hyphenation.

◊ Makes the paragraph left aligned, rather than justified.

◊ Applies hanging indentation.

Furthermore, all of these changes are applied consistently to any paragraph with the Heading 2 style. You can change the paragraph to another style in the same manner. All this works seemlessly as long as you do not apply formatting directly to the text. Styles are the fastest way to format a document.

After applying the Heading 2 style, Word updates all the style indicators to match that selected using the **Styles** pane. If you added the **Style** combo box to the Quick Access toolbar (as suggested in Chapter 2), it displays the **Heading 2** style in its text box.

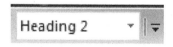

The **Quick Style** list also highlights **Heading 2** to match the selected style.

All the controls that set styles are linked together. Typing "Heading 2" into the Style combo box or selecting **Heading 2** from the **Quick Access** toolbar has the same effect as selecting **Heading 2** from the **Styles** pane.

4.4.2. Character Style Example

Assume you wanted to apply emphasis to the party names in a case citation. That kind of formatting applies to a range of characters; not the entire paragraph. For that, you need to use a character style. Word has a built in character style called Emphasis whose default behavior is to change text to italics. Try typing some text with a case citation into a Word document. To emphasize the party names, the first step is to select the text. This can be done with either the mouse or by using keys to move the caret while holding down the **Shift** key.

> Applying "a presumption of prejudice as opposed to a specific analysis does not change the ultimate inquiry:" whether pretrial publicity or community animosity resulted in actual bias on the jury that decided petitioner's case. United States v. Olano, 507 U.S. 725, 739 (1993). Such a presumption would simply reverse the ordinary

The second step is to select the Emphasis style. With Word's default template, this places the text in italics, like this:

> Applying "a presumption of prejudice as opposed to a specific analysis does not change the ultimate inquiry:" whether pretrial publicity or mmunity animosity resulted in actual bias on the jury that decided petitioner's case. *United States v. Olano*, 507 U.S. 725, 739 (1993). Such a presumption would simply reverse the ordinary

It is no more difficult to apply a character style than it is to format using the *I* or *u* buttons.

4.4.3. Mixing Style and Direct Formatting

The style formatting advantage comes when styles are used consistently to format document text. That advantage starts to evaporate when a document is formatted using a mixture of styles and direct formatting. This is most likely to occcur when when multiple people work on the same document.

Assume you have five lawyers working on the document and four of them correctly use styles for formatting but one insists on using the formatting buttons. That one idiot screws up things for everyone else.

52

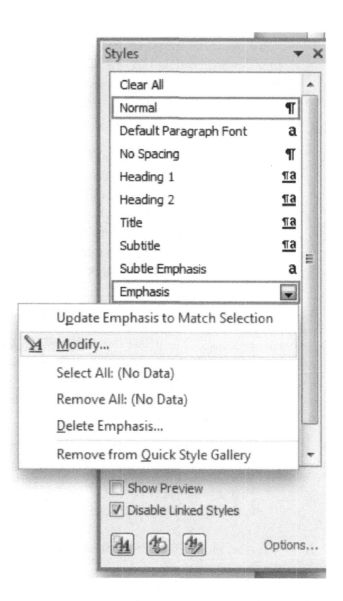

Figure 4.6
Modifying a style

4.5. How to Modify a Style

Most template configuration involves modifying existing styles. If you are creating a brief template for a document type for the first time, you will probably be able to use predefined Word styles by modifying them. Once you have a good brief template, copying that template and modifying the styles can create new brief templates for other courts.

To modify an existing style:

1. Display the style in the **Styles** pane [Windows] or **Styles** window [Mac].

2. Position the cursor over the ¶ or **a** to display a down arrow button.

3. Click on that button to display the dropdown list shown in Figure 4.6.

   You can display this same dropdown list by right clicking on the style name in the **Styles** pane (**Styles** window on Mac) or by right clicking on a button in the **Quick Style** list. These all have the same effect.

4. Select **Modify** from the dropdown list.

   This displays the **Modify Style** dialog box (Figure 4.7). This dialog box is the central location for modifying the attributes style. It is described in detail later on.

FIGURE 4.7
The Modify Style
dialog box.

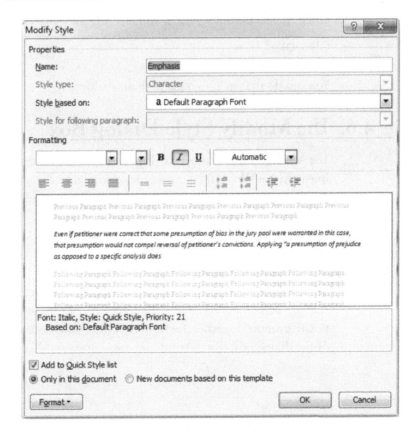

5. Make the desired changes then click **OK** to save.

Changes to styles affect the entire document. If you change a style, Word automatically updates the formatting of all text that uses the style. This keeps the formatting consistent throughout the document—but only if the document is formatted with styles. If you follow the bad practice of applying formatting directly to the text, those changes only apply to the selected text or paragraph.

The beginning of this chapter claimed that it is possible to change all the italics in a document to underlining in 4 seconds when styles are used. If the Emphasis style is consistently used for emphasis throughout the document, five clicks of the mouse changes all italics in a document of any size to underlining:

1. Click the <u>a</u> button next to the Emphasis style in the **Styles** pane.
2. Click **Modify** on the dropdown menu.
3. Click the *I* button on the **Modify Style** dialog box to toggle off italics.
4. Click the <u>u</u> button to toggle underlining on.
5. Click **OK**.

You can do that in 4 seconds without rushing.

4.6. The Modify Style Dialog Box

The **Modify Style** dialog box (Figure 4.7) is the central location for modifying a style in Word. It has two types of controls: Style management settings and Formatting settings. These are covered separately in the following sections.

4.6.1. Style Management Settings

Style management settings control how Word interacts with the style. These settings do not directly affect the formatting of the style. These settings are not all grouped together. Instead, they are found both at the top and bottom of the dialog box. The settings are are:

Name

This is the key used to identify the style. Names must be unique within a document. Style names are case sensitive. However, Word has problems when a document contains styles with names that differ only in case. You should name styles as Word does with initial capitals. You can change style names to correct mistakes or to reorganize you template.

Style type

The **Style type** is a dropdown list that can be set to **Paragraph, Character, Table** or **List** (or **Linked** on Windows). This value cannot be changed after the style is created. When modifying a style, the dropdown list is grayed out, as shown in Figure 4.7. If you make a mistake and need to change the style type, you must delete the style and recreate it.

Style based on

This dropdown list contains all the styles defined in the current document. It defines the style that the one being modified is based on. A style inherits all its formatting settings from the based on style. It uses the inherited settings unless a different value is assigned to the style. Use this setting to organize your styles to that you can make formatting modifications to as few styles as possible in your templates.

The based on style may be changed after the style has been created. This ability is useful if you want to modify the behavior of built-in styles or to restructure your own styles.

This is the only style management setting that can change the appearance of text. Changing the based on style will change any inherited formatting settings to match those of the newly selected style.

Style for following paragraph

This setting only applies to character styles. It is grayed out in Figure 4.7 because a character style is being edited. This dropdown list contains all the paragraph styles defined in the current document. It defines the style Word should use when starting a new paragraph after a style of this type. Its purpose is to minimize the amount of style changes that must be applied manually. Its value should be set to the paragraph style that is most likely to follow the current style.

Add to Quick Style list

Checking this box causes the style to be added to the **Quick Style** list on the **Home** tab of the **Ribbon**.

Only in this document

This radio button causes the changes to the style to be made in the document only. The alternative setting, **New documents based on this template,** modifies the template. The recommendation here is that this should always be set to **Only in this document**.

4.6.2. Formatting Settings

The changes you will need to make most frequently to a style are formatting settings. The **Modify Style** dialog box has controls that can change a few basic style settings. Without leaving this dialog box, you can change the style's:

◊ Typeface

◊ Type size

◊ Combinations of bold, italic and underlining

◊ Text color

◊ Line spacing

◊ Spacing before and after the paragraph

◊ Indentation

These basic controls are sufficient for formatting most character styles. Paragraph styles invariably require additional settings not found on this dialog box. The paragraph settings on the **Modify Style** dialog box are too coarse to format a document well. To access the full gamut of settings available, click the **Format** button. This displays the dropdown menu shown in Figure 4.8.

The functions of this menu are:

Font

The menu item displays the **Font** dialog box (see Chapter 6). This changes the typeface settings of the style.

FIGURE 4.8
Style settings
accessible from the
Format button

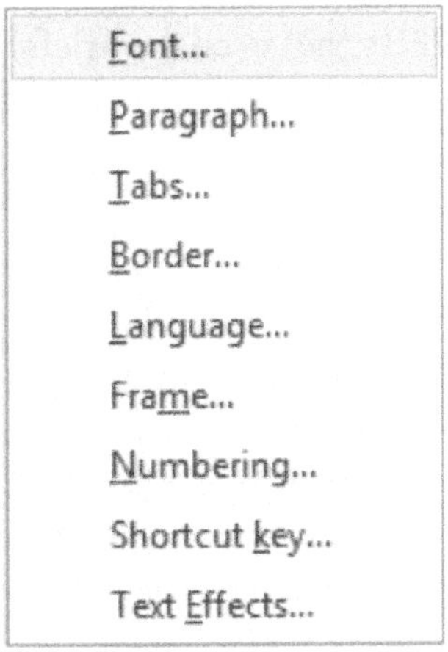

```
 ┌─────────────────────────────┐
 │  Font...                     │
 │                              │
 │  Paragraph...                │
 │                              │
 │  Tabs...                     │
 │                              │
 │  Border...                   │
 │                              │
 │  Language...                 │
 │                              │
 │  Frame...                    │
 │                              │
 │  Numbering...                │
 │                              │
 │  Shortcut key...             │
 │                              │
 │  Text Effects...             │
 └─────────────────────────────┘
```

Paragraph (paragraph styles only)

The menu item displays the **Paragraph** dialog box (Chapter 8). This changes the indentation, line spacing, and line break behavior of the style.

Tabs (paragraph styles only)

This displays the **Tabs** dialog box (see Chapter 8). It controls the placement of tabs and leader lines in the style.

Border (not used for briefs)

This defines borders that surround the text.

Language (not used for briefs)

This changes the language associated with the text. This affects spell checking. It should always be set to **English (US)** for briefs.

Frame (paragraph styles only; not used for briefs)

These settings allow a style to be placed in a separate frame (or box), outside the main text flow.

Numbering (paragraph styles only)

This controls the placement of numbers and bullets before the text (see Chapter 8). This tends to be of limited use in briefs. It is very useful for formatting pleadings.

Shortcut Key

This is used to define shortcut keys for the style (see Chapter 14).

Text Effects (not used for briefs)
This dialog box varies the appearance of text in ways that should never occur in a brief.

Word uses the same dialog boxes to format styles and to apply formatting directly to text. The behavior of (for example) the **Font** and **Paragraph** dialog boxes depends upon how they are accessed. Using them from the **Modify Style** dialog box, changes the formatting for the style and all the text in the document with that style. Accessing them from the **Ribbon** [Windows] or system menu [Mac] causes any formatting changes to be made to the currently selected text or paragraph.

4.7. How to Create a New Style

While most style changes involve modifying existing styles, there are times where you will need to create new styles for a template.

To create a new style:

1. Make sure the **Styles** pane (Styles window on the Mac) is visible:

Windows	Mac
ALT/CTRL/SHIFT/S or click the ▩ button at the lower right corner of the **Quick Style** list on the **Home** tab.	**View>Styles**

2. Click the **New Style** button—[Windows] at the bottom left. [Mac] at the top.

   This displays the **Create New Style from Formatting** dialog box. This dialog box is identical to the **Modify Style** dialog box (Figure 4.7) except for the title bar text and the **Style type** dropdown list is not disabled.

3. Set the **Name** for the style.

   Style names are case sensitive. However, having multiple styles with names that differ only in letter case causes problem. You should name styles the way Word does with its predefined styles: use all lower case with initial capitals.

4. Set the **Style type** to either **Character** or **Paragraph**.

For other types of documents you may want to create List or Table styles. However, you should *never* create linked styles [Windows only].

5. Set **Style based on** to the parent style for the new style. For character styles, this will most likely not have to be changed.

6. For a paragraph style, set **Style for following paragraph** to the style that is most likely to follow the style being created. This value should never be **Normal**.

7. Set the style formatting

8. Click **OK** to save.

Any of the style settings (except for the style type) be changed using the modify style procedure. If you need to change the style type, delete the style then recreate it with the correct type.

4.8. How to Delete a Style

You may find that you have accidentally created a style that you no longer need or that you mistakenly created a paragraph style when you wanted to create a character style. To correct, you will need to delete the style.

To delete a style:

1. In the **Styles** pane, click at the right side of the style you want to delete (same as modifying a style, Figure 4.6).

2. Select **Delete** from the dropdown menu.

Word does not allow you to delete its own, pre-defined styles.

4.9. How to Change the Style Set

There may be times where you want to reformat a document. For example, you may have a document that was created using a brief template for one court and you decide that you want to use it in another court. You can accomplish this task by changing the template associated with a document.

60

When you change the template, Word applies the style formatting defined within the new template to the existing document. Figure 4.9 shows two versions of a brief. At the top is the original version. The one on the bottom shows how the brief appears after changing templates.

FIGURE 4.9
An original brief (top) and the same with a new template (bottom).

ARGUMENT

The government's supplemental brief is tantamount to a confession of error.

The government banned Citizens United's Video On Demand distribution of *Hillary* on the strength of its asserted interest in preventing corporations from deploying "immense aggregations of wealth" to "influence unfairly the outcome of elections." *Austin v. Mich. State Chamber of Commerce, 494 U.S. 652, 660, 669 (1990).*

But now that the Court has expressed a willingness to reexamine that rationale, the government, astoundingly, has abandoned it. *Nowhere* in the government's supplemental brief will the Court find any mention of the "different type of corruption"—"the corrosive and distorting effects" purportedly accompanying any corporate or union participation in electoral politics—on which both *Austin* and *McConnell* relied. 494 U.S. at 660; 540 U.S. 93, 205 (2003). Indeed, the very word "distortion"—so prominent in *Austin*—now seems to have fallen out of the government's vocabulary altogether; it appears not once in the government's supplemental brief.

ARGUMENT

The government's supplemental brief is tantamount to a confession of error.

The government banned Citizens United's Video On Demand distribution of <u>Hillary</u> on the strength of its asserted interest in preventing corporations from deploying "immense aggregations of wealth" to "influence unfairly the outcome of elections." <u>Austin v. Mich. State Chamber of Commerce</u>, <u>494 U.S. 652, 660, 669 (1990)</u>.

There are a couple of issues with this kind of reformatting. First, Word only updates the style definitions. The page layout (*e.g.*, margins) remains the same. Second, the style names in use need to be the same in the two templates. If you call the block quotation style Quote in one template and Block Quotation in the other, Word does not know how to match the two styles up.

This process for changing templates is slightly different in Windows and the Mac. The following sections address each system separately.

4.9.1. How to Change the Template on Word 2010

To change the document template:

1. Select **File>Options** from the **Ribbon** to displays the **Word Options** dialog box (Figure 4.10).

FIGURE **4.10**
Word Options
dialog box

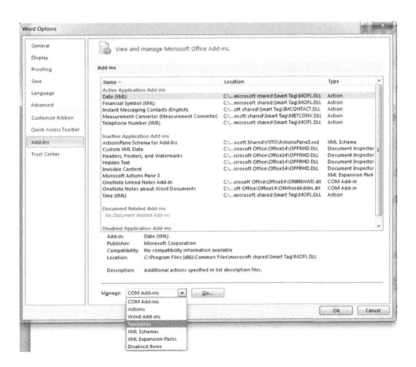

2. Select **Add-Ins** from the list at the left.

3. Set the value of the **Manage** dropdown list to **Templates**. then click the **Go** button to display the **Templates and Add-ins** dialog box (Figure 4.11).

FIGURE 4.11
Changing the document template [Windows]

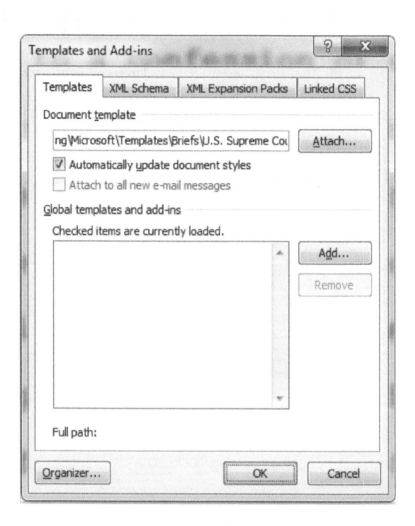

4. Check the **Automatically update document styles** box.

5. Click **Attach**.

6. Select the desired template and then click **Open**.

7. Click **OK** to apply the style settings from the selected template to the document.

4.9.2. How to Change the Template on Word 2011 for Mac.

To change the template:

1. Select **Tools>Templates and Add-Ins** from the system menu.

This displays the **Templates and Add-ins** dialog box (Figure 4.12).

FIGURE 4.12
Changing the
document template
[Mac]

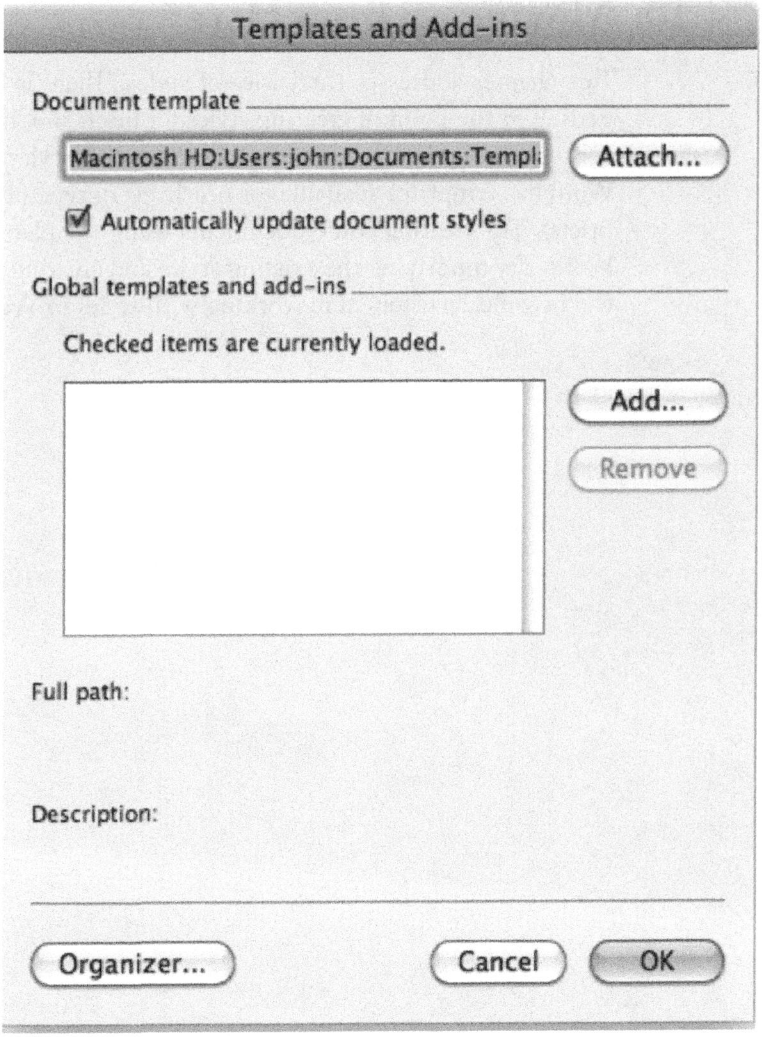

2. Check the **Automatically update document styles** box.

3. Click **Attach**.

4. Use the file selection dialog box to select the desired template, then click **Open**.

5. Click **OK** to save.

This should apply the style settings from the selected template to the document.

4.10. Moving on from Here

This chapter addresses the basics of styles. There is lot of material before getting to the point of creating styles for briefs in Chapter 9. At this point, it is recommended that you explore the use of styles in existing templates. Word has templates available for nearly every type of document (except for briefs). Try creating some documents using templates already available in Word. Try modifying the existing styles and creating new styles so that you can become accustomed to working with styles in Word.

Chapter 5
A Brief Style Set

The objective of this chapter is to show how to determine the types of styles needed for a given brief template. Before creating a template, it is a good idea to identify the major styles that it will contain. This does not have to be an exhaustive list; just sufficient to get an idea of the basic structure. Styles can be added, modified and deleted later on. As a general rule, every change in font or spacing in the text represents a change in style.

The set of styles illustrated in this chapter has been created by identifying the different formatting elements found in briefs. The examples shown come from actual briefs. This style set is used as the basis for demonstrating formatting in subsequent chapters. The set of styles described here represents just one example of how things can be organized. One principle followed here is that extra space is always added before paragraphs.

Your own templates should incorporate styles that represent the type of formatting you use in your briefs. The objective is to show a possible structure for styles within a template and illustrate why certain styles may be needed. You can use any structure that fits your needs and use style names that are most convenient. A rule to follow is that any variation in typeface, type style, type size, indentation or numbering represents a distinct style.

When you define the style set, keep in mind the following guidelines:

1. Feel free to add whatever styles you need to your templates. At the same time;

2. Try to keep the number of styles to a minimum. Avoid duplicate and unlikely to be used styles. It is perfectly acceptable to have multiple styles with the same formatting if they are used for different purposes. This can make reformatting easier.

3. A style's names should describe its function—not its formatting.

4. Use the same names for styles across templates. If you use different names, you cannot reformat a document by changing templates.

5.1. Body Text

We start by considering the formatting needs for body text. Most text in a brief is likely to be formatted using first line indented paragraphs.

> The district court sentenced Abbott to 20 years in prison. Judgment 2. The court concluded that, under the ACCA, Abbott was subject to a 15-year term of imprisonment for his Section 922(g) conviction. Abbott Pet. App. 28a-29a. The court imposed the ten-year stat-

This style formatting is called Body Text in the sample style set. Word has a predefined style using this name that can be used for this purpose.

A formatting variation that occurs frequently in briefs is body text that resumes after a block quotation. Word treats this as a distinct paragraph even though it is not a paragraph grammatically.

> aquatic resources that results from replacing water with dredged material or fill material; and (2) the contamination of water resources with dredged or fill material that contains toxic substances.
>
> S. Rep. No. 95-370, at 74 (1977). As Congress, the courts, EPA, and the Corps have all long recognized, the Section 404

The style set defines this formatting in a new style called Body Text Continue. It differs from Body Text by having space before and having no first line indent. Word predefines styles called Body Text 2 and Body Text 3 that could possibly have been used here. We have chosen not to use them because those style names are not descriptive of the function.

Another formatting variation in body text is a paragraph with a first line indentation that follows a quotation.

> action for damages arising from any occurrence at a location mentioned or addressed in such reports, surveys, schedules, lists, or data.
>
> Pertinent constitutional provisions are reproduced in the appendix to the certiorari petition (Pet. App. J1-J2).

The style set calls this Body Text Continue Indent. This style differs from Body Text formatting by inserting space above the paragraph.

The style set incorporates one additional style whose existence is driven primarily by function rather than appearance. This is for body text paragraphs that immediately follow a heading: Body Text First. This style serves two purposes. First, it allows space to be added before a heading. This can be useful when you want to have headings that occur sequentially to be spaced closer to each other than to the surrounding body text. Second, it allows paragraphs after a heading to be formatted differently than other body text paragraphs.

5.2. Block Quotations

A major formatting element in many briefs is block quotations. These are indented on the left or both sides and often with space above and below. These are two common variations on how a block quotation starts. One has the first line flush with the rest of the quotation. This indicates a quote that does not start a paragraph.

> and a small portion of it happens to fall back." *Id.* at 1403-1404. The court, however, expressly stated:
>
> > [W]e do not hold that the Corps may not legally regulate some forms of redeposit under its §404 permitting

This style of formatting is called Block Quotation in the style set. If differs from the Body Text style by being indented from the margin and lacking first line indentation.

When the quotation occurs at the start of a paragraph, the first line is usually indented.

> drainage," "plowing," and "seeding." 33 C.F.R. 323.4(a)(1)(iii); 40 C.F.R. 232.3(d). With respect to plowing, the regulations state:
>
> > *Plowing* means all forms of primary tillage, including moldboard, chisel, or wide-blade plowing, discing, har-

This variation produces another style called Block Quotation Indent in the style set. It differs from they Block Quotation style by having a first line indentation.

Sometimes a block quotation will extend over multiple paragraphs. A second paragraph in a quotation will have to be indented and will probably not have additional space above as at the start of the block quotation. This style set includes a Block Quotation Continue style that represents additional, indented paragraphs in a quotation.

5.3. Numbered Paragraphs

Numbered paragraphs are the staple of pleadings. Sometimes a few numbered list paragraphs occur in briefs.

> 1. Whether the decision of the Supreme Court of Washington was a final judgment of that court that this Court has jurisdiction to review by certiorari under 28 U.S.C. 1257(a).
>
> 2. Whether respondent may pursue a challenge that the privilege of Section 409 exceeds Congress's powers under Article I of the Constitution, given that the State of Washington and petitioner do not object to that provision.

Word's built-in style Numbered List can be used for such lists. You can modify this style for your formatting needs.

5.4. Examples of Possible Additional Styles

The scope of a brief template should match your needs. There are many other possible styles that could occur within brief text. These are some examples that could be added to a template. They are mentioned here as possibilities but will not be discussed further.

One of the features that you may want to add at some point is styles to formatted hierarchical quotes of statutes:

> (1) Except as provided in paragraph (2) of this subsection, the discharge of dredged or fill material–
>
> (A) from normal farming, silviculture, and ranching activities such as plowing, seeding, cultivating, minor drainage, harvesting for the production of food, fiber, and forest products, or upland soil and water conservation practices;

Another possible style could format quotations from transcripts:

> auctioning the licenses—the FCC insisted that the bankruptcy court should return the licenses to it. C.A. App. 589.
>
> Court: So, the FCC might get more money for the American public under a new license or it might get less?
>
> [Gov't]: Money is not the end goal. * * *
>
> Court: Money is not the objective.
>
> [Gov't]: No. * * * Congress told us what the objective was. * * * A fair and efficient allocation of the limited resource of radio spectrum.
>
> Court: All right, I hear the words. They have no content for me.
>
> *Id.* at 590-591. See note 14, *infra*.

These examples represent just some of the possibilities. Others include, unnumbered subheadings, section dividers (* * *) and signature lines. For the sake of simplicity, the example style set does not include styles for these constructs. You should have no inhibition about adding styles to your templates to support constructs you use in your documents.

5.5. Footnotes

Word predefines a Footnote Text style. This style is adequate for briefs with basic footnotes. Sometimes, footnotes get much more elaborate. Here is a footnote with a quotation.

> [4] The legislative history reveals that Section 404(f) was a compromise formulated by the Conference Committee, in response to divergent House and Senate proposals, that struck a balance between the concerns of agriculture and the congressional goal of wetlands protection. H.R. Conf. Rep. No. 95-830, at 100-101 (1977). As Senator Muskie, the Senate manager in conference, explained in the debate on the conference bill:
>
> > New subsection 404(f) provides that Federal permits will not be required for those narrowly defined activities that cause little or no adverse effects either individually or cumulatively. While it is understood that some of these activities may necessarily result in incidental filling and minor harm to aquatic resources, the exemptions do not apply to discharges that convert extensive areas of water into dry land or impede circulation or reduce the reach or size of the water body.
>
> 3 CRS, Library of Congress, *A Legislative History of the Clean Water Act of 1977*, at 474 (1978) (*Leg. His.*), (Sen. Muskie, Dec. 14, 1977).

All the quotation variations that can occur in body text are possible in footnotes.

> [22] In their reply brief at the petition stage, petitioners claimed that "[t]he government's statement that *Akers* involved "rippers" is **false**." Pet. Reply Br. 4 (emphasis in original). Petitioners' accusation is incorrect. The district court's decision in *Akers* makes clear that a ripper was used:
>
> > Various sections of the southern wetlands were disced with farm equipment. Prior to the discing, the areas were ripped with a chisel

If a brief has to support these types of quotations in footnotes, there needs to be footnote styles that are analogous to the Body Text Continue, Body

Text Continue Indent, Block Quotation, Block Quotation Indent and Block Quotation Continue styles.

Keep in mind that any construct that can occur within body text or quotations can occur within footnotes as well. For example, here is a nested statute in a footnote.

---

[4] Section 2244(d)(1) provides:

A 1-year period of limitation shall apply to an application for a writ of habeas corpus by a person in custody pursuant to the judgment of a State court. The limitation period shall run from the latest of—

(A) the date on which the judgment became final by the conclusion of direct review or the expiration of the time for seeking such review * * *.

5.6. Headings

Briefs are traditionally organized around hierarchical headings that use different numbering schemes (sometimes with type variations) to indicate structure.

A. The Full-Time Employee Rule Reflects A Reasonable Interpretation Of The Student Exemption

1. The statutory text supports the full-time employee rule

Word defines 9 styles (Heading 1–Heading 9) that should serve this purpose. A number of Word features (including document maps and table of contents generation) are tied to these heading styles. Therefore, these styles should be modified, rather than creating your own styles. As a practicable matter, brief headings rarely exceed five levels. This style set applies that limit and only uses Heading 1–Heading 5.

It may be useful to restructure the heading styles so that each heading level is based upon the previous heading level. This makes it easier to adjust spacing. The down side is that it makes other formatting more difficult. Spacing tends to be the hardest part of formatting headings so this tradeoff may be beneficial.

The style set defines one special heading that is used for the table of contents. The table of contents heading is usually formatted like a top level heading. However, one generally does not want this heading to appear in the table of contents. A way to get around this is to define a style based on Heading 1 that is set up so that it does not appear in the table of contents. We call this style Heading 1 NoTOC.

5.7. Table of Contents

Most briefs have a table of contents. When Word creates a table of contents it uses the built-in styles TOC 1–TOC 9 to build it. By default, these styles map to Heading 1–Heading 9. In other words, a heading using the style Heading 2 has a table of contents entry in the style TOC 2. The table of content styles must be formatted as part of the style set.

5.8. Table of Authorities

For a simple table of authorities, a template only needs styles for the sections (*e.g.*, statutes, cases) and the entries. More complex tables of authorities can have multiple levels of entries. Three levels of entries, as shown in the following example, tend to be the limit.

Constitution, statutes and rule:
U.S. Const:
Art. I 28
§ 6, Cl. 2 29
§ 8 .... 22, 24

The style set uses the style TOA Section to format sections. The styles TOA 1, TOA 2 and TOA 3 format entries.

5.9. Cover Text

It is suggested that you have a style dedicated to text that appears on the cover of your brief. This style serves to isolate the cover from changes to styles made in the rest of the document.

5.10. Character Styles

The scope of character styles is much more limited than that of paragraph styles. All briefs will need a style for emphasis (italics or underlining). As shown in Chapter 4, Word predefines the Emphasis style that will serve that purpose. Sometimes briefs use bold in addition for emphasis (although that is often discouraged[1]). Word's built-in Strong style handles that formatting.

> "[t]he government's statement that *Akers* involved "rippers" is **false.**"

5.11. Moving on from Here

Figure 5.1 on the following page shows the structure of the sample style set. The styles are indented to show their based on relationships. Word's built-in styles are marked with an asterisk. Remember, this chapter shows just one way to do things. Feel free to set up your templates in the way that best meets your needs.

Examine your briefs and identify the formatting variations that you use. Follow the process shown in this chapter to identify the types of styles that you will need for your briefs. Compare your needs with the sample style set to identify what you will need to add, delete or modify while setting up the styles within your template.

[1] Scalia, p. 122

74

FIGURE 5.1
The completed style
set

Normal*
  Body Text*
   Body Text First
   Body Text Continue
   Body Text Continue Indent
   Block Quotation
    Block Quotation Indent
    Block Quotation Continue
  Footnote Text*
   Footnote Text Continue
   Footnote Text Continue Indent
   Footnote Quotation
    Footnote Quotation Indent
    Footnote Quotation Continue
  List Number*
  Heading 1*
   Heading 2*
    Heading 3*
     Heading 4*
      Heading 5*
TOC 1*
 TOC 2*
 TOC 3*
  TOC 4*
  TOC 5*
TOA Section
 TOA 1
 TOA 2
  TOA 3
Cover Text

Default Character Font
  Emphasis
  Strong

Chapter 6
Typefaces

The use of typefaces is one of the factors that has the greatest impact on the appearance of a brief. The typeface used sets the overall tone of the brief. The objective of this chapter is for you to learn:

◊ The basics of typefaces, type styles and fonts

◊ How to select typefaces, including how court rules drive this selection.

◊ How to use Word's typeface features

6.1. Typefaces Communicate

The typeface you use in a brief communicates a message. Consider the message that each of these typefaces would convey to the court if used in a brief:

Summary of the Argument

Summary of the Argument

Summary of the Argument

Summary of the Argument

Summary of the Argument

Summary of the Argument

Summary of the Argument

Some of these typefaces are likely to present a positive message. Others are likely to turn the court against you right from the start.

Restrictions on typeface usage in court rules exist because lawyers have used clearly inappropriate ones in briefs. It should go without saying

NEW JERSEY

MANUAL ON STYLE

FOR

JUDICIAL OPINIONS

that a goofy typeface like Comic Sans should not be used in documents that are intended to be taken seriously. Unfortunately, the obvious often gets ignored (Figure 6.1).

Typefaces tend to develop associations from overexposure. Those associations become part of your message when you use a typeface. If you create your brief in Times New Roman, the message you convey is *cheap paperback book*. Using Bodoni will generate for the reader images of

VOGUE

IBM

MAMMA MIA!

If you use Futura in a brief, you better hope your judge is not a pilot. A pilot reading such a brief is not going to stop thinking

ILS or LOC RWY 22L

Some of the worst looking briefs this author has seen have been set in the Bookman font. Another author eloquently described the problem with this typeface by stating, "Bookman evokes the Ford administration. If fonts were clothing, this would be the corduroy suit."[1]

6.2. Terminology

Baseline
The *baseline* is the imaginary line which a row of text is aligned. The bottoms of upper case letters are optically aligned with the baseline. Characters may have descenders that extend below the baseline (*e.g.*, g, j, p, q, y).

Typeface
A *typeface* is a set or family of related fonts having the same basic design. Times New Roman, Century Schoolbook and Courier New are examples of typefaces. There is a tendency to conflate the terms *typeface* and *font* (see below).

Type Style
A *type style* is a classification of type appearance. The basic Word type styles are:

◊ regular (sometimes called roman, normal, book, or medium)

◊ italic

◊ bold

◊ bold italic

◊ small capital

There are many other common types styles that do not have direct support in Word. Such type styles include

◊ Oblique (Sometimes called slanted)—Similar to italic, except that the characters are merely sloped and not stylized.

◊ Light—Upright text with a lighter weight than regular.

◊ Extra Light—Upright text with a lighter weight than light

---

[1] Butterick, p. 131.

◊ Semibold (Sometimes called demibold)

◊ Extra Bold—Upright text with a heavier weight than bold.

◊ Condensed—Narrower than normal characters.

◊ Expanded—Wider than normal characters

A type designer may combine these to produce other styles, such as *extra bold italic* or *condensed bold*.

Font

The term *font* has different meanings, depending upon the context. Until the 20th Century, nearly all printed text was created with moveable type. In moveable type systems, each glyph (or character) is created by a single piece of metal type. Printers, from Johannes Guttenberg to Benjamin Franklin, typeset pages by arranging individual pieces of metal type in the mirror image of the printed page. Starting in the late 19th century, systems started to appear that mechanically composed lines of text using keyboard mechanisms.

When applied to moveable type, a font is a complete set of metal glyphs in a single face (*e.g.*, Times, Courier), style (*e.g.*, Roman, bold, small capitals, italic or bold italic), and size (*e.g.*, 10 pt.). Moveable types fonts come in cases divided into separate compartments for each character (or character combination). A single font in its case could weigh nearly a hundred pounds.

Moveable type has largely been relegated to formal documents, such as invitations, where the texture created by type impacting on paper is desirable stylistically. During the 20th century moveable type was largely replaced by offset printing and digital printing. In offset printing, text is composed on circular printing plates that deposit ink on a page as they rotate. The text on the printing plate usually is created using light sensitive materials, similar to developing a photograph from a camera negative. Probably the most revolutionary change in printing has come from the widespread adoption of digital systems, such as laser printers, allowing anyone to print high quality documents at relatively low cost. For both digital printing and offset printing, the page composition is usually done using computer software, such as Word.

Computer fonts are software that is written rather than physically made. Each font is stored in a separate file (or, in some cases, multiple files). The type designer creates instructions to draw the lines and curves to make up each character. Since there is no physical type, a computer can scale the characters to any size. The same font file that creates 11 pt. book sized text can also produce 40 pt. text for posters. Consequently, size is not a defining characteristic of a computer font as it is with a metal font. From the perspective of a computer type designer or software developer, a font consists of a set of characters in a specific face and style. For example, Arial Roman, Arial Bold, Arial Italic, and Arial Bold Italic are four distinct fonts.

Font scaling generally only works well over limited range of sizes. A font that looks good at typical reading sizes of 10–12 pt. might not look good at 48–72 pt. Some foundries produce sets of fonts in the same face and style that are designed for different size ranges.

It is unfortunate that Word's user interface does not mimic the relationship among fonts, typefaces and type styles. Word conflates font and typeface into font and treats type styles as options. This may simplify things for the beginner, but it makes things more difficult for those who are concerned with the details of appearance. Some of the issues will become more apparent further in this chapter.

6.3. Typeface Classifications

There are a two typeface classifications that are most important in court rules. The first is the distinction between *serif* and *sans serif* typefaces. Serif typefaces have wings at the end of letters. Sans serif typefaces do not have these wings. Figure 6.2 illustrates the difference between a sans serif and serif typeface.

FIGURE 6.2 The difference between a sans serif (left) and serif (right) typeface.

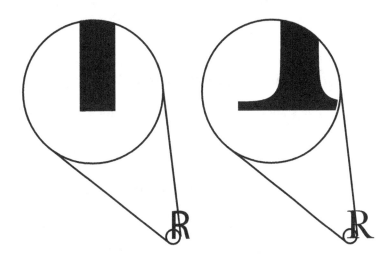

Serif typefaces are preferable to sans serif typefaces in brief text. In print, serif typefaces tend to be more readable than sans serif. However, it is common to use sans serif typefaces in headings for contrast. Some court rules (*e.g.*, Fed. R. App. P. 32(a)(5)) explicitly permit this convention. It should be pointed out that a few courts require sans serif fonts be used in briefs (*e.g.*, Conn. R. App. P. 67-2(A)).

The other important classification in court rules is the distinction between proportional and monospaced typefaces. In a proportional typeface, the width of the characters varies: I is narrower than M. Monospaced typefaces make every character the same width

Times New Roman is a proportional typeface.

```
Courier New is a monospaced typeface.
```

Monospaced typefaces are a relic of typewriters (and the continuing needs of computer programmers). The creators of typewriters found that it was simpler to make inexpensive, mechanical typing devices when every character was the same width.

Monospaced type has at least two major problems. First, it is difficult to read. Printers have known the advantage of proportional type for centuries. It would be difficult to go to a bookstore and find a book set in a monospaced type. Even in the typewriter era, books were set with proportional type. Second, there are few monospaced typefaces available that are suitable for briefs. Courier New, the leader in monospaced brief fonts, is one of the worst looking typefaces in existence (on the Mac, Courier is available as a better alternative). Monospaced fonts should only be used for the dwindling number of courts that require them.

6.4. Type Measurement

The standard unit of measurement for type is a *point*. Historically, point was an approximate unit of measure that varied in size depending upon the geography and among vendors. The computer industry has standardized on a fixed measure where a point is exactly $\frac{1}{72}$ of an inch. There are various ways of measuring fonts. Figure 6.3 shows the major measurements of font size.

FIGURE 6.3
Typeface
measurement

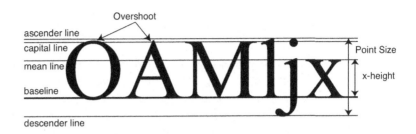

Point size is most commonly used measurement of type size. It is the distance from the highest point of the tallest character to the lowest point on any descender of a lower case character.

The point size measures the physical range that characters of the font can occupy. This is important when laying out rows of text. Unfortunately, point size does not give true measure of the apparent text size.

Point size is generally a measurement of the height of capital letters. However, most characters in a document are in lower case. Lower case characters of the same point size can be different sizes.

The next example shows characters in two fonts of the same point size. The character on the left is about 20 percent larger than the one on the right.

Xx

A font's *x-height* is the height of a lowercase x in a font. This measurement gives a better indication of the apparent size of a font than point size. Unfortunately, there is no simple way to determine x-height in Word. One generally has to use relative x-heights by placing text using different typefaces side-by-size.

The differences in character sizes produce enormous variations in the physical length for the same text. The width of both lower and upper case letters of the same font size vary among typeface. Therefore, merely changing the typeface changes the length of the text.

The following examples show the same text set in Century Schoolbook and then in Times New Roman:

> We the People of the United States, in Order to form a more perfect Union, establish Justice, insure domestic Tranquility, provide for the common defense, promote the general Welfare, and secure the Blessings of Liberty to ourselves and our Posterity, do ordain and establish this Constitution for the United States of America.

> We the People of the United States, in Order to form a more perfect Union, establish Justice, insure domestic Tranquility, provide for the common defense, promote the general Welfare, and secure the Blessings of Liberty to ourselves and our Posterity, do ordain and establish this Constitution for the United States of America.

The version in Times New Roman is a line shorter. As the name suggests, Times New Roman was designed for newspapers. Narrow newspaper columns dictated the need for narrow characters. Using Times New Roman in place of Century Schoolbook has a significant effect on text length.

The variations in character sizes affects compliance with court rules. For exampke, Alaska R. App. P. 513.5(c) permits Times New Roman and Century Schoolbook in briefs. R. 212(c)(4) limits the length of an initial or response brief to 50 pages. A complying, 50-page brief set in Times New Roman is likely to be a non-complying 60-page brief if the same text is set in Century Schoolbook.

This is not intended to be an endorsement of Times New Roman. On the contrary, Times New Roman is a typeface that should be avoided whenever possible. However, these examples do illustrate how typefaces can affect brief size and compliance with court rules.

Many courts have eliminated this problem by using Word counts to set brief limits, for example Rules of the U.S. Supreme Ct. R. 33(1)(g). Chapter 14 addresses word counts.

Pitch is a measurement that is often used with monospaced fonts. Pitch is the number of characters per inch in the font. A larger pitch means smaller characters in a font. Pitch is never used to measure proportional fonts.

Two related measurements affect the spacing of lines. *Leading* (as in the metal) is the amount of space between lines of text. Some court rules (*e.g.*, U.S. Supreme Ct. R. 33(1)) specifies the minimum leading. *Line spacing* is the space between corresponding positions of adjacent lines. The sum of the point size and the leading gives the line spacing. The spacing between lines is set using line spacing in Word.

6.5. Space Between Characters

Word has two mechanisms for adjusting the spacing between characters. The first of these is called *character spacing*. The very same concept is called *letter-spacing* or *tracking* in typography. The other mechanism is called *kerning*.

6.5.1. Character Spacing

Character spacing is the amount of space consistently inserted between letters. These examples show text with reduced character spacing, normal character spacing and expanded character spacing.

> Character spacing controls the amount of space between letters.
> Character spacing controls the amount of space between letters.
> Character spacing controls the amount of space between letters.

The general rule is that text in all capitals or small capitals should have increased character spacing and that lower case text is not changed.[2] This shows a heading with default spacing and slightly expanded spacing.

SUMMARY OF THE ARGUMENT
SUMMARY OF THE ARGUMENT

There is no set rule for the amount of spacing to add. You just adjust for best appearance. Generally, the amount of increase is relatively small.

Sometimes justified text can create absurdly wide gaps, as in the third line of this example:

> Current DHS regulations permit aliens to work on student visas under five different programs: 1) On campus employment, 8 C.F.R. § 214.2(f)(9)(i);   2) Off   campus   employment,   8 C.F.R. § 214.2(f)(9)(ii); 3) Internship with an international organization,

---

[2] Bringhurst, p. 30.

Judicious adjustments in spacing can eliminate such gaps:

> Current DHS regulations permit aliens to work on student visas under five different programs: 1) On campus employment, 8 C.F.R. § 214.2(f)(9)(i); 2) Off campus employment, 8 C.F.R. § 214.2(f)(9)(ii); 3) Internship with an international organi-

One should make such adjustments sparingly. Word simply is not a typesetting program. Trying to use it like one can cause trouble.

You should not use character spacing to circumvent page limits. Some court rules explicitly prohibit this. This should be considered an implicit prohibition under all court rules.

Some typefaces have condensed styles (*e.g.*, condensed, condensed bold, condensed italic) where the characters are narrower than normal. Condensed styles are great for printing warning labels on electonic devices that must fit in a confined space. Condensed styles should never be used in briefs.

6.5.2. Kerning

Kerning is the process of optimizing space between letter pairs. The font designer can spacify how to space specific character sequences, based upon the shape of the characters. Kerning is used to create a more appealing spacing across the entire height of characters. With metal type, typesetters kerned letter pairs by cutting off the corners of letter pairs.

Normally, characters are spaced based upon their overall width. This works well as long as the letter shapes are generally vertical.

HUN

Compare the following example to the one above:

AVA

The horizontal spacing of these letters is the same as in the example before. However, the shape of the letters creates larger space between them. Kerning, creates more uniform spacing by allowing letters to overlap vertically:

AVA

Unlike character spacing, kerning has little effect on the overall length of text. Some court rules confuse kerning with character spacing. They prohibit the former when they probably intended to ban the latter.

There is no real downside to enabling kerning. However, Word disables it by default. The urban legend explanation is that kerning would cause problems with ancient, slow computers. You can enable kerning globally by modifying the Normal style.

6.6. Number Formats

There is a growing trend for fonts to include two types of number forms (lining and old style) with two types of spacing (proportional or tabular). These combine to give four different type of numbers. Word allows you to choose which number format from those available in the font.

Lining figures are drawn entirely over the text baseline like upper case characters. *Old Style figures* descend below the base line like lower case letters. Compare

Lining 1776 1234567890
Old Style 1776 1234567890

Lining figures are analogous to capital letters and old style figures are analogous to lower case letters. Old style figures can give a more formal look to body text. However, they tend to look out of place in headings. The choice of which to use is up to personal preference. A template can use both number forms in different styles.

The term *tabular* means *monospaced*. In general, proportionally spaced figures should be used with proportional typefaces. However, tabular figures can be used in special situations where digits need to align vertically:

$ 19,456.78
$ 2,111.11
$ 21,567.89 Tabular

$ 19,456.78
$ 2,111.11
$ 21,567.89 Proportional

6.7. Ligatures

Ligatures are symbols that represent multiple letters. The most familiar ligatures are in foreign words, such as Cæsar or Baß. Ligatures are used commonly in printing English text as well. However, English ligatures tend to be subtle and designed to eliminate collisions between certain letter sequences. The following example shows the same text set without ligatures and with ligatures. In the text without ligatures, the ball of the letter f runs into the letters l and i. The bottom text combines ffl and fi into single characters.

Sniffle finger
Sniffle finger

Some typefaces are designed so that they do not need ligatures. The characters in such typefaces are designed so that no letter pairs come close or overlap. Palatino is an example of such a typeface. Notice that the letters below do not collide.

Sniffle finger

Ligatures only work with fonts that are designed to use them. Enabling ligatures has no effect with many fonts.

Word allows you to enable or disable ligatures for a style. The decision whether to use ligatures or not is one of appearance. If ligatures convey the effect you desire, use them. Otherwise, leave them out. Ligatures can be enabled globally by modifying the Normal style.

6.8. Typeface Selection

Typeface selection for briefs is a function of three factors applied in this order:

1. Compliance with court rules

2. Availability

3. Appearance

Each step in the process reduces the number of candidates. In many cases, court rules alone may effectively limit you to one choice. Appearence, in that case, never enters the equation.

6.8.1. Court Rules and Type Faces

The first consideration in selecting a typeface is the court rules. Courts define permitted typefaces with different levels of specificity:

1. No restrictions—*e.g.*, Rules of the Supreme Court and Court of Appeals of the State of Arkansas

2. General specification—*e.g.*, California Supreme Court and Courts of Appeal, California Rules of Court, R. 8.204(b)(2)("Any conventional typeface may be used.").

3. Related typefaces—*e.g.*, U.S. Supreme Court requires a Century Family typeface. R. 33(1)(a).

4. Substantially Similar to—*e.g.*, Maine R. of App. P. 9(f) "Appropriate type styles to use include Bookman, Courier, Geneva, Georgia, or other similar type styles."

5. Specific typefaces—*e.g.*, Conn. R. App. P. 67-2(A) "Only the following two typefaces, of 12 point or larger size, are approved for use in briefs: arial and univers." Alabama R. App. P. 32(a)(7) "The font of all documents filed in the appellate court must be set in Courier New 13".

The set of fonts that come with Word allow you to comply with the typeface requirements of any court. In some cases, you may have a choice of only one typeface. However, there will always be at least one. Word is so widely used that no court is going to adopt rules that hinder creating a compliant brief with it.

There are implicit typeface rules that apply to all courts. First, all court rules implicitly specify that a plain text typeface should be used. Script fonts, decorative fonts, poster fonts, blackletter fonts and anything similar should not be used, even if the rules do not explicitly prohibit them. Second, body text should be written in roman (normal, regular, book) style.

6.8.2. Font Availability

After court rules, the next practicable limit on typeface choice is font availability. In the final analysis, you can only use fonts you actually have. For most people, the selection range is the fonts that come with their operating system and Word. Others may have text processing applications installed that have added additional fonts. A few brave lawyers have purchased additional fonts.

This analysis of font availability is more complicated than Word's user interface might suggest. Briefs using proportional serif typefaces nearly always use regular, italic and bold fonts (those using sans serif or monospaced typefaces generally only use regular and bold). Many people like to use bold italic as well. Each of these is a distinct font. When you choose a typeface, you need to select one with fonts for all the type styles you will use.

Many of the typefaces shipped with Word do not include all of the basic type styles (regular, bold, italic, bold italic). For example, Word includes the Baskerville Old Face Regular font. This looks like a perfectly acceptable typeface for a brief. Unfortunately, Word includes no other type styles to go with this font, making it unusable for briefs. The Bell MT typeface comes with regular, bold and italic style. This will work in a brief as long as there is no need for bold italic type.

6.8.2.1. Simulated Type Styles

Word's user interface obscures the problem of missing type styles by masking the underlying typeface and type style relationships of fonts. Word uses a three-step selection process (see Figure 6.7). First, you select the type typeface (called a *font*). Second, select the type style (regular, bold, italic or bold italic). Finally, select whether small capitals are used. Word always allows you to select from among eight distinct styles for *every* typeface—regular, italic, bold, bold italic, regular small capitals, italic small capitals, bold small capitals, and bold italic small capitals—without regard to whether the corresponding font is installed on the system.

Word gets around this problem by simulating type styles when they are not available. This simplifies the font selection process for beginning Word users at the cost of producing dreadful text. Look carefully at the letters in a typeface with real italics and bold available. Theis example shows Century Schoolbook regular, Century Schoolbook italic, and Century Schoolbook bold; three fonts that ship with Word:

Century Schoolbook regular.
Century Schoolbook real italic.
Century Schoolbook real bold.

Notice that that the letter shapes vary among the different styles. The letter shapes in the regular and italic versions are quite different. The italics have curved strokes at the bottom of many lower case letters and the italic k is closed at the top. The regular and bold characters are different as well but the changes are more subtle. One example is that the tops of the bold characters are nearly horizontal in places where they are sloped in the regular font.

Now look what Word does when the font is unavailable:

Baskerville Old Face regular.
Baskerville Old Face simulated italic.
Baskerville Old Face simulated bold.

Word has created the italics by sloping the regular font. There is no other difference in letter shape. These fake italics give very little emphasis. Likewise, Word has created bold text by making the letter strokes heavier. There is no change in letter shape. The letter spacing of the bold text is simply odd. Simulated bold, italic and bold italic type styles simply look terrible. They should never be used within briefs.

6.8.2.2. **Small Capitals**

Small capitals are a distinct type style in which the lower case letters are smaller versions of their upper case counterparts. In a quality small capital font, the strokes of the lower-case letters are adjusted to fit their smaller size. They are not merely smaller version of the upper-case letters. However, Word simulates small capitals by doing just that. The example below shows real small capitals (top) compared to Word's simulated version (bottom). Notice the strokes of the real small capitals are somewhat heavier than the simulations so that they are in better proportion with the capital letters.

RONALD WILSON REAGAN
RONALD WILSON REAGAN

The real small capitals look better than the simulated version. However, unlike with simulated bold, italic or bold italic, the difference is subtle.

Small capitals present an interesting problem in Word. Word's small capitals option *always* creates simulated small capitals—even if real small capitals are available. Word creates the small capitals by using ordinary capital letters of a smaller size.

This problem of using small capitals in Word is compounded by the way small capitals are stored in font files. With the older TrueType font format that once dominated the industry, small capitals were stored in a separate file. In Word, this shows up in the **Font** dialog box as a distinct font that can be selected to use real small capitals. The TrueType format has now been superceded by the OpenType format. With the new OpenType font format, the trend is to have small capitals stored as alternative characters within a font. For example, regular small capitals will be stored in the same font file as the regular font. There is no way to automatically access these small capital characters in Word. You can usually insert small capitals character by character with such fonts, but it is a tedious process.

There is also a problem of availability of real small capitals. None of the typefaces that ship with Word or Windows have small capitals. There are only a few Mac system fonts that have small capitals.

The view here is that small capitals are one of the places one has to yield to the limitations of Word. Real small capitals look better than the simulated version. However, simulated small capitals tend to look close to the real version, unlike simulated italics and bold. Unless you have small capitals available for your typeface in a separate font file, just go with Word's simulated version. The only place small capitals are likely to occur in a brief are on the cover page, so this should not be a problem. However, do not use simulated bold, bold italic and italic small capitals.

6.8.2.3. Ensuring needed fonts are available

You can see the available typefaces on the **Font** dialog box (below) and in the font dropdown list on the **Home** tab. Unfortunately, these give no indication of what font styles are actually available. To find whether a specific typeface and style combination is available, use the Control Panel [Windows] or Font Book [Mac]. Remember that you only need to have the styles that you actually are going to use.

6.8.2.3.1. How to Check Fonts on Windows.

Windows manages fonts through the Control Panel:

1. Select **Control Panel** from the Windows system start menu.

2. Select **Appearance and Personalization.**

3. Select **Fonts**.

4. Double click on a typeface to see the available fonts.

Figure 6.4 shows the fonts available for the Bell MT typeface: regular, bold and italic. If you do not want to use bold italic text in your brief, this typeface has all the needed styles.

FIGURE 6.4
The Control Panel shows Bell MT has regular, bold and italic styles available [Windows].

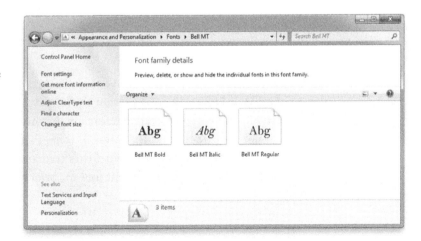

6.8.2.3.2. How to Check Fonts on the Mac

On the Mac you can find the available fonts directly from within Word. The **Font** menu displays the typefaces installed and the available type styles.

If you want to browse in a more leisurely manner, you can use the Font Book application. Font book is the utility the Mac uses to manage fonts. It is started from the Application stack. Once running, you can use Font Book to display samples from each font.

Figure 6.5 shows how some typefaces appear in Font Book. The Baskerville font that ships with the Mac has regular, bold, semibold and italic versions of these. However, the Baskerville Old Face font that ships with Word only has the regular style available.

FIGURE 6.5
Use Font Book to check for available fonts [Mac].

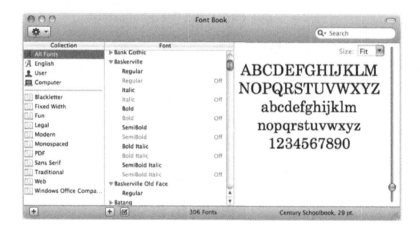

6.8.2.4. Buying Fonts

The gamut of fonts extends well beyond those that come with Word. In fact, the standard Word fonts do not represent the best available for brief writing. You can extend the range of available fonts by buying them. Because most people will not venture beyond the range of fonts that comes with Word, a typeface that you buy can became your firm's trademark. One word of caution: You are not going to find a decent font for brief text on a *5000 Greatest Fonts* disk.

6.8.3. Font Appearance

The final consideration (after court rules and availability) for typeface selection is appearance. This consideration is a bit more challenging than the others because the choice is primarily subjective. You should use a typeface that *you* feel comfortable putting before a court.

6.8.3.1. Basic Rules

Here are three basic rules for typeface selection:

1. Always prefer proportional typefaces over monospaced.

   Florida R. App. P. 9.210 states, "Computer-generated briefs shall be submitted in either Times New Roman 14-point font or Courier New 12-point font." That means use Times New Roman.

2. Always prefer serif typefaces to sans serif.

   Oregon R. App. P. 5.05(4)(f) states, "If proportionally spaced type is used, the style shall be either Arial or Times New Roman". That also means use Times New Roman.

3. Do not use non-Latin fonts.

   Many fonts are designed for languages that do not use Latin characters, such as Arabic, Chinese, Hebrew and Korean. These fonts usually have Latin characters defined as a convenience. On Windows, such fonts are sometimes indicated in the Font dropdown by non-Latin characters to the right in the **Home>Font** dropdown list. In Figure 6.6, one can see that

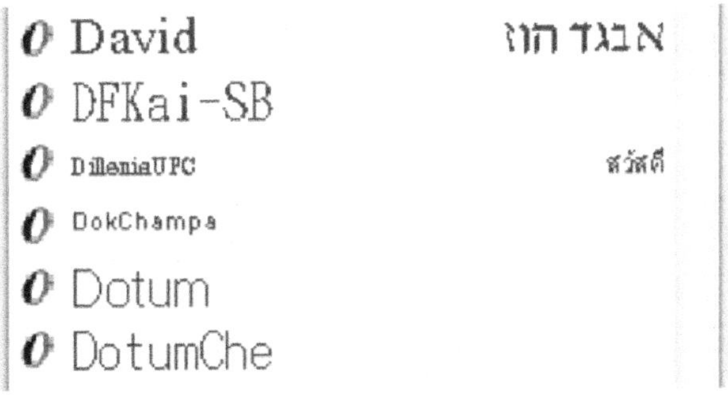

FIGURE 6.6
Non-Latin fonts are sometimes indicated in the Font dropdown list.

David is a Hebrew font. Usually, you have to go by the name to identify a non-Latin font. DFKai-SB is a Japanese font, DokChampa is a Lao font, and Dotum and DotumChe are Korean fonts.

6.8.3.2. Font Size and Appearance

Always test fonts at the size you intend to use in the brief. Type size affects appearance of a font. For example, the Century Schoolbook font that comes with Word looks fine at 10–12 pt. At 14 pt. the letters appear clunky.

One area where court rules conflict with readability is on font size. Fonts tend to be most readable around 9–12 pt. size range, depending upon the font.[3] Larger font sizes tend to force the reader to look at words rather than sentences, reducing comprehension. Printers had settled on font sizes of about 10 pt. for books long before scientists started to experiment with readability and confirmed that this is the best size.

Court rules generally specify a minimum font size that usually ranges from 11–14 pt. Generally, you should use the smallest font size allowed. The only exception would be if you planned to use a font with a small x-height under rules that permit an 11 pt. font. In that case you might want to bump up to 12 pt.

Some courts have recognized that requiring excessively large type can be counterproductive. The Seventh Circuit's Cir. R. 32(b) permits a 12 pt. font for use in the body text and 11 pt. in footnotes, compared to the 14 pt. requirement of Fed. R. App. P. 32(a)(5).

One way to compensate for large fonts in court rules is to use a typeface with a smaller x-height, such as Caslon or Garamond. At 14 pt., Garamond will have an x-height that is close to that of 12.25 pt. Times New Roman.

6.8.3.3. Test Printed Output

Always evaluate fonts using printed samples. A font that looks good on the screen may not look good in print. Likewise, a font that does not look good on a screen may look exceptional on print. The reason for this is pixel density. Laser printers have about 1.5 million pixels per square inch. Computer monitors tend to have about 15,000 pixels or fewer per square inch. The details of serif fonts tend to be obliterated on low-resolution computer monitors. Strokes that appear normal on a computer screen can appear too

---

[3] Swanson, p. 102.

heavy on the printed page. Strokes that appear normal on a printed page may appear faint on a computer monitor.

Some serif typefaces have been optimized for computer monitors by muting the serifs. Such typefaces include Cambria, Constantina and Georgia. These compromise typefaces should be avoided in briefs.

6.8.3.4. Evaluate Punctuation

Once you have your printed output, examine the characters closely in the fonts you are considering. One area where fonts vary considerably is in punctuation. Some fonts may contain stylized punctuation that you may not like. Here are three examples that show differences in punctuation:

> "[N]one of [the exceptions to the rule against nonparty pre-clusion] extend generally to the situation of a would-be absent class member with respect to a denial of class certi-fication"); 18A Wright & Miller § 4455, at 457–458. Century Schoolbook

> "[N]one of [the exceptions to the rule against nonparty preclu-sion] extend generally to the situation of a would-be absent class member with respect to a denial of class certification"); 18A Wright & Miller § 4455, at 457–458. Palatino Linotype

> "[N]one of [the exceptions to the rule against nonparty preclusion] extend generally to the situation of a would-be absent class member with respect to a denial of class certification"); 18A Wright & Miller § 4455, at 457–458. Bell MT.

Start by looking at the quotation marks. In Century Schoolbook and Bell, they have distinct balls at the end. In Palatino, they are rather straight, like pen strokes. In Bell, the brackets are highly stylized. Some people may find the quotes in Palatino and the brackets in Bell unattractive. Others may have no problems with these attributes.

6.8.3.5. Evaluating Italics

Fonts vary in how they treat italics. The following example shows text in Times New Roman (top) and Galliard (bottom) in Roman and italic. While the italics in Times New Roman differ from Roman by being lighter and sloped, in Galliard the italic characters are more stylized. Many of the italic characters are shaped quite differently from their roman counterparts, notably in this example g and a. If you want much emphasis in italics, Galliard is a good choice. If you want italics to be subtler, Galliard is the wrong way to go.

> Bennington Foods LLC v. St. Croix Renaissance Group
> *Bennington Foods LLC v. St. Croix Renaissance Group*
> Bennington Foods LLC v. St. Croix Renaissance Group
> *Bennington Foods LLC v. St. Croix Renaissance Group*

6.9. Using Word's Typeface Features

This section is a reference for using the **Font** dialog box. The **Font** dialog box is the central point for making typeface changes in Word (Figure 6.7). Word permits change to basic typeface settings in other locations (*e.g.*, on the Home ribbon tab). The **Font** dialog box is the only place where all the settings are found together. As you set up the styles in your briefs, refer back to this section when you need to make changes to the typeface settings,

In most cases, you will access the **Font** dialog as part of modifying a style (by selecting **Format>Font** on the **Modify Style** dialog box). When you make typeface changes in this manner, they are applied to all text with the style. The best way to set the main font for a brief is to modify the Normal style. Because all predefined styles are based on Normal, this usually sets the font for all styles other than headings.

In a very few situations, such as formatting a cover page, you will access the **Font** dialog box directly to modify text:

Windows	Mac
CTRL/D	**Command/D**; or **Format>Font**

When used in this manner, changes made on the **Font** dialog box only affect the currently selected text.

The settings on the **Font** dialog box are divided across two tabs: **Font** and **Advanced**. These are described in the following sections.

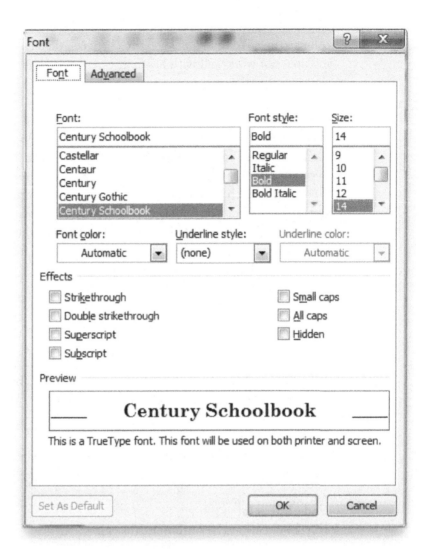

6.9.1. Font Tab Controls

The **Font** tab contains the basic typeface, type style and type settings as well as the most common font settings.

Font
This selects the typeface. At the top of the list, Word shows **+Headings** and **+Body** [Windows] or a typeface name followed by **(Theme Body)** or **(Theme Headings)**[Mac]. These are used by a Word feature called *Themes*. Themes function like mini-templates where you can define typeface and

color settings. You can quickly switch between themes. This kind of switching does not work well with briefs. It is recommended that you do not use themes with briefs

Font Style

This selects the type style. Some commercial fonts do not work well with the **Font** dialog box. The typeface may appear in multiple groups (such as Book, Medium, Semibold) but within the groups you have to select the type style. In such cases be sure that you only select combinations that exist so that you do not get simulated typefaces. With either of these conditions, it is possible to select an italic font listed under **Font** then select **Italic** under **Font Style**. This causes Word to start with an italic font and slant it even more—resulting in very bizarre text.

Size

This sets the type size in points.

Font color

This should always be **Automatic** (meaning black). Brief text should be black only. That means no shades of gray as well.

Underline style

This should always be **(none)** or set to a single line when using underlining for emphasis.

Underline color

This should always be **Automatic** (black).

Strikethrough

Checking this box causes the text to be drawn with ~~a line through it.~~ This is always unchecked for briefs.

Double Strikethrough

Checking this box causes the text to be draw with a ~~double line through it.~~ This should always be disabled for briefs.

Superscript

Checking this box causes the text to be drawn as a superscript: smaller size and raised above the baseline.

A *googol* is 10^{10}.

Superscripts are rarely used in briefs (other than footnotes) but do appear on occasion. They should be used where appropriate.

Subscript
This causes the text to be drawn as a subscript: smaller size and lowered below the baseline.

The molecular formula for sulfuric acid is H_2SO_4.

Subscripts are rarely used in briefs but should be used where appropriate.

Small Caps
Checking this box causes the text to be drawn using simulated small capitals.

All Caps
This box causes the text to be displayed in all capital letters. This is useful in headings because it allows the heading to appear in mixed case within the table of contents; something not possible if the heading is typed in all upper case letters.

Hidden
This causes the text not to be visible. This should always be left unchecked.

6.9.2. Advanced Font Features

The **Advanced** tab of the **Font** dialog box contains additional settings (Figure 6.8). These settings are for more advanced Word users. The Advanced tab is divided into two panes: **Character Spacing** and OpenType Features.

6.9.2.1. Character Spacing

As the name suggests, the **Character Spacing** pane adjusts the spacing of text. Each setting is described below.

FIGURE 6.8
The Advanced
tab of the Font
dialog box contains
additional typeface
settings.

FIGURE 6.8
The Advanced tab of the Font dialog box contains additional typeface settings.

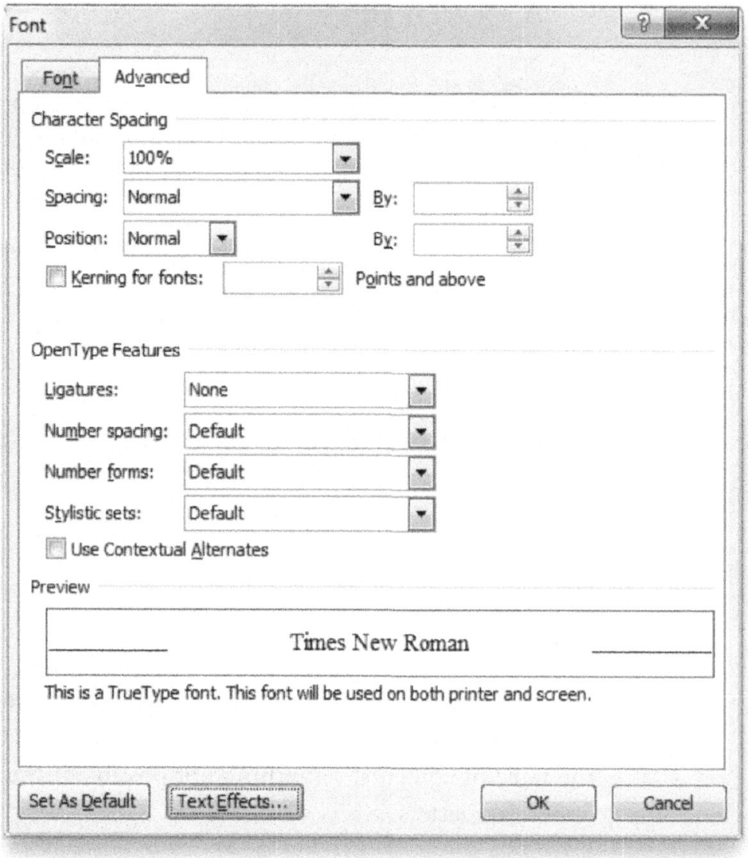

Scale

The Scale setting stretches or shrinks the text horizontally using a percentage scale. Value larger than 100% stretch the text horizontally.

United States Supreme Court

Values smaller than 100% shrink the text:

United States Supreme Court

The height of the text does not change. There is rarely any reason to use this feature in briefs. It is occassionally useful for modifying ornamental characters that can occur on cover pages.

Spacing and By

The **Spacing** control adjusts the amount of space within the text. This is called *tracking* in some applications. The effect of this setting is to expand or control the text. The Spacing dropdown list has three values:

1. **Normal**—The default character spacing is used.

2. **Condensed**—The character spacing is reduced by the amount specified in the **By** value.

3. **Expanded**—The character spacing is increated by the amount specified in the **By** value.

The **By** value is ignored when **Spacing** is set to **Normal**. The **By** setting should be changed in small increments. The minimum increment is 0.05 pt. One point in the **By** setting is approximately the normal letter spacing for a 10 pt. font.

Position and By

The **Position** can be set to **Raised** or **Lowered**. This raises or lowers the text relative to the baseline. The **By** setting specifies the amount in points. There is little use for this feature in briefs.

Text at the baseline with ^raised text^ and ₗₒwered text·

There is rarely any need to raise or lower text in briefs. It is occassionally useful for positioning ornamental characters that are sometimes used on cover pages.

Kerning

Check the **Kerning for fonts** box to enable kerning.

6.9.2.2. OpenType Features

OpenType is a format for storing fonts. Nearly all new fonts are in this format. These settings control features that are available in OpenType fonts but not with older font formats (TrueType and Postscript). These settings are not found in versions of Word prior to 2010 [Windows] and 2008 [Mac].

Ligatures

This setting disables ligatures or specifies which types of ligatures should be enabled. This value should be set to **None** (ligatured disabled), **Standard** or **Standard and Contextual**. Do not use the **Historical and Discretionary** or **All** settings for briefs. These settings can create text like this

Boston

instead of

Boston

Number Spacing

This selects the number spacing for the font. This can be **Default**, **Proportional** or **Tabular**. **Default** selects the number spacing that the font designer has selected for the default (usually **Proportional**).

Number Forms

This value can be **Default**, **Lining** or **Old Style** and controls which number form is used for the font. **Default** uses the number form the font designer has selected as the default (usually **Lining)**.

Stylistic Sets

Stylistic sets are effectively fonts within a font. They can be used to create effects like these within the same font.

Supreme Court

Supreme Court

There is no need to use stylistic sets within a brief. Leave **Stylistic sets** set to **Default**.

Contextual Alternates

Contextual alternates are characters that can be used within certain patterns of surrounding characters. Generally, these are only used with script fonts. **Contextual alternates** can be enabled or disabled, as desired.

6.10. The Font Dialog Box with Character Styles

The **Font** dialog box has a slightly different behavior when modifying a character style. For a character style, the various controls on the dialog box can have a no value setting. A no value setting means that the character style leaves in place the corresponding setting from the paragraph style applied to the text. Figure 6.9 shows how the **Font** dialog box appears when creating a character style. The **Font**, **Font style** and **Size** text boxes can be empty. The check boxes have an additional, unselected position. An empty text box or an unselected check box means that the character style does not modify that attribute.

FIGURE 6.9
The Font dialog box
when modifying a
character style

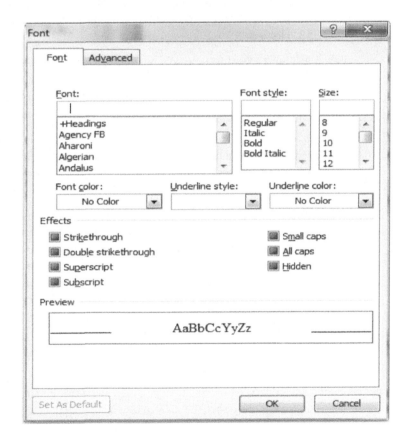

6.11. Typeface Comparisons

This section contains a side-by-side comparison of some fonts that come with Word, Windows or the Mac and are common in briefs.

Katz found a search because a person who uses a telephone booth seeks "to exclude * * * the uninvited ear" from the conversation, 389 U.S. at 352, and the government's interception of the conversation "violated the privacy upon which [the defendant] justifiably relied," *id.* at 353. Arial

Katz found a search because a person who uses a telephone booth seeks "to exclude * * * the uninvited ear" from the conversation, 389 U.S. at 352, and the government's interception of the conversation "violated the privacy upon which [the defendant] justifiably relied," *id.* at 353. Helvetica

Katz found a search because a person who uses a telephone booth seeks "to exclude * * * the uninvited ear" from the conversation, 389 U.S. at 352, and the government's interception of the conversation "violated the privacy upon which [the defendant] justifiably relied," *id.* at 353. Baskerville

Katz found a search because a person who uses a telephone booth seeks "to exclude * * * the uninvited ear" from the conversation, 389 U.S. at 352, and the government's interception of the conversation "violated the privacy upon which [the defendant] justifiably relied," *id.* at 353. Cochin

Katz found a search because a person who uses a telephone booth seeks "to exclude * * * the uninvited ear" from the conversation, 389 U.S. at 352, and the government's interception of the conversation "violated the privacy upon which [the defendant] justifiably relied," *id.* at 353. Courier

Katz found a search because a person who uses a telephone booth seeks "to exclude * * * the uninvited ear" from the conversation, 389 U.S. at 352, and the government's interception of the conversation "violated the privacy upon which [the defendant] justifiably relied," *id.* at 353. Courier New

Katz found a search because a person who uses a telephone booth seeks "to exclude * * * the uninvited ear" from the conversation, 389 U.S. at 352, and the government's interception of the conversation "violated the privacy upon which [the defendant] justifiably relied," *id.* at 353. Bell MT

Katz found a search because a person who uses a telephone booth seeks "to exclude * * * the uninvited ear" from the conversation, 389 U.S. at 352, and the government's interception of the conversation "violated the privacy upon which [the defendant] justifiably relied," *id*. at 353. Bookman Old Style

Katz found a search because a person who uses a telephone booth seeks "to exclude * * * the uninvited ear" from the conversation, 389 U.S. at 352, and the government's interception of the conversation "violated the privacy upon which [the defendant] justifiably relied," *id*. at 353. Century Schoolbook

Katz found a search because a person who uses a telephone booth seeks "to exclude * * * the uninvited ear" from the conversation, 389 U.S. at 352, and the government's interception of the conversation "violated the privacy upon which [the defendant] justifiably relied," *id*. at 353. Didot

Katz found a search because a person who uses a telephone booth seeks "to exclude * * * the uninvited ear" from the conversation, 389 U.S. at 352, and the government's interception of the conversation "violated the privacy upon which [the defendant] justifiably relied," *id*. at 353. Garamond

Katz found a search because a person who uses a telephone booth seeks "to exclude * * * the uninvited ear" from the conversation, 389 U.S. at 352, and the government's interception of the conversation "violated the privacy upon which [the defendant] justifiably relied," *id*. at 353. Goudy Old Style

Katz found a search because a person who uses a telephone booth seeks "to exclude * * * the uninvited ear" from the conversation, 389 U.S. at 352, and the government's interception of the conversation "violated the privacy upon which [the defendant] justifiably relied," *id*. at 353. Palatino Linotype

Katz found a search because a person who uses a telephone booth seeks "to exclude * * * the uninvited ear" from the conversation, 389 U.S. at 352, and the government's interception of the conversation "violated the privacy upon which [the defendant] justifiably relied," *id*. at 353. Perpetua

Katz found a search because a person who uses a telephone booth seeks "to exclude * * * the uninvited ear" from the conversation, 389 U.S. at 352, and the government's interception of the conversation "violated the privacy upon which [the defendant] justifiably relied," *id*. at 353. Times New Roman

If you did not notice a difference between Arial and Helvetica, look closely again at how the strokes end. In Helvetical they are all horizontal or vertical. In Arial the strokes and at arbitrary angles.

6.12. Moving on from Here

At this point, you should identify the typefaces that you have available and are suitable for briefs. Create a Word document containing a lengthy sample of each typeface to use for comparison and reference. Once you have identified candidate typefaces, try reformatting an old brief with each one, print them out and compare.

Chapter 7
Page Layout

The objective of this chapter is for you to learn how to set up pages within a brief template. This chapter describes how to implement various aspects of page layout, including margins, headers and footers, page numbers, rules and line numbers. These page layout elements should be added to your document templates and saved to those templates.

7.1. Paper Size

Paper size is the first step in defining the page layout. In most cases you have to do nothing here. It is most likely that the page size is already set to **Letter**. Even if you are using a commercial printer to create a booklet sized brief, it is most likely the printer will want the page laid out on a letter-sized sheet of paper (see below).

If you have to change the paper size (such as to legal):

1. Display the **Page Setup** dialog box [Windows] or **Document** dialog box [Mac].

Windows	Mac
a. Click the small button at the lower right corner of the **Page Layout>Page Setup** group.	a. Click **Format>Document**.
	b. Click **Page Setup** (Figure 7.2)
b. Select the Paper tab (Figure 7.1).	

2. Select the desired value from the **Paper size** dropdown list.

3. Click **OK** to save.

7.2. Margins

Margin settings are the next step (after page size) for laying out the page. The rest of the page setup depends on the combination of page size and margin settings. Word allows you to set the left, right, top and bottom margins as desired.

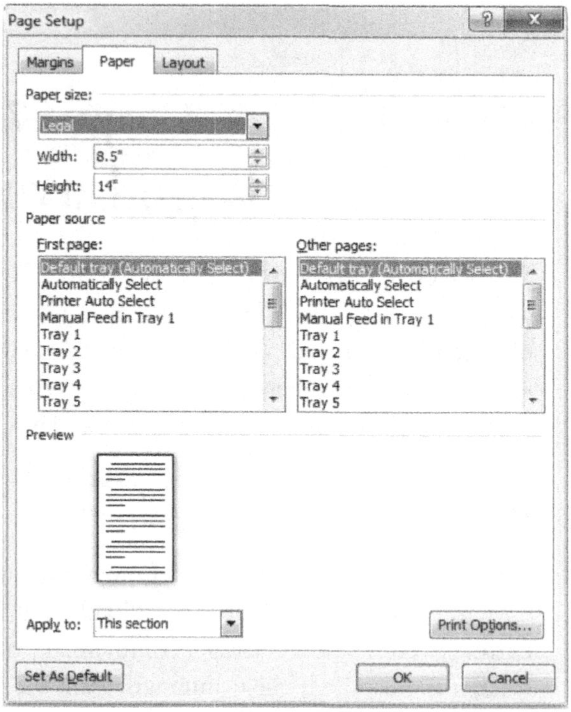

108

FIGURE 7.1
Page size settings
[Windows]

In addition, Word allows you to control the placement of the header and footer. By default, the header and footer are ½″ from the top and bottom margins. This is normal for 1″ margins. When the top or bottom margins are wider or smaller, this header and footer location usually needs to be adjusted as well.

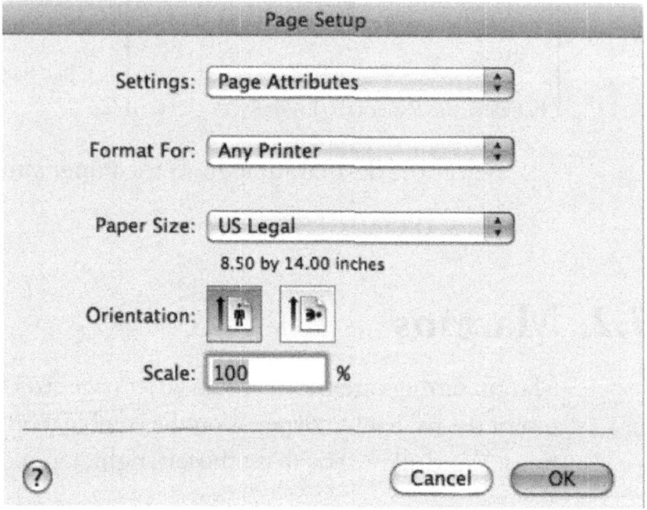

FIGURE 7.2
Page size settings
[Mac]

7.2.1. **Court Rules**

Courts rules usually have margin requirements for briefs. Some courts give requirements for all four margins. Other courts specify only one or two. Most rules specify minimum margins, allowing narrow text, if desired.

There are three ways in which courts specify margins: stating the margin width, the text field size or a combination of both:

◊ Texas Rules of Appellate Procedure R. 9.4(c), "Margins. Papers must have at least one-inch margins on both sides and at the top and bottom."

◊ Minnesota Rules of Appellate Procedure R. 132.01, "Pages shall be 8 ½ by 11 inches in size with written matter not exceeding 6 ½ by 9 ½ inches."

◊ Kansas Rules Relating to Supreme Court, Court of Appeals, and Appellate Practice R. 6.07(a), "Text, excluding pagination, shall not exceed 6 inches by 9 inches. The left margin shall be no less than 1 ½ inches and the top, bottom and right margins shall be no less than 1 inch."

The use of a text field gives the brief writer some flexibility in formatting. It allows the text to be moved outward to account for binding, for example.

7.2.2. **Line Lengths**

Ideally, a line of text should have about 66 characters (including spaces) and no more than 75.[1] When lines get longer than this they become difficult to read. When the eye has to travel a long distance to get to the next line, rereading the same line again becomes more likely.

Getting 66 characters per line on a letter-sized sheet of paper is likely to require a wider margin than dictated by court rules. At 12–14 pt. text, one may need side margins that are 1-½" to 2". Most court rules specify minimum margins, so this adjustment is usually (but not always) permitted. One should not be afraid of using margins wider than the minimum unless you are hitting page limits.

---

[1] Bringhurst, p. 26.

7.2.3. Binding

The binding method should be taken into account when setting margins. The amount of paper obscured by binding depends upon the type used. Spiral binding tends to obscure very little of the page. Stapled bindings can obscure quite a bit. If you are using a binding method that obscures part of the page, you may wish to have a narrow inside margin than outside margin if permitted by the court rules.

7.2.4. Working with Booklet-Sized Paper

The U.S. Supreme Court requires and some other courts permit briefs printed on booklet sized (9-¼" × 6-⅛") paper. This is created by printing 32 pages on both sides of a standard 38" × 25" sheet, folding in half four times and trimming. Booklet sized sheets are not normally available unless custom cut at a paper store. The court's formatting and binding requirements effectively require that a commercial printer be used for briefs.

FIGURE 7.3
Margin settings
[Windows]

Commercial legal printers normally want briefs laid out on letter-sized paper. They will specify the margins in such a way that trimming the pages will leave the text properly laid out for booklet sized paper. An issue here is that the desired location of the text on the page varies among printers. Some printers allow the text field to be anywhere on the page. Other printers want the text to be at a specific location. For example, one printer specifies 2.2″ left and right margins, a 2.15″ top margin and a 1.8″ bottom margin with the header 1.84″ from the top edge to comply with U.S. Supreme Court R. 33(1)(c) that limits the text field to 4-⅛″ × 7-⅛″.

You must contact your printer for its specifications before laying out the pages. The printer's settings will specify the margins and the location of the header and footer.

7.3. How to Set the Margins

To set the margins:

1. Display the **Page Setup** dialog box [Windows Figure 7.3] or **Document** dialog box [Mac Figure 7.4]:

Windows	Mac
Page Layout>Page Setup>Margins> Custom Margins	**Format>Document**

FIGURE 7.4
Margins Settings
[Mac]

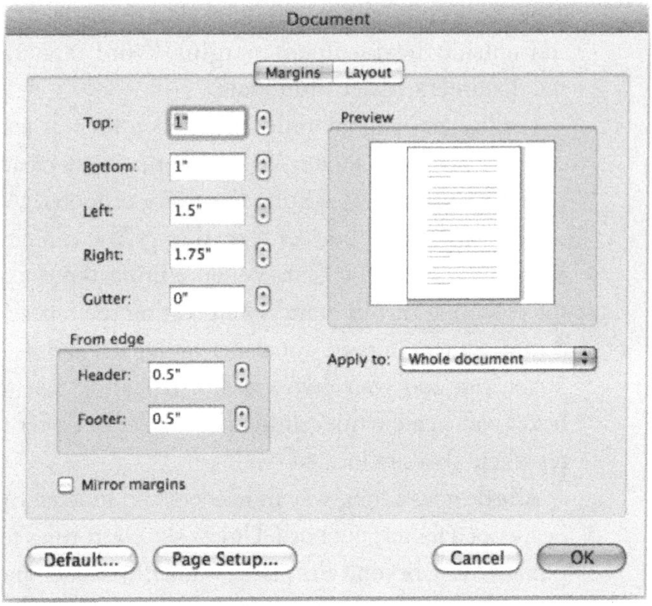

Set the **Top, Bottom, Left** and **Right** margins. Leave **Gutter** at 0″.

1. [Windows Only—Mac settings are on the same tab] Go to the **Layout** tab.

2. Set the **From edge** value for the **Header** and **Footer**, if necessary. These values should be about ½″ less than the corresponding margin.

3. Only if you need two-sided printing: Check **Different odd and even** [Windows] or **Mirror margins** [Mac].

   When this box is checked, the Right value sets the inside margin and the Left value sets the outside margin.

4. Click **OK** to save.

7.4. Headers and Footers

The *header* and *footer* are text boxes whose content repeat across multiple pages. The header is located above the top margin, extending from the left and right margin. The footer is at the bottom of the page below the bottom margin. The location of the top of the header and bottom of the footer is configurable.

The header and footer take precedence over the document margins. They grow to accommodate any text placed inside. If a header or footer cannot stay outside the document margins, Word expands the margins and shrinks the document to accommodate.

The header or footer only exists when there is text within them. When you edit the header or footer, Word automatically creates it, if it does not already exist. When you stop editing the editor or footer, Word deletes it if it is empty.

Word has two modes of text editing. You can either edit the document text or edit the repeating text. When editing the document text, Word displays the repeating text in gray. When editing the repeating text, Word displays the document text in gray. You can switch back and forth between the two modes.

You can add your own areas of repeating text to the document. Any text boxes you create while editing the header or footer repeat across pages, no matter where they are located.

A little goes a long way in headers and footers. Briefs generally have either a header or a footer; not both. Unless the court rules require it, there is no need to put anything beyond the page number in header and footer.

7.4.1. How to Edit the Header or Footer

Double click on the header or footer to edit it. When editing the header and footer area, Word displays a blue line with tabs that indicate their extent and turns the document text gray (Figure 7.5). Anything you add to the document while editing the header and footer repeats across pages. The process for creating headers that differ among sections is described in Chapter 11.

Double click on the document text to return to editing it. This returns the document text to black and the header text gray.

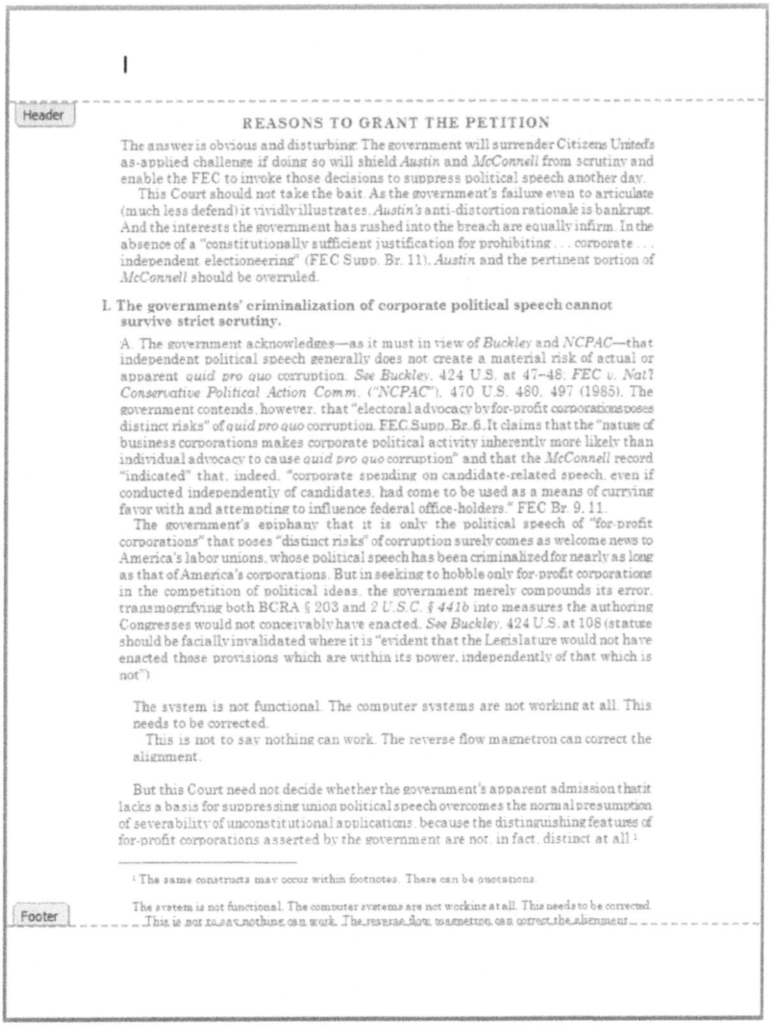

Header

REASONS TO GRANT THE PETITION

The answer is obvious and disturbing: The government will surrender Citizens United's as-applied challenge if doing so will shield *Austin* and *McConnell* from scrutiny and enable the FEC to invoke those decisions to suppress political speech another day.

This Court should not take the bait. As the government's failure even to articulate (much less defend) it vividly illustrates. *Austin's* anti-distortion rationale is bankrupt. And the interests the government has rushed into the breach are equally infirm. In the absence of a "constitutionally sufficient justification for prohibiting . . . corporate . . . independent electioneering" (FEC Supp. Br. 11). *Austin* and the pertinent portion of *McConnell* should be overruled.

I. The governments' criminalization of corporate political speech cannot survive strict scrutiny.

A. The government acknowledges—as it must in view of *Buckley* and *NCPAC*—that independent political speech generally does not create a material risk of actual or apparent *quid pro quo* corruption. *See Buckley*. 424 U.S. at 47–48; *FEC v. Nat'l Conservative Political Action Comm.* ("*NCPAC*"). 470 U.S. 480. 497 (1985). The government contends, however, that "electoral advocacy by for-profit corporations poses distinct risks" of *quid pro quo* corruption. FEC Supp. Br. 6. It claims that the "nature of business corporations makes corporate political activity inherently more likely than individual advocacy to cause *quid pro quo* corruption" and that the *McConnell* record "indicated" that, indeed, "corporate spending on candidate-related speech, even if conducted independently of candidates, had come to be used as a means of currying favor with and attempting to influence federal office-holders." FEC Br. 9. 11.

The government's epiphany that it is only the political speech of "for-profit corporations" that poses "distinct risks" of corruption surely comes as welcome news to America's labor unions, whose political speech has been criminalized for nearly as long as that of America's corporations. But in seeking to hobble only for-profit corporations in the competition of political ideas, the government merely compounds its error, transmogrifying both BCRA § 203 and *2 U.S.C. § 441b* into measures the authoring Congresses would not conceivably have enacted. *See Buckley*. 424 U.S. at 108 (statute should be facially invalidated where it is "evident that the Legislature would not have enacted those provisions which are within its power, independently of that which is not")

The system is not functional. The computer systems are not working at all. This needs to be corrected.

This is not to say nothing can work. The reverse flow magnetron can correct the alignment.

But this Court need not decide whether the government's apparent admission that it lacks a basis for suppressing union political speech overcomes the normal presumption of severability of unconstitutional applications, because the distinguishing features of for-profit corporations asserted by the government are not, in fact, distinct at all.[1]

[1] The same constructs may occur within footnotes. There can be quotations.

Footer

The system is not functional. The computer systems are not working at all. This needs to be corrected.

This is not to say nothing can work. The reverse flow magnetron can correct the alignment.

FIGURE 7.5
Editing the Header and Footer

114

7.4.2. How to Create Odd and Even Headers

You may want to have different headers and footers for even and odd pages. This is very common when using two-sided printing. Suppose you wanted to have the page number at the outside margin. With two-sided pages you need the page number at the right for odd pages and at the left for even pages.

To create odd and even headers and footers:

1. Edit the header or footer.

2. Enable odd and even headers and footers:

Windows	Mac
Check **Header & Footer Tools>Design> Options>Different Odd & Even Pages**	Check **Header and Footer>Options> Different Odd & Even Pages**

FIGURE 7.6
The Header and Footer set up for odd and even pages

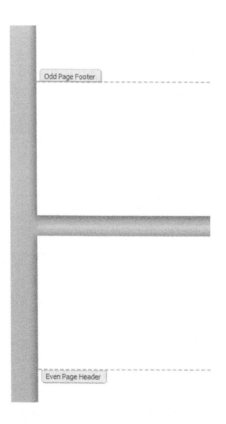

The visible indication of the change is that the blue tabs on the header and footer are updated to indicate odd or even (Figure 7.6). Scroll through the document to edit the even or odd pages. Text that you enter into the odd page header or footer only shows up on odd numbered pages. Likewise, text placed in the even page header or footers only shows up on even pages. Note that the document must have at least two pages in order to edit header or footer for even pages.

7.4.3. How to Insert a Page Number

Page numbers generally occur within the header or footer of a document. However, you can place a page number anywhere within a Word document.

1. Position the caret where the page number should appear.

Windows	Mac
	CTRL/SHIFT/P; or
ALT/SHIFT/P; or	
Insert>Header & Footer>	a. Select Insert>Field.
Page Number>Current Position>	b. Select Page (Figure 7.7).
Plain Number	c. Click OK.

FIGURE 7.7
Inserting a page
number [Mac]

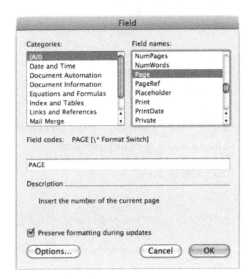

After you insert the page number, you can format it by adding additional text or using the controls on the home tab. The header and footer is one of the areas where it makes sense to format the text directly rather than using styles. Figure 7.8 shows a footer containing page numbers that have been

FIGURE 7.8
A footer containing
page number
text formatted in
various ways

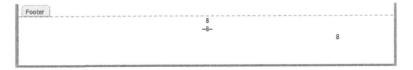

formatted in different ways. The recommendation here is that you use un-adorned page numbers unless the court rules require something different.

7.4.4. How to Change the Page Number Format

Word can insert page numbers using different forms of numbering: arabic, upper and lower case roman numerals, and upper and lower case latin letters.

To change the page number format:

1. Display the **Page Number Format** dialog box (Figure 7.9).

Windows	Mac
Header & Footer Tools>Design>	a. **Insert>Page Numbers**.
Header & Footer>Page Number>	
Format Page Numbers	b. Click **Format**.

2. Select the page **Number format**.

3. This will be **1, 2, 3 ..., I, II, III, ...** or **i, ii, iii, ...** (for front matter).

4. Select either **Continue from previous section** or **Start at** and set a value (usually 1) as appropriate.

5. Click **OK** to save.

FIGURE 7.9
Page Number
Format dialog box

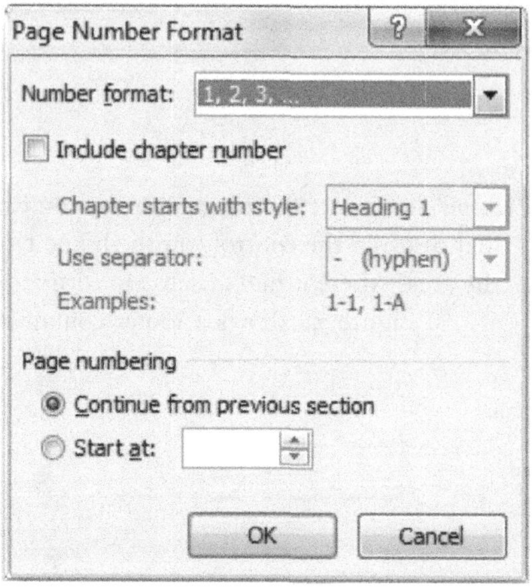

7.5. A Footer Example

California Trial Court Rules provide an example of an elaborate footer in court rules. R. 2.210 specifies:

Rule 2.110. Footer

(a) Location
Except for exhibits, each paper filed with the court must bear a footer in the bottom margin of each page, placed below the page number and divided from the rest of the document page by a printed line.

(b) Contents
The footer must contain the title of the paper (examples: "Complaint," "XYZ Corp.'s Motion for Summary Judgment") or some clear and concise abbreviation.

(c) Type size
The title of the paper in the footer must be in at least 10-point type.

Figure 7.10 shows a footer that complies with this rule.

FIGURE 7.10
A footer formatted according to California trial rules

To create a this kind of footer:

1. Double click the footer to edit it.

2. Insert the page number (using the procedure above).

3. Position the caret after the page number.

4. Press **Return** to start new line.

5. Type in the title of the paper on the new line.

6. Center the text.

7. Select the title of the paper

8. Add the separator line::

Windows	Mac
Click the down arrow next to the **Home>Paragraph>Borders** button ( ) and select **Top Border** from the dropdown menu.	**Home>Paragraph>Borders( )>Top**

The footer should now look similar to the one shown in Figure 7.10

7.6. Firm Contact Information Example

Word predefines header and footer text boxes for adding repeating text across pages. However, you can insert additional text boxes to create repeating text anywhere on the page. Whenever you enter a text box while editing the header and footer, the text box appears across multiple pages. When you create a text box while editing the document, it only appears on the page where it was inserted.

FIGURE 7.11
Contact information in the document margin

This example adds a text box that prints the firm contact information on each page. In some courts, it is local custom to have such a contact box. It should be pointed out that some courts (*e.g.*, N.C. R. App. P., Appendix B) explicitly ban this practice in their rules and that it can create unnecessary clutter in the document.

To create the contact box shown in Figure 7.11:

1. Edit the Header and Footer.

2. Insert a text box:

Windows	Mac
Insert>Text Box>Draw Text Box	**Insert>Text Box**

3. Use the mouse to adjust the size and position of the text box.

On Windows you can also right click on the text box and select **More Layout Options** in the popup menu to explicitly set the size and position. On the Mac you can also right click on the text box and select **Align** or **Distribute or Format Shape** to set the size and position.

4. Right click on the text box and select Format Shape from the popup menu.

5. Select **Text Box**.

6. Set **Text direction** to **Rotate all text 270°** [Windows] or **Rotate text 90° counter clockwise** [Mac].

7. Type in the firm contact information

8. Format the text as desired

The following steps remove the borders around the text box. On the Mac there may not be a border. If so, these steps may be skipped.

9. Right click on the border

10. Select **Format Shape** from the popup menu.

11. This displays the **Format Shape** dialog box (Figure 7.12).

12. Select **Line Color** at the left.

13. Select **No Line**.

14. Click **Close**.

FIGURE 7.12
Disabling borders
around the text box

120

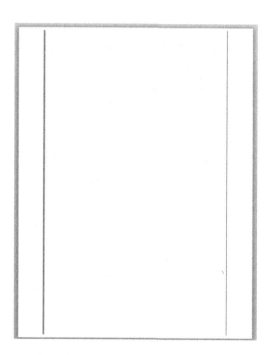

FIGURE 7.13
A page with rules.

7.7. How to Create Page Rules

Do not place rules (lines) at the margins unless court rules require them. However, some courts require ruled brief pages. Usually, rules are used in conjunction with line numbering (see below), For example, Nev. R. App. P. 32(a)(4) requires the page to be lined at the left margin.

Figure 7.13 shows a page with rules. In this example, there is a double line at the left and a single line at the right.

To create page rules:

1. Display the **Borders and Shading** dialog box (Figure 7.14):

Windows	Mac
Page Layout>Page Background> Page Borders	**Layout>Borders**

1. Select the line style for the left margin in the **Style** list.

2. Click at the left size of the page on the **Preview** pane.

3. Do the same for the right line.

FIGURE 7.14
Borders and
Shading dialog box

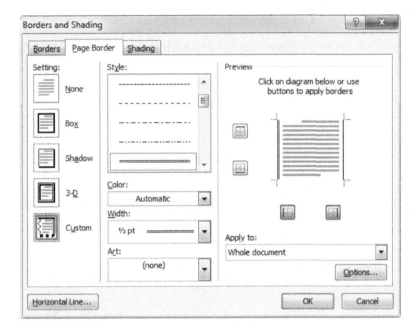

4. Click **Options** to display the **Borders and Shading Options** dialog box (Figure 7.15).

5. Set **Measure from** to **Text**.

6. You can set **Left** and **Right** to adjust the distance between the rules and the text margins.

7. Return to the document.

FIGURE 7.15
Borders and
Shading Options
dialog box

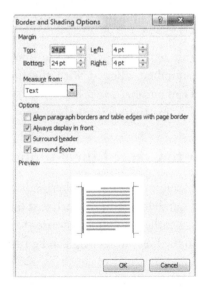

8. Double click in the header or footer.

9. Place some text in both the header and footer. This can be just a space in each.

Having text in the header and footer ensures that Word does not delete them when you return to editing the text. The default settings on the **Borders and Shading Options** dialog box have **Surround header** and **Surround footer** checked. This causes the borders to go past the margin to the start of the header or footer. Changing the location of the header or footer (Figure 7.2) changes the location of the borders. Setting the header and footer distance from the edge to zero causes the border to go all the way to the top of the page.

7.8. How to Set up Line Numbers

Do not number lines unless required by the rules. Some courts require lines to be numbered in briefs. California Trial Court Rules R. 2.208(4) gives the requirement:

> Line numbers must be placed at the left margin and separated from the text of the paper by a vertical column of space at least ⅕ inch wide or a single or double vertical line. Each line number must be aligned with a line of type, or the line numbers must be evenly spaced vertically on the page. Line numbers must be consecutively numbered, beginning with the number 1 on each page. There must be at least three line numbers for every vertical inch on the page.

This rule explicitly permits the line numbers to be done in two different ways: numbers aligned with the lines of text or numbers evenly spaced. Word can number pages either way, with the former being much simpler to do. The next two sections show how to use both methods.

7.8.1. How to Create Line Numbers Aligned With the Text

Word's automatic line numbering is the easiest way to number lines. When Word numbers the lines, each text line has a number next to it. The vertical spacing of the line numbers varies to match the text as shown in Figure **7.16**. Automatic line numbering can be turned on and off easily.

FIGURE 7.16
A brief with numbers aligned with the text

1   The statutory subsection now codified at Section

2   1512(g) originated in a House bill in 1982. H.R. 7191,

3   97th Cong., 2d Sess. (128 Cong. Rec. 26,357 (1982))

4   ("In a prosecution for an offense under this section,

5   no state of mind need be proved with respect to the

6   circumstance * * * that the law enforcement officer is

7   an officer or employee of the Federal Government.").

8   Representative Rodino, one of the sponsors of the

9   House bill, explained the purpose of including that

10   provision:

11   This provision is necessary because of the con-
12   vention that the state of mind applicable to the
13   conduct required for the offense also applies to
14   any circumstances or results that are required.
15   Because the term[] * * * "law enforcement of-
16   ficer" [is] defined in section 1515 to mean * * * a
17   Federal officer * * * it would be necessary for the
18   prosecution, absent this provision, to prove that
19   the defendant knew the * * * law enforcement of-
20   ficer was * * * a Federal officer * * * . Since the
21   * * * Federal status of the officer * * * [is a] mat-
22   ter[] that go[es] to the power of the Federal gov-
23   ernment to assert jurisdiction over conduct, ra-
24   ther than to the criminal nature of the conduct, it
25   is neither necessary nor appropriate to require
26   proof that the defendant knew the * * * officer
27   * * * was a Federal* * * officer.

28   128 Cong. Rec. at 26,351. That explanation confirms

To automatically number lines:

Windows	Mac
Page Layout>Page Setup Layout> Text layout>Line Numbers> Restart Each Page	**Layout>Text layout> Line Numbers>Restart Each Page**

To disable automatic line numbers:

Windows	Mac
Page Layout>Page Setup Layout>Text layout>Line Numbers>None	**Layout>Text layout>Line Numbers>None**

124

FIGURE 7.17
A brief with
uniformly spaced
line numbers

1	The statutory subsection now codified at Section
2	1512(g) originated in a House bill in 1982. H.R. 7191,
3	97th Cong., 2d Sess. (128 Cong. Rec. 26,357 (1982))
4	("In a prosecution for an offense under this section,
5	no state of mind need be proved with respect to the
6	circumstance * * * that the law enforcement officer is
7	an officer or employee of the Federal Government.").
8	Representative Rodino, one of the sponsors of the
9	House bill, explained the purpose of including that
10	provision:

> This provision is necessary because of the convention that the state of mind applicable to the conduct required for the offense also applies to any circumstances or results that are required. Because the term[] * * * "law enforcement officer" [is] defined in section 1515 to mean * * * a Federal officer * * * it would be necessary for the prosecution, absent this provision, to prove that the defendant knew the * * * law enforcement officer was * * * a Federal officer * * * . Since the * * * Federal status of the officer * * * [is a] matter[] that go[es] to the power of the Federal government to assert jurisdiction over conduct, rather than to the criminal nature of the conduct, it is neither necessary nor appropriate to require proof that the defendant knew the * * * officer * * * was a Federal* * * officer.

128 Cong. Rec. at 26,351. That explanation confirms

Line numbers for the quoted block: 11 12 13 14 15 16 17 18 19 20 21 22

Word applies the Line Number style to the numbers. You can modify this style to change the appearance of the numbers.

7.8.2. How to Create Uniformly Spaced Line Numbers

Another way to number lines in a brief is to have the numbers evenly spaced. The interval between the line numbers remains constant, even when the vertical spacing of the text changes, as shown in (Figure 7.17). This approach for creating line numbers is the same as used for the firm contact information box shown above.

To create fixed line numbers:

1. Double click in the header or footer to edit it

2. Insert a text box to the left of the text using the procedure in the Firm Contact Information example above. Align the text box so it is slightly to the left of the left margin and that the top margin matches the text box margin.

   The next steps remove the internal margin of the text box to that the numbers can go right next to the edge of the text box:

3. Right click on the text box.

4. Select **Format Shape** from the popup menu.

5. Select **Text Box** on the **Format Shape** dialog box (Figure 7.18).

6. Set the **Internal margin** values to 0.

7. Type the line numbers into the text box using the same style as the body text. You may wish to right align the numbers.

8. Double click within the body text to finish.

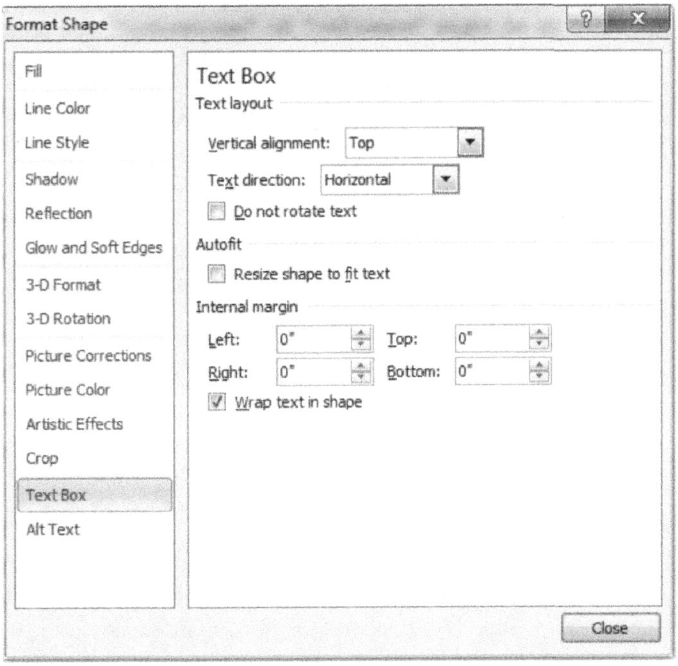

FIGURE 7.18
Removing the internal margin of the text box

7.9. Moving on from Here

After reading this chapter, you should be able to start modifying your brief templates to incorporate a page layout that follows court rules. Start by setting the margins. Next add the header or footer. Finally, add any other elements (such as line numbers or page rules) that are required. Save your template with these changes.

Afterwards, be sure to test. Try creating a new document from your template. Make sure that page layout in the new document matches your intentions with the template.

Chapter 8
Paragraph Formatting

The objective of this chapter is for you to learn how to perform paragraph formatting in Word. Most style changes made while setting up a template involve modifications to paragraph formatting. This chapter covers the three groups of style settings used in briefs that apply exclusively to paragraphs styles:

1. **Paragraph**—Alignment, indentation and control over line break within paragraphs.

2. **Tab**—Setting the position, alignment and leaders for tab stops.

3. **Numbering**—Setting up automatically numbered paragraphs or paragraphs that begin with bullets.

These settings are accessible from **Modify Style** dialog box by clicking the **Format** button.

There are two additional groups of style settings needed for brief. **Font** was covered in Chapter 6 and **Shortcut key** is in Chapter 14. Refer back to this chapter and those when you are setting up your styles.

8.1. Paragraph Settings

Word places paragraph settings on the **Paragraph** dialog box. You generally access the **Paragraph** dialog box while modifying a style (see Chapter 4) by selecting **Format>Paragraph** from the **Modify Style** dialog box.

You also use the paragraph dialog box to format text directly, for example to format a cover page.

Windows	Mac
Click the ⬜ button at the lower right corner of the **Home>Paragraph** group.	**Format>Paragraph**

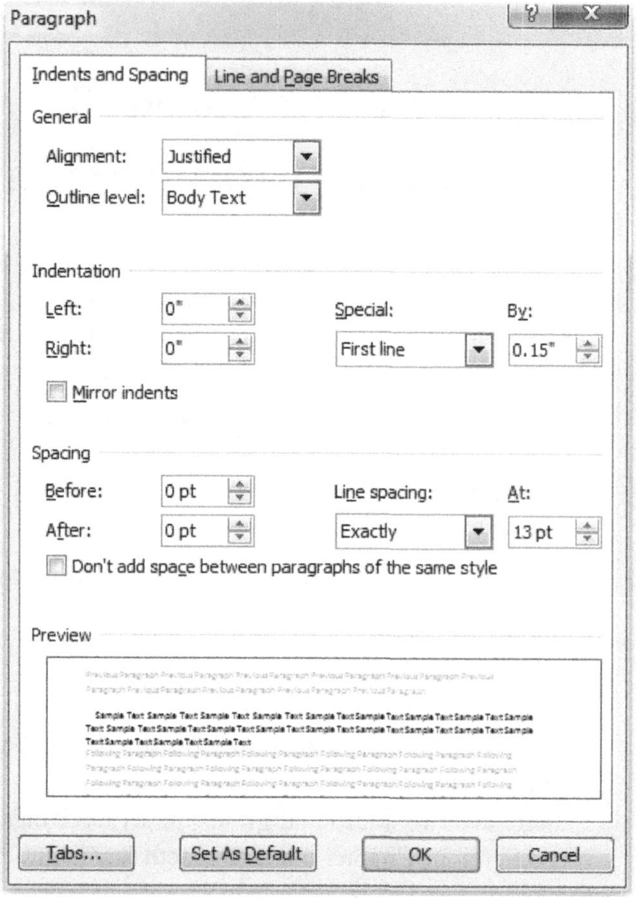

FIGURE 8.1
The Indents and
Spacing tab

The **Paragraph** dialog box's controls are spread over two tabs: the **Indents and Spacing** tab and the **Line and Page Breaks** tab. The next sections describe the features of each tab.

8.1.1. Indents and Spacing

The **Indents and Spacing** tab (Figure 8.1) contains the most frequently used paragraph settings. A number of the fields specify offsets. The unit of measurement for horizontal offsets is inches while points are used for vertical offsets. You can enter a value in inches or points into any field by appending the unit of measurement. For example:

Word converts **18 pt** entered in a horizontal offset into **0.25"**.
Word converts **0.5"** entered into a vertical offset into **36 pt**.

These are the settings on the **Indents and Spacing** tab:

Alignment

This controls the paragraph alignment relative to the margins. There are four possible settings:

1. **Left**—The text is left aligned and not justified.

2. **Centered**—The text is centered

3. **Right**—The text is right aligned.

4. **Justified**—The text is aligned to the left and justified.

For body text, the setting should be either **Left** or **Justified** (see Hyphenation and Justification below). **Centered** is often used in top level headings. The **Right** setting is rarely used within brief styles but it is frequently used for formatting cover pages (Chapter 13).

Outline level

Determines how Word maps the style to the document's table of contents struture. The possible values are **Body Text, Level 1, Level 2, ... Level 9**. The **Body Text** settings indicates that the style does not represent a heading within the document structure. The other settings map the style to the corresponding heading level within the table of contents structure. The value of **Outline level** rarely needs changing.

Indentation Left

Sets the indentation of the paragraph relative to the document's left margin. For body text in briefs, this value will be zero. Positive values indent the text. Negative values place text outside the margin.

Indentation Right

Specifies the indenation of the paragraph relative to the right margin. For most styles this value remains zero. It is possible to set tab stops past the right indentation. When this is done, tabs can be used to position text past the right indentation.

Special and **By**

Control the indentation of the first line of a paragraph relative to the subsequent lines. There are three posible values for **Special**:

1. **(none)**—The first paragraph line is flush with the remaining lines.

2. **First line**—The first paragraph line is indented the amount specified in the **By** text box. This is the setting for normal, indented paragraphs.

3. **Hanging**—Lines after the first are indented by the amount specified in the **By** text box.

The value in the **By** text is ignored when the **Special** is set to **(none)**.

This is one of the most frequently used paragraph settings. The following examples show the effect of the various settings:

The relevant statutory and regulatory provisions are reproduced in the appendix to this petition. App., *infra*, 49a–79a.—**(none)**

The relevant statutory and regulatory provisions are reproduced in the appendix to this petition. App., *infra*, 49a–79a.—**First line**

The relevant statutory and regulatory provisions are reproduced in the appendix to this petition. App., *infra*, 49a–79a.—**Hanging**

Mirror Indents

When checked, this setting switches **Left** and **Right** to **Inside** and **Outside**. This is not needed for briefs.

Spacing Before

The amount of space to add before the paragraph. If the **Don't use HTML autospacing** setting has been enabled (as suggested in Chapter 2), the total space added between paragraphs is the sum of the previous paragraph's **Spacing After** setting and the current paragraph's **Spacing Before** setting. If this option has not been enabled, the amount of space added is the larger of the two values.

Spacing After

The amount of space to add after the paragraph. You may find setting up styles easier if you only use **Before** spacing in your templates and always leave **After** set at zero.

Line spacing and **At**

Determine how lines are spaced in the paragraph. There are six possible values for **Line spacing**:

1. **Single**—Lines are spaced at the internal leading of the font.

2. **1.5 lines**—Lines are spaced at 1-½ times the internal leading of the font.

3. **Double**—Lines are spaced at twice the internal leading of the font.

4. **At least**—Lines are spaced at least the amount specified by the **At** value but may be increased to accomodate elements contained in the line.

5. **Exactly**—Lines are spaced the amount specified by the **At** value.

6. **Multiple**—Lines are spaced the internal leading of the font times the amount specified by the **At** value.

The **At** value is only used when **Line spacing** is set to **At least**, **Exactly** or **Multiple**. Otherwise, it is ignored.

You should use the **Exactly** (or possibly **At least**) setting for briefs. The other settings are based upon the internal leading defined in the font. This varies widely among fonts of the same size and can be absurdly large at times, especially for double spacing (Figure 8.2). Chapter 9 addresses line spacing for specific situations.

FIGURE 8.2 Various fonts using Word's Double spaced setting	Garamond	Times	Century	Didot
	Garamond	New	Schoolbook	Didot
	Regular	Roman	Regular	Regular

Don't add space between paragraphs of the same style

When checked, Word does not add the space specified by the **Before** and **After** settings between paragraphs that have the same style. For example, this setting allows a style the use of a style for a sequence of bulleted paragraphs to be grouped together with space above and below without creating extra space between each bullet item.

FIGURE 8.3
The Line and Page
Breaks tab

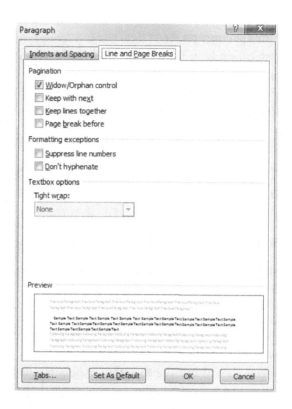

8.1.2. Line and Page Breaks

The remaining paragraph settings are on the **Line and Page Breaks** tab. These settings are check boxes that toggle features on and off. They control how Word inserts page breaks within or before a paragraph (Figure 8.3).

Widow/Orphan control

Widows and orphans are stubs of paragraphs that appear on a single page. The first line of a paragraph is called *orphan* when the rest of the paragraph appears on the following pages. The last line of a paragraph is called a *widow* when it appears at the start of a new page. Some style guides consider widows or ophans undesirable.

When this box is checked, Word automatically eliminates widows and orphans by moving text to the next page. The drawback of enabling widow and orphan control is that it tends to add extra blank space at the bottom of the page. Such extra space may look worse than widows and orphans. You can enable or disable this setting depending upon what you think looks best for a particular document.

Keep with next

When this box is checked, the paragraph is placed on the same page as the next paragraph. This is normally enabled for headings.

Keep lines together

Causes Word to place all the lines of the paragraph on the same page. This is normally enabled for headings.

Page break before

Causes Word to insert a page break before the paragraph. This is useful for heading styles in some types of documents. For example, it can ensure that a book chapter always starts on a new page. With briefs, it is generally easier to manually insert page breaks where needed.

Supress line numbers

Disables automatic line numbering for the paragraph (Chapter 7). This allows some paragraph styles to be unnumbered when the rest of the document is numbered.

Don't hyphenate

Disables hyphenation for the style. There are often places where hyphenation may be undesirable, such as on a cover page or in headings. Use this setting to disable hyphenation where it is not wanted. Whenever this setting is used, the paragraph **Alignment** should not be set to **Justified**.

Type wrap

This controls the text position within a text box. This is not used in briefs.

8.2. Justification and Left Alignment

There is no requirement that text be justified. Left aligned and justified text are both acceptable, just as they are both used in professionally typeset documents. Some court rules explicitly prohibit justified text. Colo. R. Civ. P. 10 (d)(2)(I) states, "a left-justified margin shall be used for all material." However, most court rules are silent about justificiation.

There are several reasons why you should not justify a particular brief:

◊ Text set in a monospaced font is never justified.

◊ Text set in a sans serif font is usually not justified.

◊ Text containing certain lengthy constructs (such as Internet addresses) may may look strange if it is justified.

One could add to this list the fact that it is simply easier to create properly formatted left aligned text than justified text. That said, the choice of whether to justify the text is up to personal preference.

There is a firm rule that applies to justified text: If you justify you must hyphenate as well. There are no exceptions to this rule. Justified text that is not hyphenated is one of the most obvious signs of slipshod formatting. It makes Word's relatively poor justification look even worse.

8.3. How to Enable Hyphenation

Word has two methods of hyphenation: automatic and manual. The automatic hyphenation method uses an algorithm to insert hyphens (some systems use a dictionary for automatic hyphenation). The advantage of automatic hyphenation is that it is easier to do than manual. The problem is that Word's hyphenation algorithm tends to insert odd breaks. For example, it transforms "these" into "the-se" even though it is a one-syllable word. The alternative is manual hyphenation. Under this method Word asks you where to break the word at the end of a line. Word inserts a special character called an *optional hyphen* into potential break points. An optional hyphen is not visible unless it becomes a break point (see Chapter 9 for more information). The recommendation here is that you use manual hyphenation, at least as part of the final proofreading of a brief.

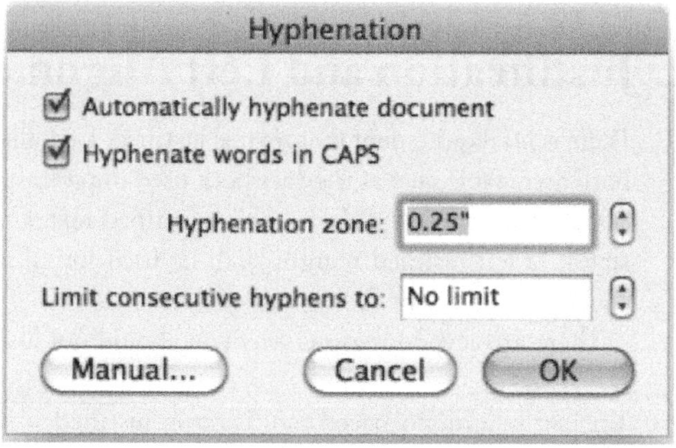

FIGURE 8.4
The Hyphenation
dialog box [Mac].

To hyphenate a document:

Windows	Mac
a. Select **Page Layout> Page Setup>Hyphenation**.	a. Select **Tools>Hyphenation**.
b. Select **Manual** or **Automatic** from the dropdown menu.	b. This displays the **Hyphenation** dialog box (Figure 8.4).
	c. Check the **Automatically hyphenate document** box or click the **Manual** button to manually hyphenate.

If you choose manual hyphenation, Word goes through the document to look for potential hyphenation points. When it finds one, Word displays the **Manual Hyphenation** dialog box (Figure 8.5). Click **Yes** to approve the suggested hyphenation point or **No** to reject it. Using this method you can ensure that the break points occur in proper locations. In addition, you can prevent technically correct but ambiguous breaks that make text hard to read, such as hyphen-ation—rather than hyphena-tion. Hyphenated line breaks should have at least two characters before the hyphen and three after. You can bypass or supplement the manual hyphenation process by inserting optional hyphen characters (see Chapter 10). The drawback to manual hyphenation is that it takes much longer to do than automatic hyphenation.

FIGURE 8.5
The Manual
Hyphenation
dialog box.

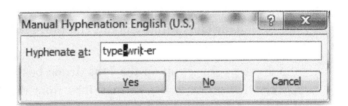

8.3.1. How to Disable Hyphentation for a Style

Word enables hyphenation for the entire document. You may have some styles that you do not want hyphenated. For example, some people do not like the appearnace of hyphenated headings. You can disable hypenation any style by checking the **Don't hyphenate** box on the **Paragraph** dialog box (Figure 8.3). If you disable hypenation for a style you must set **Alignment** to **Left**.

8.4. Tabs

There is generally little need to use tabs in briefs. You should never make the leftmost indentations of text using tabs. Always use paragraph settings for that purpose. That said, tabs are useful in certain circumstances. For example, Tabs are essential when you need to right align page numbers in a table of contents or table of authorities.

In many situations you do not even need to set tab stops yourself. Word creates an implicit tab stop at hanging indentations. If you are trying to set up a brief style to handle transcript quotations, you can set up a hanging indentation like this:

> Court: So, the FCC might get more money for the American public under a new license or it might get less?
> [Gov't]: Money is not the end goal. * * *

This text can be properly aligned by inserting **Tab** characters:

> Court: ↪ So, the FCC might get more money for the American public under a new license or it might get less?
> [Gov't]:↪ Money is not the end goal. * * *

Tabs stops are set up on the **Tabs** dialog box (Figure 8.6). To display the **Tabs** dialog box, select **Format>Tabs** from the **Modify Style** dialog box. This dialog box has three function: add a tab stop, clear a tab stop, clear all tab stops.

In addition to the position of the tab stop, there are two groups of radio buttons that control how Word displays the tab: **Alignment** and **Leader**. The behavior of each is described below.

Alignment

This radio button group sets and displays the tab alignment. There are five possible settings:

1. **Left**—The text after the tab character is aligned to the left of the tab stop position.

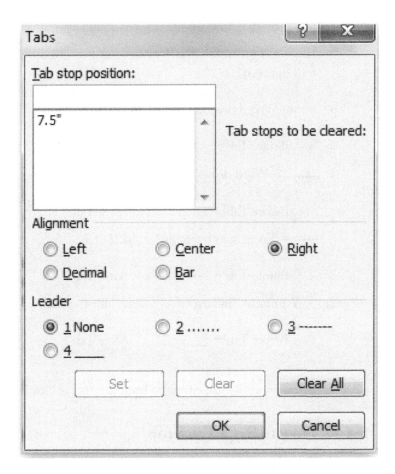

FIGURE 8.6
The Tabs dialog box

2. **Center**—The text after the tab character is aligned so that it is centered on the tab stop position.

3. **Right**—The text after the tab is aligned to the right of the tab stop position. Use this to right align numbers in a table of contents or table of autorities.

4. **Decimal**—Used to align numbers. The tab position specifies the location of the decimal point. If the text does not contain a decimal point, it is right aligned to the stop position.

Airframe↦	1,233.3 lbs
Engine↦	456.75 lbs
Avionics↦	55.125 lbs

5. **Bar**—This does not set up a tab stop but rather causes Word to draw a vertical bar at the position specified for the tab stop.

Leader

This setting controls the type of leader inserted before the text. There are four options:

1. **none**—Word does not draw a leader with the tab.

    Before Tab↪   After Tab

2. ....—Word draws a leader using periods.

    Before Tab↪ .... After Tab

3. ------ —Word uses hyphens for the leader.

    Before Tab↪ ------------ After Tab

4. _—Word uses underscore characters for the leader.

    Before Tab↪ _____ After Tab

Briefs generally use either no leaders or period leaders.

8.4.1. How to Set a Tab Stop

To add a tab stop:

1. Display the **Tabs** dialog box (Figure 8.6).

2. Enter the offset from the left margin for the tab stop into the **Tab stop position** text box.

3. Select the **Alignment** for the tab stop.

4. Click **Set**.

The tab stop should now appear in the list box. If you select a tab in that list box, Word updates the **Alignment** and **Leader** radio buttons to shows the settings for the selected tab stop.

8.4.2. How to Delete a Tab Stop

To delete all tab stops, simply click **Clear All**. To delete a single tab stop:

1. Select the tab stop to be deleted from the list box.

2. Click **Clear**.

The tab should now be removed from the list box.

8.5. Bullets and Numbering

Bulleted and numbered paragraphs do not occur regularly wthin briefs. However, they do appear from time to time, with numbered paragraphs being more common. Use numbers when the items follow a sequences or when the text indicates a fixed number of items. Use bullets when the items do not follow a sequence. In general, you do not need to create styles for bulleted or numbered list. Word predefines List Bullet and List Number styles that can be modified.

FIGURE 8.7
The Numbers and
Bullets dialog box

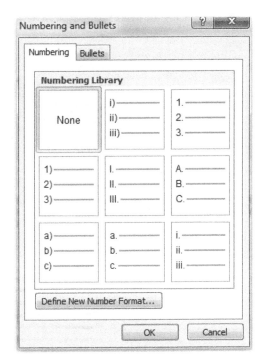

8.5.1. How to Modify a Numbered List

To modify the paragraph numbereing:

1. Select **Format>Numbering** from the **Modify Style** dialog box.

    This displays the **Numbering and Bullets** dialog box (Figure 8.7).

2. Go to the **Numbering** tab (**Numbered** tab on the Mac).

3. If the desired numbering format is available, select it and click **OK**.

    Use the following steps to set up a different numbering format:

4. Click the **Define New Number Format** button (**Customize** button on the Mac).

    This displays the **Define New Number Format** dialog box (Windows Figure 8.8) or **Customize Numbered List** dialog box (Mac Figure 8.9).

5. Select the desired number style (*e.g.*, **1, 2, 3, ..., I., II, III, ...**)

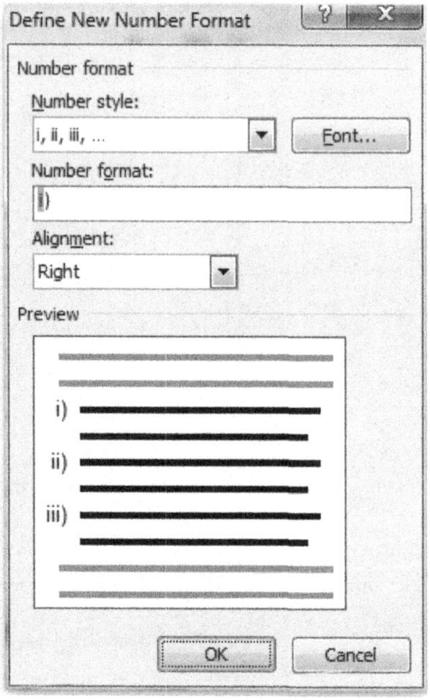

FIGURE 8.8
Defining
numbering
[Windows]

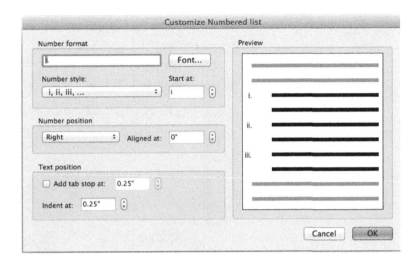

6. Set the number alignment (**Right** or **Left**).

7. Edit the **Number format** box as desired, *e.g.*, **1)** or **1.**

8. On the Mac you can set the number position and indentation at this point. On Windows, you have to return to the **Paragraph** dialog box to make these settings.

9. Click **OK** to save.

When you create a numbered list paragraph within a document, Word numbers it by incrementing the number of the previous numbered paragraph. This allows numbered paragraphs to be interrupted with unnumbered paragraphs. To start a new list, right click on the desired pargraph and select **Restart Numbering** from the popup menu.

8.5.2. How to Edit a Bulleted List

The process for formatting a bulleted list is very similar to that of creating a numbered list. The major difference is that you select a character to use a bullet rather than a number format. You may have to try various fonts in order to find one with a character suitable for the bullets.

To modify bullets for a style:

1. Select **Format>Numbering** from the **Modify Style** dialog box.

This displays the **Numbering and Bullets** dialog box.

142

FIGURE **8.10**
Selecting a bullet

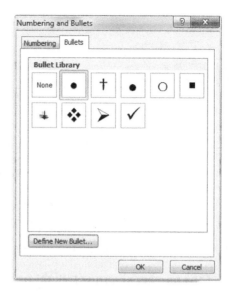

2. Go to the **Bullets** tab (**Bulleted** tab on the Mac) shown in Figure 8.10.

3. If the desired numbering format is available, select it and click **OK**.

FIGURE **8.11**
Selecting bullets
[Windows]

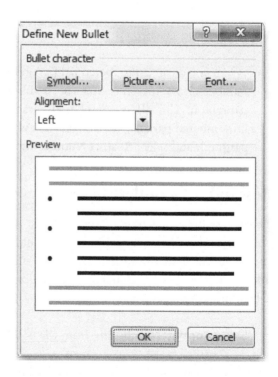

Use the following steps to set up a different bullet format.

4. Click **Define New Bullet** (**Customize** on the Mac).

   This displays the **Define New Bullet** dialog box (Figure 8.11 [Windows]) or **Customize Bulleted list** dialog box (Figure 8.12 [Mac]).

5. Click the **Symbol** button [Windows] or **Bullet** button [Mac] and select the desired symbol to use for the bullets. If you cannot find the symbol you want, click the **Font** button to select a font containing a suitable character.

6. On the Mac you can set the position of the bullet and the paragraph text. On Windows, you have to return to the **Paragraph** dialog box to set the paragraph indentation.

FIGURE 8.12
Selecting bullets
[Mac]

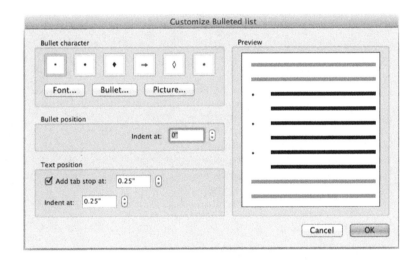

8.6. Moving on from Here

The next chapter covers how to set up specific types of brief styles. As you work the building the styles in your template, refer to this chapter for how to make specific paragraph formatting settings.

Chapter 9
Setting Up Brief Styles

Previous chapters covered the building blocks for styles:

◊ Chapter 4—How to create and modify styles

◊ Chapter 5—The styles needed for brief writing

◊ Chapter 6—Typeface settings

◊ Chapter 8—Paragraph setttings

This chapter brings together material covered in those chapters to show how to set up specific styles used in briefs. It goes though how to set up body text, block quotations, footnotes, headings and tables of contents and authorties styles. The style names used in this chapter match those from Chapter 5. These range of techniques shown through these examples should be sufficient to create nearly any style used in a brief.

9.1. Style Preliminaries

There are a few prerequisites that need to be in place before setting up your document styles. You need to have:

1. Determined the typefaces to be used.

2. Determined the type size.

3. Set up the page margins.

   These elements have been covered in Chapter 6 and Chapter 7. The recommendation here is that you set the body text typeface and size in the Normal style. This will allow you set the document font in one location. In addition you need to:

4. Determine the vertical spacing of the brief.

5. Determine the horizontal spacing of the brief.

9.1.1. Vertical Spacing

Ideally, lines in the body of text should occur at regular, consistent intervals.[1] When the body text is interrupted by quotations or headings, the text should resume on the same interval. When two-sided printing is used, body text lines on facing pages should match up.

Maintaining this interval is only practicable in Word with single spaced text or when all the lines are double-spaced. If the body text is double-spaced and quotations are single-spaced the alignment of the body text depends upon whether there is an odd or even number of lines in the quotation. In theory, one could set up additional styles to handle the odd and even situations. However, this is really not practicable. You are better off just letting Word do the best it can with vertical spacing.

If the court rules require double-spaced text, use twice the font point size as the line spacing. When the rules specify 1-½ spacing, use 1.5 times the font size.

The rules for a few courts specify leading for single spaced text. For example, Wis. R. App. P. 809.19(8)(b) specifies 13 pt. body text with 2 pt. of leading. That gives a line spacing of 15 pt. In such cases, follow the court rules.

If the rules simply specify single-spacing without indicating line spacing, there are a number of approaches to take. The simplest is to use a leading of 2 or 3 pt. This will usually work for the font sizes used in briefs. Another approach is to follow the method used by typesetting applications. Such programs tend to use a default line spacing of 1.2 times the font point size. This gives a leading of about 2.2 pt. to 2.8 pt. in brief font sizes. The expert method is to use whatever line spacing looks good with the font you are using. A few fonts are even designed to be set without any leading at all.[2] Longer lines tend to require more leading. Figure 9.1 shows 11 pt. text with various leading settings. Longer line lengths tend to require a larger line spacing than shorter lines.

Sometimes setting the line spacing to **Exactly** can cause Word to display the text with the bottoms of descenders in each line cut off. These cut off lines tend not to appear when printing or creating a PDF file. If it looks like Word is chopping the bottom off of g, j, p and q, print a sample using your settings. If the printed text looks fine, ignore the problem on the screen. Otherwise, try increasing the line spacing.

[1] Bringhurst, pp. 36–39.
[2] Lawson, pp. 256, 288, 290

FIGURE 9.1
11 pt. text set with
different leading

0 pt.
The privacy interests implicated by the government's collection of information here are minimal. The government seeks only limited, employment-related information, and the information provided is protected from public disclosure by the Privacy Act of 1974, 5 U.S.C. 552a, and by policies adopted by the relevant agencies.

2 pt.
The privacy interests implicated by the government's collection of information here are minimal. The government seeks only limited, employment-related information, and the information provided is protected from public disclosure by the Privacy Act of 1974, 5 U.S.C. 552a, and by policies adopted by the relevant agencies.

2.2 pt.
The privacy interests implicated by the government's collection of information here are minimal. The government seeks only limited, employment-related information, and the information provided is protected from public disclosure by the Privacy Act of 1974, 5 U.S.C. 552a, and by policies adopted by the relevant agencies.

2.5 pt.
The privacy interests implicated by the government's collection of information here are minimal. The government seeks only limited, employment-related information, and the information provided is protected from public disclosure by the Privacy Act of 1974, 5 U.S.C. 552a, and by policies adopted by the relevant agencies.

3 pt.
The privacy interests implicated by the government's collection of information here are minimal. The government seeks only limited, employment-related information, and the information provided is protected from public disclosure by the Privacy Act of 1974, 5 U.S.C. 552a, and by policies adopted by the relevant agencies.

5 pt.
The privacy interests implicated by the government's collection of information here are minimal. The government seeks only limited, employment-related information, and the information provided is protected from public disclosure by the Privacy Act of 1974, 5 U.S.C. 552a, and by policies adopted by the relevant agencies.

9.1.1.1. Where to Set the Line Spacing

The recommendation here is that you set the line spacing in the root style for the body text and headings. Do the same for block quotations and footnotes if their line spacing differs from the body text. Leave the line spacing for the Normal style set to **Single**. This will make it easier to lay out one-off documents elements, such as cover pages, where there may be a number of variations in font size.

9.1.2. Horizontal Spacing

Horizontal indentations should be based upon a common indentation increment. All indentations should be multiples of this increment. Consistent indentation helps prevent paragraphs, headings and block quotations from appearing haphazardly placed on the page.

Indentation is often based upon a unit called an *em*. The name refers to the width of the letter but its size is the font height. For a 9 pt. font, an em is ⅛″. The indentation increment can be rounded for simplicity. For example, a 12 pt. font gives an em of $^{12}/_{72}″ = 0.1666666666666 \approx 0.15″$.

Em based indentations may not be appropriate if the court rules require a monospaced typeface. When the rules require a typewriter look, typewriter-style indentations of ¼″ to ½″ may be more appropriate stylistically.

Some courts specify the amount of indentation. For example, N.C. R. App. P., App. B specifies tab stop locations at ½″, 1″, 1-½″, 2″, 4-¼″ and 5″. Indentation specifications like this are very rare, however, in court rules.

9.2. Body Text Paragraphs

Body text makes up the bulk of a brief. Therefore, body text is the best place to start building styles for a template. This style is called Body Text in the style set. As shown in Chapter 5, body text needs to be formatted in various ways to accomodate interruptions in text, such as headings and block quotations.

The start of a paragraph may be indicated in one of two ways. The most common method is to indent the first line by the indentation increment. The paragraph indentation usually is one em.[3]

---

[3] Bringhurst, p. 38

> After weighing the equities of respondent's situation, the IJ granted respondent cancellation of removal in the exercise of discretion. App. 17a–20a.
>
> The Board of Immigration Appeals (Board) reversed, vacated the grant of cancellation of removal, and ordered respondent removed from the United States. App. 4a–10a.

The other method to mark the start of a paragraph is to add space above. It is more common with text set in sans serif type and only works with single-spaced text. The amount added above is usually the line spacing or ½ the line spacing.

> After weighing the equities of respondent's situation, the IJ granted respondent cancellation of removal in the exercise of discretion. App. 17a–20a.
>
> The Board of Immigration Appeals (Board) reversed, vacated the grant of cancellation of removal, and ordered respondent removed from the United States. App. 4a–10a

Pick one method or the other to start paragraphs. Using both methods together is redundant.[4]

The following table summarizes how to set up both types of body text styles:

	First Line Indented	Space Above
Alignment	Left or Justified	Left or Justified
Special	First line	(none)
By	Horizontal Increment	N/A
Spacing Before	0	>0
Line spacing	Exactly	Exactly
At	Line Spacing	Line Spacing

9.2.1. Space Before Paragraphs

Briefs normally use indentation to indicate a paragraph. Most of this chapter assumes that this method will be used. If you use space before paragraphs,

[4] Williams, p. 44

you will probably need fewer styles. There is no need for separate indented and flush styles with varying spacing before. Consider this example:

> The ADA's legislative history indicates that the statute's defenses for religious entities were to be interpreted in the same manner as the parallel defenses in Title VII. See, e.g., H.R. Rep. No. 485, 101st Cong., 2d Sess. Pt. 2, at 76–77 (1990). The House report provides an illustrative example:
>
> > [A]ssume that a Mormon organization wishes to hire only Mormons to perform certain jobs. If a person with a disability applies for the job, but is not a Mormon, the organization can refuse to hire him or her.
> >
> > However, if two Mormons apply for a job, one with a disability and one without a disability, the organization cannot discriminate against the applicant with the disability because of that person's disability.
>
> Id. at 76; see 29 C.F.R. Pt. 1630, App. § 1630.16(a) (EEOC guidance making same distinction).

Notice that the continuation of body text after the quotation can be formatted the same as the text before the quotation. In addition, all the quotation paragraphs can be formatted the same. This means that the template does not require separate styles for these constructs as is necessary with documents using indented paragraphs. The remainder of this chapter addresses style settings in the content of the more complex requirements of indented paragraphs.

9.2.2. Body Text After a Block Quotation

When body text resumes after a block quotation, it is formatted differently from other body text. The resumption may be flush to indicate the continuation of a grammatical paragraph (Body Text Continue) or indebted (Body Text Continue Indent) to start a new grammatical paragraph. If the text is single-spaced, there is usually additional space above the resumption text to separate the body text from the quotation.

You need to determine how much space will separate quotations before setting up continuation of body text styles. If the text is double spaced, it is best to rely on the line spacing and do not add any additional space around the quotation. When the text is single-spaced, the gap above and below the quotation is usually a full line or ½ the line spacing. This gives three possible combinations for calculating the **Before** spacing for the style:

1. Body text and quotation single-spaced—**Before** = the **Before** setting for the quotation.

2. Body text and quotation double-spaced—**Before** = 0.

3. Body text double-spaced and quotation single-spaced—**Before** = **At** (line spacing) setting for body text minus the **At** setting for the quotation.

The first two cases are straight forward but the last may need a bit of explanation. Assume that the text is 12 pt. and double spaced at 24 pt. with single-spaced quotations at 14 pt. line spacing. When the text shifts from body text to a block quotation, Word adds 12 pt. of leading after the last line of body text (line spacing minus the font size). Shifting back from the quotation to the text, Word inserts 2 pt. of leading after the quotation. The result is a much larger gap above the quotation than below. 10 pt. (= 24 pt. - 14 pt.) needs to be added before the body text to even out the gaps.

In nearly all respects, the continuation styles (Body Text Continue and Body Text Continue Indent) are the same as that of Body Text. The only deviations are in the **Before** space and possibly the indentation. These styles should be derived from Body Text with the following paragraph settings:

	Body Text Continue	Body Text Continue Indent
Special	(none)	Unchanged
Before	> 0	> 0

9.2.3. Body Text Before Headings

It is useful to have a body text style that occurs after a heading (Body Text First). This style can vary from the Body Text style in:

◊ The **Before** spacing—To set the text off from the heading. Relying on **Before** spacing exlusively is generally easier than using rather than a mixture of **Before** and **After**.

◊ Indentation—Paragraph indentations following heading are superfluous.[5]

Even if you do not plan to make paragraphs following headings flush or with additional **Before** space, you may wish to use a distinct Body Text First style. Doing so consistently in your documents will make reformatting easier if you need to change the spacing around headings later on.

---

[5] Bringhurst, p. 39

9.3. Block Quotations

Court rules generally require block quotations be indented. Block quotations may be indented on both sides or just the left side. The latter method is the better choice when the text field is narrow. The amount of indentation can be one or more indentation increments. Block quotations usually are separated from single-spaced body text as described in the previous section.

The style set from Chapter 5 has three quotation styles:

1. Block Quotation—Flush left start of quotation

2. Block Quotation Indent—Indented start of quotation

3. Block Quotation Continue—Subsequent quotation paragraphs (indented)

The Block Quotation style is derived from Body Text with the following modifications:

Left	>0
Right	Same as **Left** or 0
Before	>0
Special	**(none)**

The Block Quotation Continue and Block Quotation Continue Indent styles can be derived from Block Quotation with the following modifications:

	Block Quotation Continue	Block Quotation Indent
Before	0	Unchanged
Special	First line	First line
By	>0	>0

9.4. Footnotes

Format footnote styles in the same way as with body text (and other styles that appear within body text, such as quotations). Word uses the style Footnote Text when it creates footnotes. If footnotes are different size from the body text, set the font size and line spacing in this style.

Word has a number of settings that control the appearance of footnotes. These are not style settings but rather global configuration settings for the document.

9.4.1. Footnote Styles

Footnotes are formatted similarly to body text. It is easiest to use Word's built in Footnote Text style for normal footnotes. This is what Word uses automatically when it inserts a footnote. If you change this style so that it is based on Body Text, footnotes can track the body text formatting. Many court rules permit footnotes in a smaller font than the body text. If so, the font size can be changed in Footnote Text.

Although not routine, footnotes can contain block quotations and similar styles analogous to those that can appear within body text. If you have a need for such constructs in your footnotes, create footnote-specific analog styles with the same formatting changes. Base these on Footnote Text rather than Body Text.

FIGURE 9.2
Footnote settings

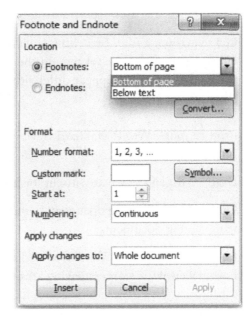

9.4.2. How to Set the Footnote Location

Word can place footnotes in one of two places: immediately after the text or at the bottom of the page. The appearance is different only on the last page of a section where the text does not fill the page. Under the former setting, the empty space appears below the footnotes. Under the latter, the empty space appears between the footnote and the text.

To set the footnote location:

1. Display the **Footnote and Endnote** dialog box (Figure 9.2).

Windows	Mac
Click the ▣ button at the bottom right of the **References>Footnotes** group.	**Insert>Footnote**

2. Set **Footnotes** to **Bottom of page** or **Below text**, as desired.

3. Click **Apply**.

9.4.3. Document Views

A *view* is a way of looking at a document though Word. Word supports several types of views. Word's set of views is analogous to multiple cameras in a television studio. Switching cameras makes the set appear differently but the contents of the set remain the same. Likewise, changing the view makes the document appear differently but the contents remain the same. Words views are:

◊ Print Layout—Word's standard view. It shows how the text appears on the printed page.

◊ Draft—Displays raw text without formatting to a page.

◊ Outline—Displays the document in outline format. This view is helpful for reorganizing documents.

◊ Full Screen Reading [Windows] or Full Screen [Mac]—Similar to Print Layout view with a larger viewing area for the document but limited editing capabilities. This view can be useful for proofreading documents.

◊ Web Layout—Displays the page in the manner of a web page. This is not useful for formatting briefs.

Word for Mac has additional views. Unlike those listed above, these change the format of the document and should not be used for briefs.

◊ Publishing Layout—This functions like the separate Publisher application in Office for Windows.

◊ Notebook Layout—This functions like the separate OneNote application in Office for Windows.

There are several ways to change the view. On Windows, you can select the view on the **View>Document Views** ribbon group or by clicking one of the view icons at the lower right of the status bar. On the Mac, you can select the view from the **View** menu or by clicking a view icon at the bottom of the Sidebar (when it is visisble).

Nearly all brief editing takes place in Page Layout view. The topic of views is almost an unnecesary diversion. However, some of the configuration settings for footnotes can only be made in Draft View.

9.4.4. How to Change the Footnote Layout

Word allows you to edit three elements of the footnote layout: the footnote separator, footnote continuation separator and a continuation notice. The footnote separator appears before the start of a footnote. By default this is a line that runs ⅓ of the way across the page. The continuation separator appears before a footnote that continues to a second or subsequent page. By default, this is a line that runs across the page.

Generally, there is no need to change the length of these lines. However, you can adjusted the thickness by selecting the line and changing the point size. You can also change the amount of space between the body text and the line.

The continuation notice is text that appears at the bottom of a page when the footnote extends to an additional page. By default, there is no continuation notice. Figure 9.3 shows how a footnote continuation notice can appear. There is no need to change the continuation notice unless your document contains many long footnotes.

To change the footnote layout:

1. Ensure that there is at least one footnote in the template. If necessary, you can create a dummy footnote then delete it after this procedure.

FIGURE 9.3
A footnote with a
continuation notice

"some day" intentions—without any description of concrete plans, or indeed even any specification of *when* the some day will be—do not support a finding of the "actual or imminent" injury that our cases require. See *supra*, at 560.[1]

---

[1] The dissent acknowledges the settled requirement that the injury complained of be, if not actual, then at least *imminent*, but it contends that respondents could get past summary judgment because "a reasonable finder of fact could conclude . . . that . . . Kelly or Skilbred will soon return to the project sites." *Post*, at 591. This analysis suffers either from a factual or from a legal defect, depending on what the "soon" is supposed to mean. If "soon" refers to the standard mandated by our precedents—that the injury be "imminent," *Whitmore* v. *Arkansas*, 495 U. S. 149, 155 (1990)—we are at a loss to see how, as a factual matter, the standard can be met by respondents' mere profession of an intent, some day, to return. But if, as we suspect, "soon" means nothing more than "in this lifetime," then the dissent has undertaken quite a departure from our precedents. Although "imminence" is concededly a somewhat elastic concept, it cannot be stretched beyond its purpose, which is to ensure that the alleged injury is not too speculative for Article III purposes—that the injury is " ' "*certainly* impending," ' " *id.*, at 158 (emphasis added). It has been stretched beyond the breaking point when, as here, the plaintiff alleges only an injury at some indefinite future time, and the acts necessary to make the injury happen are at least partly within the plaintiff 's own control. In such circumstances we have insisted that the injury proceed with a high degree of immediacy, so as to reduce the possibility of deciding a case in which no injury would have occurred at all. See, *e. g.*, *id.*, at 156–160; *Los Angeles* v. *Lyons*, 461 U. S. 95, 102–106 (1983).

There is no substance to the dissent's suggestion that imminence is demanded only when the alleged harm depends upon "the affirmative actions of third parties beyond a plaintiff's control," *post*,

(cont.)

2. Switch to Draft View:

Windows	Mac
View>Document Views>Draft	**View>Draft**

3. Display the footnotes (Figure 9.4).

Windows	Mac
References>Footnotes>Show Notes	**View>Footnotes**

FIGURE 9.4
Footnote display in
Draft View.

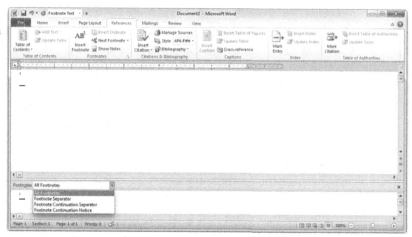

4. Choose the element you want to edit from the **Footnotes** dropdown list (**Footnote Separator, Footnote Continuation Separator** or **Footnote Continuation Notice**).

5. Edit as desired.

   Click the **Reset** button if you want to revert to the default setting.

6. Return to Print Layout View:

Windows	Mac
View>Document Views>Print Layout	**View>Print Layout**

9.5. Headings

Briefs use headings like no other type of document. As with most documents, they serve as a navigation guide establishing a document outline. Uniquely, headings tend to be lengthy and an integral part of the argument. The reader should be able to look at the brief table of contents and get an overall view of the argument. You should use Word's built-in heading styles (Heading 1–Heading 9) for your brief headings. Not doing so will cause certain Word features (including table of contents) from working properly.

Headings are the most complicated part of the template to set up because of the number of attributes. Heading attributes include:

◊ Heading Levels

◊ Numbering

◊ Indentation

◊ Alignment

◊ Character format

◊ Justification and Hyphenation

◊ Vertical spacing

9.5.1. Heading Levels

Briefs use multiple levels of headings. The levels are nested so that they form a tree-structured document outline. Making the heading structure clear is a key part of the template design. How many heading levels should there be? This depends upon the size of the brief. A lengthy opening brief generally requires more heading levels than a short reply brief. That said, a brief becomes inherently hard to follow if there are too many levels of headings. Three levels of headings handle most situations and five levels is about the most a reader can follow.

There are a couple of oddities in brief numbering. First, top-level headings (*e.g.*, Argument) generally are not numbered. This is not the custom in all jurisdictions but is followed in most. Second, only one top-level heading (*i.e.*, Argument or its equivalent) is subdivided by other headings. If another top level section is lengthy and has to be subdivided, a different heading system normally is used. For example, a lengthy Statement of the Facts, may be divided using unnumbered subheadings while the Argument section is divided using numbered headings.

9.5.2. Heading Numbering

The main indicator of heading structure is numbering variations. Each heading level uses a different number format. This is the ordering that is generally used:

1. Capital Roman: I., II., III.

2. Capital Letters: A., B., C.

3. Arabic: 1., 2., 3.

4. Lower Case Letters: a., b., c.

5. Lower Case Roman: i., ii., iii.

If additional heading levels are absolutely necessary, one can repeat these number styles using a right parenthesis following the number characters.

9.5.3. Heading Indentation

Indentation tends to be the next most important indication of heading structure (after numbering). Each numbered heading level is uniformly indented greater than the previous level. Figure 9.10 shows a numbered heading that has been indented. Notice that the heading lines up with the paragraph indenation.

9.5.4. Heading Alignment

Numbered headings can be aligned in two different ways. First the heading can be flush with the number.

> **I. Ineffective assistance leading to the rejection of a plea offer does not deprive a defendant of a substantive or procedural right that renders a subsequent trial unfair as to undermine confidence in the trial's outcome.**

The other way to align the headings is use a hanging indentation so that lines after the first are aligned with the heading text.

> **I. Ineffective assistance leading to the rejection of a plea offer does not deprive a defendant of a substantive or procedural right that renders a subsequent trial unfair as to undermine confidence in the trial's outcome.**

Either method is acceptable.

Flush headings are much easier to set up than hanging indentation. Hanging indentation creates two alignment points. The numbering, especially with Roman numerals or letters, can easily throw off the alignment.

> **III. Ineffective assistance leading to the rejection of a plea offer does not deprive a defendant of a substantive or procedural right that renders a subsequent trial unfair as to undermine confidence in the trial's outcome.**

There are a number of ways to get around the alignment problems with hanging indentations. An elegant method is right-align the number and only worry about the alignment of the text with the rest of the document.

> **I. Individuals have no reasonable expectation of privacy in information that is exposed to public view.**
>
> **III. Individuals have no reasonable expectation of privacy in information that is exposed to public view.**

The brute force method is to use a large indentation increment.

I.   **Individuals have no reasonable expectation of privacy in information that is exposed to public view.**

III.   **Individuals have no reasonable expectation of privacy in information that is exposed to public view.**

You can also format the number differently from the rest of the text, using a smaller font or narrower typeface.

I.   **Individuals have no reasonable expectation of privacy in information that is exposed to public view.**

III.   **Individuals have no reasonable expectation of privacy in information that is exposed to public view.**

9.5.5. Heading Character Format

Word processors have opened the door to all kinds of character formatting of headings. The availability of roman, bold, italic, bold italic, small capitals and the dreaded all capitals make it possible to put each heading level in separate type style. Heading levels also can use different sized fonts or even different typefaces. Just because you can do it does not mean you have to do it. Finally, using every type style available can make a document look garish and may limit your typeface choices.

This example shows a series of headings that are all set in bold:

I. Plaintiffs Fail to Satisfy the Requirements for a Preliminary Injunction.

A. Plaintiffs Cannot Demonstrate Likelihood of Success on the Merits.

1. Plaintiffs fail to establish standing, a threshold constitutional issue going to the heart of "Likelihood of Success on the Merits."

a. Plaintiffs cannot show "injury in fact" that is "concrete and particularized."

Here is the same with the headings formatted using a common sequence of varying type styles to indicate structure:

I. Plaintiffs Fail to Satisfy the Requirements for a Preliminary Injunction.

A. Plaintiffs Cannot Demonstrate Likelihood of Success on the Merits.

1. *Plaintiffs fail to establish standing, a threshold constitutional issue going to the heart of "Likelihood of Success on the Merits."*

a. Plaintiffs cannot show "injury in fact" that is "concrete and particularized."

Some court rules (*e.g.*, Fed. R. App. P. 32(a)(5)(A)) explicitly permit sans serif fonts in headings. Should you choose to do so, the trick becomes finding a combination of fonts that provides a contrast without creating a conflict. Creating consistent vertical alignment with different sized headings can be a challenge in Word.

The recommendation here is that you start out simple—at least to start. Try setting all the headings in bold so that they stand out from the rest of the text. If you find that indentation and numbering alone are not sufficient to indicate structure, then you can add character style variations to headings.

9.5.5.1. Centered Text

Centered text is generally harder to read than left aligned text because the eyes have to move to a different position to read each line. Compare:

A defendant who pleads guilty in exchange for a specific sentence pursuant to a Rule 11(c)(1)(C) agreement is not eligible for a sentence reduction under 18 U.S.C. 3582(c)(2) because the sentence is not "based on" a Guidelines range

A defendant who pleads guilty in exchange for a specific sentence pursuant to a Rule 11(c)(1)(C) agreement is not eligible for a sentence reduction under 18 U.S.C. 3582(c)(2) because the sentence is not "based on" a Guidelines range

The latter is generally easier to read. Like all capitals, reserve centered text for short headings where understanding does not require careful reading. Headings like these do not cause problems when centered:

Argument

Table of Contents

9.5.6. Yelling

The most baffling practice in legal writing is the use of *yelling*. Yelling is writing in all upper case letters. It makes lengthy text nearly unreadable. Yet lawyers persist in yelling in headings. Compare

I. INEFFECTIVE ASSISTANCE LEADING TO THE REJECTION OF A PLEA OFFER DOES NOT DEPRIVE A DEFENDANT OF A SUBSTANTIVE OR PROCEDURAL RIGHT THAT RENDERS A SUBSEQUENT TRIAL UNFAIR AS TO UNDERMINE CONFIDENCE IN THE TRIAL'S OUTCOME.

I. Ineffective assistance leading to the rejection of a plea offer does not deprive a defendant of a substantive or procedural right that renders a subsequent trial unfair as to undermine confidence in the trial's outcome.

The latter is much more readable than the former.

In reading briefs, one can sense a tendency in some quarters to avoid natural sentence formatting. Some people try to get around the problem of unreadable yelling text by using small capitals instead. This is, at best, a marginal improvement over all capitals.

I. INEFFECTIVE ASSISTANCE LEADING TO THE REJECTION OF A PLEA OFFER DOES NOT DEPRIVE A DEFENDANT OF A SUBSTANTIVE OR PROCEDURAL RIGHT THAT RENDERS A SUBSEQUENT TRIAL UNFAIR AS TO UNDERMINE CONFIDENCE IN THE TRIAL'S OUTCOME.

Another method used to avoid sentence capitalization is to use title capitalizations:

I. Ineffective Assistance Leading to the Rejection of a Plea Offer Does Not Deprive a Defendant of a Substantive or Procedural Right That Renders a Subsequent Trial Unfair as to Undermine Confidence in the Trial's Outcome.

This is more readable than small capitals or all capitals. However, it is not stylically appropriate for a sentence. Why not simply use sentence capitalization for an argumentative heading that is a sentence?

All capitals are fine for short section headings where the meaning is intuitive. A heading like this causes no problems in all capitals:

ARGUMENT

If you use all capitals, be sure to increase the character spacing slightly (see Chapter 6).

9.5.7. Justification and Hyphenation in Headings

Headings are a place where you might want to justify and hyphenate differently from the rest of the document. Some people do not like hyphenation in headings. If you do not want hyphenated headings, change the paragraph settings for the heading styles to right-aligned and with hyphenation disabled as shown above.

9.5.8. Vertical Spacing of Headings

Headings are usually spaced so that they are separated from the text. The body text above and below the heading is separated to form a window. The headings are usually centered within the window or with the heading positioned closer to the text.

You could use the **Before** and **After** spacing of the heading style to create this window. The problem with that method becomes apparent when two headings occur consecutively. The construct produces a large gap between the two headings. That is the reason it was suggested previously to only use the **Before** setting for headings and use the Before setting for the Body Text first to create any additional space after the the heading.

9.5.9. Setting up the Heading Styles

Always use Word's built in styles Heading 1 through Heading 9 for headings. Otherwise certain Word features will not work correctly.

It may be helpful to set up the heading styles so that Heading 2 has the **Style based on** set to **Heading 1**, Heading 3 has the **Style based on** set to **Heading 2**, and so on. The advantage is that it allows changes to all the heading styles to be made in one place. The down side is that you have to make changes twice where there need to be differences among style formatting.

9.5.9.1. How to Set up Heading Numbering

Heading numbering is not set up as part of the style definition. The numbering is set up separately on the **Define new Multilevel list** dialog box (Figure 9.4). There, the numbering is linked back to the heading styles. This separataion allows the numbering relationships for all the heading styles to be defined in one place. The name notwithstanding, this same dialog box is used to create and edit heading numbers.

On the Mac, this dialog box is called **Customized Outline Numbered list**. The layout and labels are different from the Windows equivalent. However, the functionality between the two is the same.

To access the Define new Multilevel list dialog box:

1. Place the caret within a text with a heading style.

2. Click the ⁴ₐ̄ᵢ̄▾ button on the **Home>Paragraph** group to display the dropdown menu.

3. Select **Define New Multilevel List button**.

These are descriptions of the setting on this dialog box:

More>> Button
If this button is visible, click it make all the settings visible. After clicking, the button label switches to **<<Less**.

Click level to modify
This list box allows you to select a value 1–9. These values correspond to the heading styles Heading 1–Heading 9. The selected value controls which heading level is currently being modified. You can switch among levels at any time.

Link level to style
This setting maps the selected level in the list set up to a style. Be sure that this value is always set. For briefs, the selected level should always be mapped to the corresponding heading style (Heading 1–Heading 9).

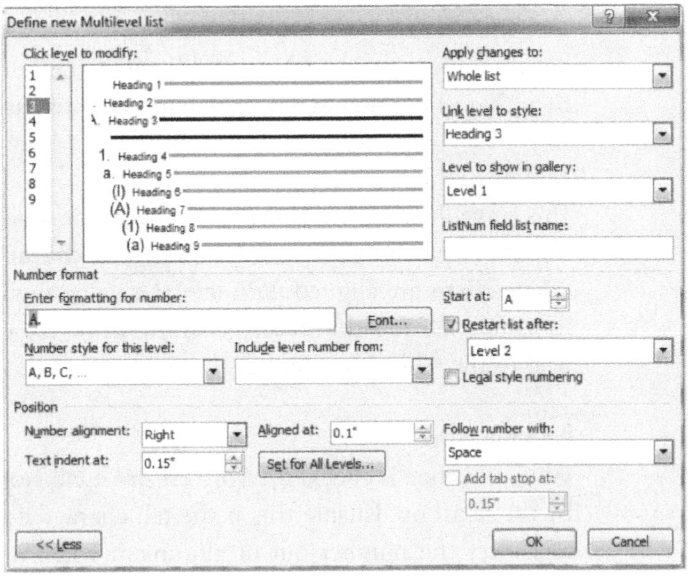

FIGURE 9.4
Define new
Multilevel list
dialog box

Enter formatting for number (Number format [Mac])
This text box controls how the heading number is formatted with surrounding text. For briefs, edit this field to add the period after the number.

Font
Click this button to change the font (typeface, size, type style) used for the number. Generally this does not need to be changed.

Number style for this level (Number style [Mac])
Use this dropdown list to specify how the heading level is numbered (*e.g.*, **1, 2, 3, ...**, **i, ii, iii, ...**, **A., B, C, ...**). Each heading level can have a different number style. For top level headings, this is often set to **(none)**.

Number alignment (Number position [Mac])
This setting controls how the number is positioned relative to the number alignment point. There are three possible values: **Left, Center** and **Right.** This should be set to either **Left** or **Right** for briefs with hanging indentations and **Left** for flush headings.

Aligned at
Specifies the offset from the margin where the heading number is aligned. Positive values indent the number. Negative values place the alignment point outside the text margins.

Text indent at

Set the indentation of the text following the number. Use a value greater then that of **Aligned at** to create hanging intentation in headings.

Follow number with

This controls what Word uses to separate the automatically generated heading number from your text. It can be **Tab character, Space** or **Nothing**. If the headings are aligned flush left, this value should be **Space**. For hanging indentations, **Tab character** generally works best. The setting here carries over to the table of contents.

Add tab stop

When this box is checked, Word creates a tab stop at the position specified by the text box. Enable this if the tab character after the number puts the text after the number out of alignment when using hanging indentation (**Follow number with** set to **Tab character**).

Set for All Levels [Windows Only]

This button displays a dialog box that allows you to set the indentation for all levels at a fixed interval.

Include level number from

Only needed if you are daring and want to use outline numbering (*e.g.*, 1.2.4) in your briefs. While editing the **Enter formatting for number** text box, use this dropdown to insert the numbers of the higher level headings. Format these numbers with periods as necessary.

Legal style numbering

In spite of the name, this setting has little relationship to legal documents. Checking this box forces the numbers to be in Arabic format. This is only useful when using outline numbering.

The remaining settings on the on the **Define new Multilevel list** dialog box apply to complex forms of numbering not used in briefs : **Apply changes to, Level to show in gallery** [Windows only], **Start at, Restart list after (Restart numbering after** [Mac]**), ListNum field name.**

The following table shows possible settings that can be used for headings with hanging indentations based upon 0.15″ increments:

	Number style	Number alignment	Aligned at	Text indent at
Level 1	(none)		0	0
Level 2	I, II, III, ...	Right	0.1	0.15
Level 3	A, B, C, ...	Right	0.25	0.3
Level 4	1, 2, 3, ...	Right	0.4	0.45
Level 5	a, b, c, ...	Right	0.55	0.6

These are settings are for the same with flush headings:

	Number style	Number alignment	Aligned at	Text indent at
Level 1	(none)		0	0
Level 2	I, II, III, ...	Right	0.1	0.15
Level 3	A, B, C, ...	Right	0.25	0.3
Level 4	1, 2, 3, ...	Right	0.4	0.45
Level 5	a, b, c, ...	Right	0.55	0.6

9.5.9.2. Formatting the Headings

Format the headings on the **Paragraph** dialog box after you set up the numbering. Set up the line spacing. If the top-level heading is to be centered, set this up in the style's paragraph settings. The numbering process may create unneeded indentation for unnumbered headings that should be set to zero.

9.5.9.3. Keeping a Heading on One Page

Headings should always appear on the same page as the first text after the heading. Unless your headings are extremely long, the headings should not cross page breaks either. This behavior is set on the Line and Page Breaks tab of the **Paragraph** dialog box (Figure 9.13). If you have set up the heading styles so that they are based upon each other (as suggested above), this change only needs to be made in the style from which the rest are derived.

9.5.9.4. Headings That Do Not Appear in the Table of Contents

Sometimes there is a need to have specific headings that do not appear in the table of contents. For example, a top level heading of "Table of Contents" probably should not appear within the table of contents. You can create a style derived from Heading 1 for that purpose. Using a derived style will allow the new style to track any formatting changes made to Heading 1. The only style setting you need to change is on the **Paragraph** dialog box. Change **Outline level** from **Level 1** to **Body Text** (see Chapter 8).

9.6. Table of Contents and Authorities Styles

Styles used in the table of contents and table of authorities styles are generally formatted very similarly. However, they tend to use styles settings that are not used by other brief styles. Word uses its built in styles (TOC 1 through TOC 9) when it creates a table of contents (see Chapter 10). You format the generated table of contents by changing these styles. Word's automatic table of authorities feature also creates styles. However, the suggestion in Chapter 10 is that you should not use this feature. Instead you should create your table authorities manually and you should create table of authorities styles in your templates. Figure 9.5 shows an entry in a table of authorities.

FIGURE 9.5
A table of authorities entry

Air Pollution Variance Bd. v. *Western Alfalfa Corp.*,
416 U.S. 861 (1974) 18

This table of authorities entry uses these formatting features:

1. Hanging indentation

2. Indented right margin

3. Tab with leader line

The first two settings are made on the **Paragraph** dialog box while modifying the style. To create a hanging indentation, set **Indentation>Special** to Hanging and set **By** to the amount of the indentation for the lines after the first. The right aligned page number with a leader is created on the **Tabs** dialog box (see Chapter 8). Subtract the left and right margins from the page width to find the location for the tab stop.

A common problem in tables of contents and authorities is that when the entry spans multiple lines it can run into the page number as shown in Figure 9.6. The solution this problem is to use the **Indentation>Right** paragraph setting for the style to indent the text from the right. A value of around ¼″ to ½″ is generally sufficient. Word permits tabs to go past the right indentation, allowing the page numbers to be separated from the text. Figure 9.7 shows how the same text appears with a right indentation.

9.7. Emphasis

The only character style that is absolutely necessary is a style for emphasis. The Blue Book and AWLD permit italics and underlining for emphasis. A document should use one method or the other. Italics and underlining should never be used in the same document.

Underlining is the poor man's form of emphasis. Italics are generally preferred over underlining. Underlining obscures descenders within lower case letters, making the text harder to read. For example, underlining <u>Lujan</u> makes the text appear a lot like Luian

The reason there is no rule to always use italics is that some typefaces do not have a real italic style. Sans serif and and monospaced fonts tend to have what is called an *oblique* style rather than italics. Oblique text is simply a slanted version of roman style.

Sans serif italics do not emphasize—they are just bent over.
`Italics in Courier do not emphasize.`

For text set in a monospaced font, underlining may be more stylistically appropriate for a consistent typewriter look.

The recommendation here is to use Word's built in Emphasis character style. Modify this style to use either underlining or italics as appropriate. This can be done directly on the **Modify Style** dialog box or by using **Format>Font** to access the **Font** dialog box.

Some court rules permit bold to be used as an additional form of Emphasis. Another recommendation is that this use of bold text be avoided. If you absolutely require bold emphasis, use Word's built in Strong style and modify it to suit your needs.

9.8. Moving on from Here

At this point you should be ready to set up the styles within your template. The easiest way to make sure your styles are set up correctly is to work on an actual brief. Copy an existing brief into your template. Apply styles to the elements of the brief. Finally, modify the styles until all their elements are adjusted properly. You can either leave the brief text in place as a placeholder or delete it before saving the template.

Chapter 10
Basic Text Formatting

This purpose of this chapter is to teach you how to use characters properly within Word. It addresses subtle issues that occur when typing the text. The theme here is to use the right character in the right situation. This chapter represents a slight detour from the main thread of the book. The focus to this point has been the creation of templates. The topics here cover things that occur while using templates.

10.1. Spaces

Two spaces should never occur consecutively in a document. Forget what you learned in typing class about using two spaces after a period. Two spaces screws up spacing, especially if you justify. Part of your proofreading process should be to do a global search and replace two spaces with a single space.

The possible exception is when you are using a monospaced font. If the court rules require you to create a document that looks like it came from a typewriter, it might be stylistically appropriate to use two spaces after a period.

Similarly, do not use the **Return** key to add vertical space. Multiple **Return** keys should not occur consecutively in a document. Using **Return** to adjust vertical spacing can produce bizarre results, especially if the document is used or printed on multiple computers. Use paragraph style settings to adjust space between paragraphs instead.

10.2. Special Characters

Special characters fall into two general categories. The first is symbols that are not found on the keyboard. Examples of such symbols include, ©, ®, ™, § and ¶. The second category is characters with special behaviors, such as nonbreaking spaces and optional hyphens.

There is a large gap between characters and available keys. A computer keyboard has about 50 character keys. With the shift key, these can produce about

100 characters. Computer fonts usually have around 250–2,000 characters.

This problem is compounded by the allocation of keys. Seemingly useless characters, like ~, |, { and }, get keyboard space. At the same time, ¶ and § do not have keys. Computer programmers, who find the former more useful, design computer keyboards—not lawyers.

```
void mergeValues (unsigned int count,
  unsigned int op1 [],
  unsigned int op2 [])
{
  const unsigned int mask = 0xFF ;
  for (unsigned int ii = 0 ; ii < count ; ++ ii)
  {
    op1 [ii] = (op1 [ii] + mask) & ~mask ;
    op1 [ii] |= op2 & mask ;
  }
}
```

Always use the appropriate character in your documents—never approximate. The full range of characters in a font is available through Word. This includes currency symbols (¢, £, ¥, €) and mathematical symbols (≈, Δ, ÷). For areas use

100mm × 73mm

not

100mm x 73mm

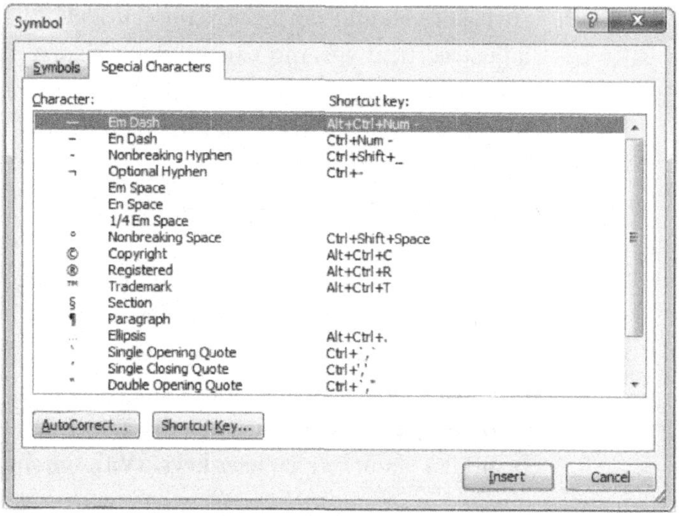

FIGURE 10.1
Insert special
characters using the
Symbol dialog box.

10.2.1. How to Insert a Special Character

To insert a special character using the mouse:

1. Display the **Symbol** dialog box (Figure 10.1):

Windows	Mac
Insert>Symbols>Symbol>	**Insert>Symbol>**
More Symbols>Special Characters	**Advanced Symbol>Special Characters**

> The **Symbol** dialog box is non-modal so you can switch back and forth between it and your document text.

2. Select the **Special Characters** tab.

3. Select the desired character from the list and click **Insert**.

Notice that, if a symbol has a keyboard shortcut, Word displays it next to the symbol. If you remember the shortcut, you can use it instead of the **Symbol** dialog box. Chapter 14 covers how to create your own keyboard shortcuts for symbols.

The **Symbols** tab on the **Symbol** dialog box gives access to additional symbols that are available in a font (Figure 10.2). On Windows, this gives access to the full range of characters available. On the Mac, only a small

FIGURE 10.2
Insert any available character from the Symbols tab [Windows].

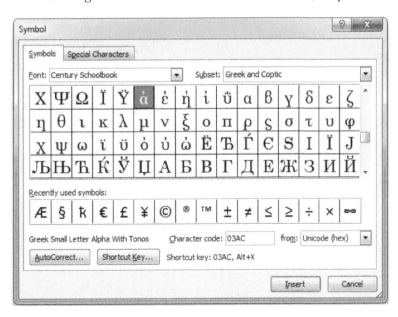

range of available characters is shown. Refer to Chapter 2 on how to use the Character Viewer to insert any available character.

You can (and should) define keyboard shortcuts for characters that you use frequently. Chapter 14 covers how to create shortcuts.

10.2.2. Symbols with Special Behavior

Manual Line Break

Default keyboard shortcut: **Shift/Return**

A manual line break character starts a new line without starting a new paragraph. These are not used frequently within brief text but they are common in headings, cover pages, tables of contents and tables of authorities.

If Word's default formatting gives something like this

United States District Court
for the District of New
Jersey

manual line breaks can be used to produce more natural breaks:

United States District Court↵
for the↵
District of New Jersey↵

Optional Hyphen

Default keyboard shortcut: **Ctrl/-** or **Command/-**

An optional hyphen is used to manually hyphenate words. An optional hyphen marks the point where a word can be broken across a line. Optional hyphens are not visible unless they are used to break a word. Always ensure that there are at least two characters before an optional hyphen and three characters after.

Nonbreaking Hyphen

Default keyboard shortcut: **Ctrl/Shift/-** or **Command/Shift/-**

Word considers a hyphen to be a location where it can always break a line, even if it violates the basic hyphenation rules of 2 characters before and 3 characters after.

> The defendant came to America on an F-
> 1 student visa.
>
> Wrong

Correct this problem by using a nonbreaking hyphen. A nonbreaking hyphen appears as a regular hyphen. However, word breaks do not occur at a nonbreaking hyphen.

> The defendant came to America on an F-1
> student visa.
>
> Correct using a nonbreaking hyphen.

Nonbreaking Space

Default keyboard shortcut: **Ctrl/Shift/Space** or **Command/Shift/Space**

A nonbreaking space appears as a space in the text but Word will not replace it with a soft line break. It is analogous to a nonbreaking hyphen. A nonbreaking space should be used where the text before and after a space should be kept on the same line.

Examples (• represents a nonbreaking space):

> 1)•is not a generalized grievance
> §•1101(a)
> p.•10
> .•.•.

10.2.3. How to Make Special Characters Visible

The ¶ button toggles the display of special character on or off. On Windows, this is located on the Ribbon at **Home>Paragraph**. On the Mac, this button is on the editing toolbar.

10.3. Abbreviations and Acronyms

Small capitals are normally used for abbreviations and acronyms except for personal names and postal codes.[1]

> AD 1066
> 10:30 PM
> NATO Headquarters
> MV Galaxy

Compare

> MLK Boulevard
> JFK Airport
> Boise ID

This usage of small capitals highlights the advantage of real small capitals. Word's simulated small capitals tend not to have good contrast.

10.4. Dashes

Three types of dashes are normally used in briefs. They are the hyphen (-), en-dash (–) and em-dash (—). Each has separate purposes and they are not interchangeable.

Hyphens

The hyphen is the only dash that has its own keyboard key. The hyphen has several functions. The most common use is for hyphenating words at the end of a line and to join compound words. Style manuals give different advice on when a hyphen should be used in compound words. One univer-

---

[1] Bringhurst, p. 48

sal rule is that one should use a hyphen in a compound word whenever it resolves ambiguity.

> I saw a man eating shark.
> I saw a man-eating shark.

The hyphen clarifies the meaning of the text.
   Another purpose of the hyphen is as a separator.

> 201-555-1212
> § 12-2

The hyphen often serves as the numeric minus sign. In text of a mathematic nature, a minus sign character is usually used instead of a hyphen. However, not all fonts contain a minus character (–). When a minus sign is not available, a hyphen is generally used instead.

En Dash

Default keyboard shortcut: **Ctrl/Num-** or **Command/Numpad-**

The en dash is a dash the width of the letter N. It is used to express ranges and relationships.

> pp. 143–51
> The New York–London route
> McCarran–Walter Act

Compare "Farah Fawcett-Majors" to "the Fawcett–Majors marriage" to illustrate the difference between a hyphen and an en dash. Briefs are likely to contain more en dashes then hyphens. En dashes tend to occur frequently within citations because of page ranges. Do not use hyphens for page ranges.
   Some government documents (*e.g.*, the Federal Register) improperly use an en-dash where a non-breaking hyphen should occur. "B-1 Visa" (hyphen) is correct. "B–1 Visa" (en dash) is not.

Em Dash

Default keyboard shortcut: **Alt/Ctrl/Num-** or
Command/Option/Numpad-

The em dash is a dash the width of the letter M. Em dashes should be used sparingly within a brief. An em dash is generally used to indicate pauses or breaks.

An aircraft—that is to say—a helicopter.

Two em dashes in sequence can be used to indicate omitted letters.

The defendant then addressed the bench, stating "F—— you."

10.5. Quotation Marks

Use curved typesetting quotation marks " " and ' ' instead of straight type-writer quotation marks (" and '). Word automatically converts straight quotes to typesetting quotation marks. This works most of the time but there can be some problems with contractions. For example, Word converts

Dartmouth Class of '75

incorrectly to

Dartmouth Class of '75

instead of

Dartmouth Class of '75

The solution is to type the quotation mark immediately after *of* then back up to add the space.

If you copy text into your document you may wind up with straight quotation marks. You can convert easily to typesetting quotation marks by using global search and replace. Changing " to " (straight quotation in both places) and ' to ' will cause Word to replace straight quotation marks with typesetting quotation marks.

There is one exception to the rule to use typesetting quotation marks. If the court rules require that you use a monospaced font, straight quotations marks may be more stylistically appropriate.

10.6. Feet and Inches

Do not use typesetting quotation marks to indicate feet and inches.

The defendant is 6'-1" tall.

Some fonts contain feet and inches marks characters. This character can be inserted using the **Symbol** dialog box or Character Viewer [Mac]. Italicized straight quotes can also be use to indicate feet and inches.

The defendant is 6′-1″ tall.

Press **Ctrl/Z** [Windows] or **Command/Z** [Mac] after typing the quotation mark to undo Word's conversion to curved quotation marks.
The same technique can be used for locations with the degree symbol.

Newark is located at 40° 44′ N 74° 10′ W.

The same character is used for minutes and feet and for seconds and inches.

10.7. Accented Characters

Accented characters are not used frequently in briefs. However, they are sometimes needed, usually in foreign, proper nouns. For example:

Comité de Apoyo a los Trabajadores Agrícolas v. Solis, 2010 U.S. Dist. LEXIS 90155 (E.D. Pa. 2010)

Accented characters can be inserted using the **Symbol** dialog box or Character Viewer [Mac]. However, Word predefines keyboard shortcuts for most common accented characters. The shortcuts are highly intuitive on Windows:

Character	Keystroke	Example
Acute accent	**Ctrl/'-LETTER**	áéíóú ÁÉÍÓÚ
Grave accent	**Ctrl/`-LETTER**	àèìòù ÀÈÌÒÙ
Circumflex	**Ctrl/Shift/^-LETTER**	âêîôû ÂÊÎÔÛ
Tréma	**Ctrl/Shift/:-LETTER**	äëïöü ÄËÏÖÜ
Cedilla	**Ctrl/,-c or Ctrl/,-Shift/C**	ç Ç
	Ctrl/Shift/&-a or Ctrl/Shift/&-Shift/A	æ Æ
	Ctrl/Shift/&-o or Ctrl/Shift/&-Shift/O	œ Œ
Eszett	**Ctrl/Shift/&-s**	ß

Unfortunately, the shortcuts are less intuitive on the Mac.

Character	Keystroke	Example
Acute accent	**Option/e--LETTER**	áéíóú ÁÉÍÓÚ
Grave accent	**Option/`-LETTER**	àèìòù ÀÈÌÒÙ
Circumflex	**Option/i-LETTER**	âêîôû ÂÊÎÔÛ
Tréma	**Option/u-LETTER**	äëïöü ÄËÏÖÜ
Cedilla	**Option/c or Option/Shift/C**	ç Ç
	Option/' or Option/Shift/'	æ Æ
	Option/q or Option/Shift/Q	œ Œ
Eszett	**Option/S**	ß

10.8. Fractions

You can create fractions using the fraction slash (or division slash character if is not available). Make the numerator a superscript and the denominator a subscript

$$^{22}\!/_{53}$$

Most fonts contain fraction characters. The range of fractions varies by font. The recommendation here is that you create your own fractions using a slash so that all fractions appear the same.

10.9. Ellipses

Most fonts have an ellipsis character. Under its default settings, Word converts three periods typed consecutively into an ellipsis character. The ellipsis character has the advantage over multiple periods that it does not break across lines.

There are two problems with using the ellipsis character in briefs. First, it conflicts with the Blue Book § 5.3. The Blue Book states that an ellipsis is created using spaces between periods. The second problem occurs when you need a period following an ellipsis. An ellipsis character followed by a period can look funny (Figure 10.1). In Century Schoolbook the period dot is smaller than those of the ellipsis character and the space before the period dot is wider.

The best solution is to use a combination of periods and non-breaking spaces to create ellipsis. This will ensure consistency between three- and four-dot versions while not breaking across lines.

FIGURE 10.1
An ellipsis character
followed by a period
(enlarged with
reference lines)

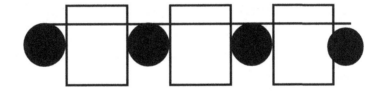

10.10. Tab Characters

There is very little need to use tab characters to format briefs in Word. Paragraph indentations should be defined using paragraph styles—never using the **Tab** key. One of the few places one routinely uses **Tab** in a brief is in tables of contents and tables of authorities to right align page numbers.

Another place tabs are useful is where there is a left alignment after the start of a paragraph. In Figure 10.4, tab characters occur after the colons to align the hanging text.

FIGURE 10.4
Tabs used to create
hanging indentation

auctioning the licenses—the FCC insisted that the bankruptcy court should return the licenses to it. C.A. App. 589.

    Court: So, the FCC might get more money for the American public under a new license or it might get less?

    [Gov't]: Money is not the end goal. * * *

    Court: Money is not the objective.

    [Gov't]: No. * * * Congress told us what the objective was. * * * A fair and efficient allocation of the limited resource of radio spectrum.

    Court: All right, I hear the words. They have no content for me.

Id. at 590-591. See note 14, *infra*.

10.11. Final Comments

In general, you should use the appropriate character from the full range available with the font you are using. One exception is when using a typewriter font, such as Courier or Courier New. In that case, it might be more appropriate stylistically only to use those characters that appear on the typewriter keyboard, including straight quotation marks.

Chapter 11
Brief Sections

Longer documents often need to have pages laid out in different ways. You may wish to number the body text differently (*e.g.*, 1, 2, 3, …) from the front matter (*e.g.*, i, ii, ii, …) and from appendices (*e.g.*, A-1, A-2, A-3, …) and not have a number on the cover page at all. The mechanism for doing this in Word is to divide a document into *sections*. Each section can have different headers and footers, margins and even different page sizes.

11.1. Types of Section Breaks

A *section break* is a special, nonprinting character that marks the start of a new document section. There are four types of section breaks:

1. Next Page—Starts a section on the next page. Any text after the section break will begin on the page after the break.

2. Continuous—Starts a section on the current page. This is useful for multi-column text. However, it has no use in creating briefs.

3. Odd Page—Starts a new section on the next odd page. Any text after the section break will begin on the first odd page after the break. This is useful when using two-sided printing to place text on the right side page of a spread. For example, an Odd Page section break after a cover page will put the following text on the next sheet of paper, rather than on the back of the cover.

4. Even Page—This has the same function as an Odd Page break except that the text starts on the next even page. Unless you are writing in a language that goes right to left (*e.g.*, Hebrew), this type of break is of limited use.

In a single-sided brief, you will only use Next Page section breaks. For double-sided briefs, you can use both Next Page and Odd Page section breaks where desired.

184

11.2. How to Insert a Section Break

To insert a section break:

Windows	Mac
a. Click Page **Layout>Page Setup>Breaks** to display the **Page Breaks** dropdown menu (Figure 11.1). b. Select the break type from the menu.	Click **Insert>Break** and select the break type.

FIGURE 11.1
The Page Breaks
dropdown list

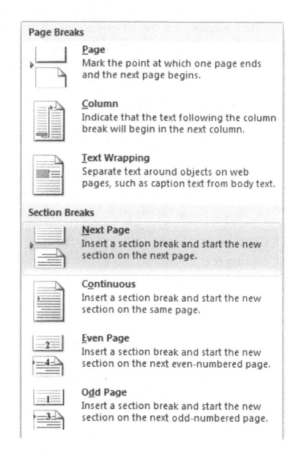

11.3. How to Delete a Section Break

The section break is merely a character within the document text. Position the caret immediately after the break and press **Backspace** [Windows] or **Delete** [Mac]. This is a bit difficult because section breaks are not normally visible. The ¶ button (Home tab [Windows], Toolbar [Mac]) toggles the visibility of nonprinting characters on and off. Figure 11.2 shows the appearance of a section break when nonprinting characters are visible. This makes deleting section breaks easier.

FIGURE 11.2
The appearance of a section break with nonprinting characters visible

Brief·on·Behalf·of·Appellee................................Section Break (Odd Page).................................

11.4. How to Change a Break Type

To change the type of break used to create a section:

1. Position the caret within the section.

2. Display the **Page Setup** dialog box [Windows Figure 11.3] or **Document** dialog box [Mac Figure 11.4].

FIGURE 11.3
Changing the section break type [Windows]

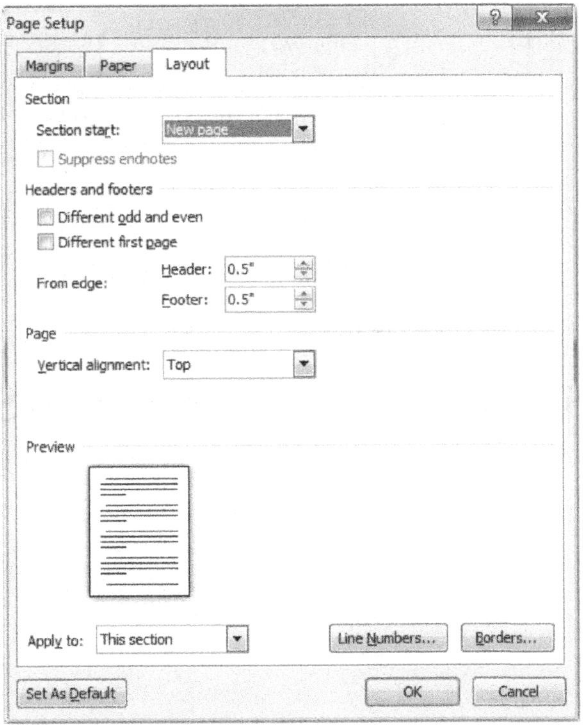

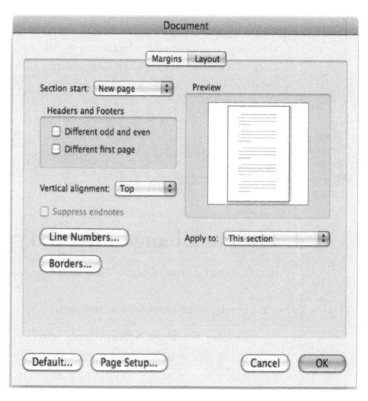

FIGURE 11.4
Changing the
section break type
[Mac]

Windows	Mac
Click the ⧉ button at the lower right corner of the **Page Layout>Page Setup** group.	**Format>Document**

1. Select the **Layout** tab.

2. Set the desired value for **Section start**.

3. Click **OK** to save.

11.5. How to Set up Headers in Sections

Word links the header and footer of a section to that of the previous section by default. A blue tab with the text "Same as Previous" indicates the header or footer is linked (Figure 11.5). When linked with the previous section, changing a header or footer in the linked section also changes it in the previous section.

FIGURE 11.5
A header set up the
same as the previous
section

FIGURE 11.5
A header set up the
same as the previous
section

To create a different header or footer, you must unlink it from the previous section (Figure 11.6).

1. Edit the header and footer.

2. Place the caret in the header or footer that you want to unlink.

3. Unlink the header or footer.

Windows	Mac
Toggle the **Header & Footer Tools> Design>Navigation>Link to Previous** button.	Uncheck **Header and Footer> Options>Link to Previous**.

This removes the blue *Same as Previous* tab from the header or footer.

Header and footers are unlinked separately. You can have one or both linked to the previous section. The same settings can be used to relink the header or footer to the previous section.

FIGURE 11.6
Controlling header
and footer linking
across sections.
Windows (top)
Mac (bottom)

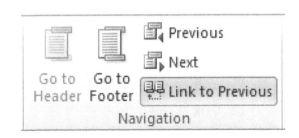

188

11.6. How to Number Pages Differently

To set the page number format for a section:

1. Display the **Page Number Format** dialog box (Figure 11.7).

Windows	Mac
Insert>Header & Footer> **Page Number>Format Page Number**	a. **Insert>Page Numbers** b. Click **Format**.

FIGURE 11.7
Formatting page
numbers for a
section

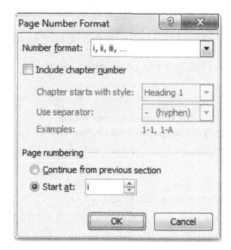

2. Set **Number format:** to the desired style of numbering for the section.

3. Set **Page numbering** to **Continue from previous section** or **Start at** with an initial value.

   Generally, you will want to set this to **Start at** with a value of **1**.

4. Click **OK** to save.

11.7. How to Set Margins for a Section

When you create a new section, Word numbers pages in the new section using the same style as the previous section. It also continues the number sequence across sections. You can change both the page number style and the initial page number (usually to 1) for the new section.

To change the page numbering in a section:

1. Position the caret within the section.

2. Display the **Page Setup** dialog box [Windows] or **Document** dialog box [Mac].

Windows	Mac
Page Layout>Page Setup> Margins>Custom Margins	**Format>Document**

3. Be sure **Apply to** is set to **This section** (Figure 11.8).

4. Set the margin values for the section.

5. Click **OK** to save.

FIGURE 11.8 Setting margins for a section.

11.8. Moving on From Here

At this point, think about how briefs are structured for the courts you submit to. You may wish to divide your template into sections to match that structure. Unless the brief lengths are measured cover-to-cover (as under Idaho App. R. 34(b)), you will probably want to have at least two sections, so that the cover page can be unnumbered. If you want front matter to be separately numbered, there needs to be a separate section for that. Try creating the needed sections with the pages properly laid out and numbered.

Chapter 12
Tables of Contents
and
Tables of Authorities

This chapter covers the process of creating a table of contents and a table of authorities in Word. Word has built features for automatically generating both of these types of tables. Chapter 9 discussed how to set up the styles for formatting these tables. As you work with tables of contents and authorizes, refer to that chapter to adjust their appearance.

For creating a table of contents, Word's automatic generation usually does a very good job. For creating a table of authorities, Word's table of authorities is a marketing feature in name only. The recommendation here is that you do not use it. However, its usage is explained in detail, so read on and you can be the judge.

12.1. Fields

A table of contents or table of authorities in Word is a *field*. A field is a document element that displays text or graphics programmatically. Word supports many different types of fields. For example, Word has a bar code field that produces something like this for envelopes:

One field that has been used previously in this book is the page number field. Places a page number field in the document heading and Word automatically updates the field to display the number of the page that it is actually on with the formatting specified for the section.

12.1.1. How to Display Fields

To toggle the display of field codes in a document:

Windows	Mac
ALT/F9	**Option/F9**

You can toggle the display of fields by pressing **ALT/F9** (**Option/F9** on the Mac). If you enable the display of fields, a page number appears something like this:

{Page }

If you know the mechanics of a specific field, you can edit the field code directly (something essential when using Word's table of authorities feature).

12.1.2. How to Unlink a Field

The process of converting a field to text is called *unlinking*. You cannot edit the text of a field directly. If you want to edit the text, you have to unlink the field first. Unfortunately, once you unlink and change the text, there is no way to go back to the field (other than undo).

To unlink a field:

1. Select the field.

2. Press:

Windows	Mac
Ctrl/Shift/F9	**Command/Shift/F9**

12.2. Creating a Table of Contents

Word can automatically create a table of contents, complete with page references. The discussion that follows takes a *need to know approach*. Word's table of content feature has capabilities that exceed the needs of legal documents. This discussion is then limited to those features that are likely to be used in these types of documents.

To create a table of contents, Word extracts text from the document body and uses it to create table of content entries. Word organizes the table of contents entries in a hierarchy of up to nine levels, similar to that used for headings. Each entry level within the table of contents is assigned a separate style, one of TOC 1, TOC 2, … TOC 9. Word initially sets up these styles with indentations to indicate the hierarchy.

Word uses styles to create a table of contents. It searches the document for text in specific styles, then copies that text to the table, followed by a tab character and the page number. By default, Word includes the text from the heading styles Heading 1, Heading 2 and Heading 3 in the table of content and maps those to the TOC 1, TOC 2 and TOC 3 styles.

12.2.1. How to Create a Table of Contents from Headings

To create a table of contents in a document:

1. Position the caret at the location where you want the table to appear.

2. Display the **Table of Contents** dialog box (Figure 12.1):

Windows	Mac
a. Click **References> Table of Contents>Table**	a. Select **Insert>Index and Tables**.
b. Select **Contents> Insert Table of Contents** from the dropdown menu.	b. Click the **Index** tab.

FIGURE 12.1
The Table of
Contents dialog
box

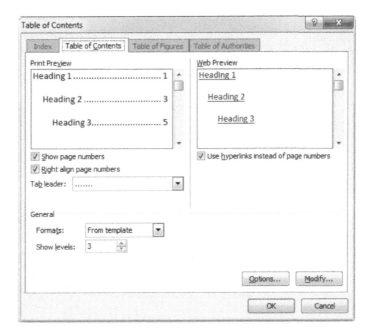

3. Set **Show levels** to the number of heading levels you want to appear in the table of contents.

   The maximum value of 9 includes all headings in the table of contents. Use a smaller value here if you want to exclude lower level headings from the table of contents. The number of heading levels to include is a matter of personal choice and may depend upon the nature of a specific brief. The table of contents gives a summary of the brief. Include enough heading levels that the the table of contents gives a full story but no so many that it becomes cluttered. Two levels of narrative headings is often sufficient.

4. Uncheck the **Use hyperlinks instead of page numbers box**.

   If this box is checked, Word assigns the Hyperlink character style to the text in the table of contents. This makes it difficult to select and format the table of contents paragraph styles.

5. Click **OK**.

The table of contents should appear at the insertion point in the document. Figure 12.2 shows an example of a table of contents created by Word.

FIGURE 12.2
A table of contents generated by Word

TABLE OF CONTENTS

Table of Contents i
Opinions below 1
Jurisdiction 1
Statutory and regulatory provisions involved 2
Statement 2
Summary of argument 2
Argument 3
I. The Council on Environmental Quality permissibly authorized alternative NEPA arrangements under 40 C.F.R. 1506.11 to address "emergency circumstances" in this case 3
   A. CEQ's interpretation of section 1506.11 comports with the plain meaning of "emergency." 4
   B. The Ninth Circuit erred in deferring to the district court's reading of section 1506.11. 8
II. The district court's preliminary injunction is inconsistent with established principles governing injunctive relief. 16

12.2.2. The Table of Contents Field

If you toggle on the displaying field codes in your document, the table of contents will shrink to one line that looks something like this:

{ TOC \o "1-3" \u }

Generally, there is no need to edit the TOC field directly because its switches reflect options that can be changed when you create the table. However, you do need to be aware that the table of contents is a field whose value can be automatically updated.

12.2.3. How to Update a Table of Contents

If you make changes to a document after you have inserted a table of contents, you may have to update the table. There are several ways to do this. You can simply insert a new table of contents using the procedure given above. This causes Word to overwrite the existing table or contents.

You can also:

1. Position the caret within the table of contents.

2. Right click and select **Update Field** from the popup menu. This displays the **Update Table of Contents** dialog box (Figure 12.3).

3. [Optional] Select **Update entire table**.

4. Click **OK**.

The default setting of **Update page numbers** causes Word to only update the page numbers in the table. If you have made changes to the table of

FIGURE 12.3
Updating a Table of Contents

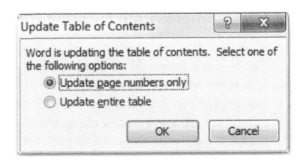

content text directly (see below), this option will preserve your changes but will not update the table to reflect any changes made to headings or fields in the document text. If you have not changed the table directly, **Update entire table** is the better choice.

12.2.4. Formatting the Table of Contents

Formatting of the table of contents should be done entirely by modifying the TOC styles if possible. You should avoid inserting text or applying formatting directly to the table of contents text. The reason for this is that changes made to the table of contents directly will be lost if you recreate the table. However, changes you make to styles will be applied whenever the table is updated.

In most cases it is possible to create a table of contents without having to resort to modifying the text directly. However, to do so, you have to accept Word's way of doing the table formatting. If you want to go outside the bounds of how Word formats the table of contents, you must format the text directly. If you do so, you should delay making such changes until the document text is completely finished and there is no possibility that you will need to update the table of contents.

12.2.5. Persistent Modifications to the Table of Contents

Word's automatic table of contents feature creates a table that will work for most people without direct editing. Style changes can handle most formatting requirements. There are some types of table of contents formatting that cannot be done without direct editing of the table. The following sections illustrate how direct editing can create table of contents formatting that is not possible to create automatically. You have to judge whether the benefits of such formatting outweigh the difficulties created by using it.

12.2.5.1. How to Right Align Heading Numbers

Word normally sets up left aligned heading numbers in a table of contents. Figure 12.2 is formatted with the heading numbers left aligned. It is possible to use right aligned numbers using a combination of numbering, style changes and manual editing, as shown in Figure 12.4.

Tabs and tab stops control placement of right aligned numbers. Modify the table of contents styles (TOC 1 to TOC 9) to set these positions. Right aligned numbers only makes sense with hanging indentation. Modify the paragraph settings so that the **Left** indentation setting is zero, **Special** to **Hanging** and **By** to the offset where the text is to be positioned. You will also need to set up a right aligned tab stop (see Chapter 8) that is slightly to the left of the hang indentation (around 0.05″–0.10″ less) to position the page number.

There needs to be a tab character before and after the heading number. One way to add the tab that follows the number is through the heading number setup on the **Define new Multilevel list** dialog box (**Customize Outline Number list** on the Mac). Set **Follow number** to **Tab character**. It is not possible to automatically add the tab character before the number using the settings on this dialog box. To manually insert the tabs, you first much unlink the table of contents field (see above) then add tabs before the numbers. You can also manually insert the tabs after the numbers.

Right aligning numbers in the table of contents requires a bit of overhead. Any changes that you make manually will be lost if you need to update the table of contents later.

12.2.5.2. How to Justify a Table of Contents

Word will not automatically hyphenate a table of contents. If you want a justified table of contents, you need to manually hyphenate it. Figure 12.5 shows a table of contents entry that has been justified and hyphenated along with one that is justified and unhyphenated. The word gaps in the unhyphenated version (note the gaps surrounding the word *on* in the first line) are ridiculously large. Many briefs filed in the U.S. Supreme Court have unhyphenated and justified tables of contents that look much worse. To hyphenate the table of contents you must unlink the table of content field. Then insert optional hyphens to manually hyphenate the table (see Chapter 8).

12.3. Creating a Table of Authorities

There are three ways to create a table of authorities (TOA) in Word:

1. Use a third party tool to create the table of authorities.

2. Use Word's built-in TOA feature.

3. Create the table of authorities by hand.

12.3.1. Using a Third Party Tool

There are several products on the market for creating tables of authorities. These are usually integrated into Word with their own ribbon tab. The advantages of such products can be found in their marketing brochures. However, specific products are outside the scope of this book.

12.3.2. Using Word's TOA Feature

Word has the ability to create a rudimentary table of authorities automatically. Using Word's TOA feature is a two-step process. First you mark the citations in the document using fields; then you generate a table of authorities from those fields. The concept is simple but in practice it is difficult to work through. One difficulty is that you must to be able to work with fields.

12.3.2.1. The TA Field

Word uses the TA field to mark entries for the table of authorities. It is nearly impossible to use Word's TOA feature without editing TA fields directly. You have to edit the TA field to correct errors in the table of authorities. Therefore in order to use the TOA feature, you need to understand the structure of this field. A TA has this general form.

> { TA \l *Munaf v. Geren*, 128 S. Ct. 2207 (2008)" \s "Munaf v. Geren" \c 1 }

The switches in this field have the following meanings:

\l

Specifies the long form of the citation. This is the text that appears in the table of authorities. If a citation appears incorrectly in the table of contents, you have to change this value.

\s

Specifies a short form of citation. TA fields may have just a \s switch in which case they share the long citation defined in another field with a matching short citation.

\c

Specifies the ordinal category the entry should be listed in the table of authorities. In the example above, "\c 1" specifies that the entry appears in the first section in the table of authorities. By default the first section is "Cases." However, you can customize the headings for each section. If a citation appears in the wrong section within the table of authorities, this is the value you need to change.

There are a few other possible switches for the TA field. However, they rarely are needed or used.

12.3.2.2. How to Mark a Citation

To mark a citation for inclusion in the table of authorities for the first time:

1. Select the citation.

2. Display the **Mark Citation** dialog box (Figure 12.6) by pressing:

Windows	Mac
Shift/ALT/i	Command/Option/Shift/I

A "preliminary injunction is an 'extraordinary a

Munaf v. Geren, 128 S. Ct. 2207, 2219 (2008) (citation

is warranted only where the party seeking the inju

o prevail on the merits" an

litigation without an injun

(1975); see *Munaf,* 128 S.

8, 972 (1997) (*per curiam*)

If you are going to use Word's TOA feature, you should memorize this keyboard shortcut because you will be using it so frequently. Figure 12.7 shows how the **Mark Citation** dialog box displays the selected text. The **Mark Citation** dialog box is non-modal so you can switch back and forth between it and the document text.

3. Edit the text in the **Selected text** text box so that it appears exactly the way you want it to appear in the table of authorities. For initial case citations, you generally will have to remove the page number. Some people like to insert a page break after the party names so that TOA entries will not wrap around the page. Select the section you want the entry to appear in from the **Category** dropdown list.

4. Edit the short citation. This can be anything you want that will uniquely identify the case. The party names are usually sufficient here unless you have to cite a case with multiple opinions.

   Figure 12.7 shows the previous citation edited and ready for marking.

5. Click **Mark**.

   This inserts the TA field for the entry in the document. Figure 12.8 shows how the field appears in the Word document.

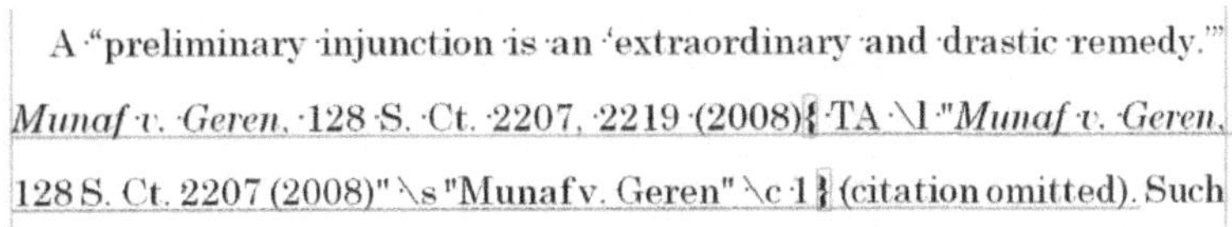
A "preliminary injunction is an 'extraordinary and drastic remedy.'"
Munaf v. Geren, 128 S. Ct. 2207, 2219 (2008){ TA \l "Munaf v. Geren,
128 S. Ct. 2207 (2008)" \s "Munaf v. Geren" \c 1 } (citation omitted). Such

Figure 12.8
The TOA entry in the document

When you mark the citation the **Mark Citation** dialog box remains open so that you can mark additional citations in your document. The only way to delete or change a citation marking is to edit the field directly. In recognition of this, Word makes hidden characters visible whenever you mark a citation. The TA field behaves differently from other fields in that it becomes visible with hidden characters. Use the ¶ button on the **Home** tab to display TA fields—not **ALT/F9** (**Option/F9 [Mac]**), as for other fields. The easier access to this one particular type of field reflects the fact that, unlike other fields, TA fields routinely must be edited directly.

Some citations may be significantly different in the text from how they should appear in the table of authorities. Figure 12.9 is an example of a text

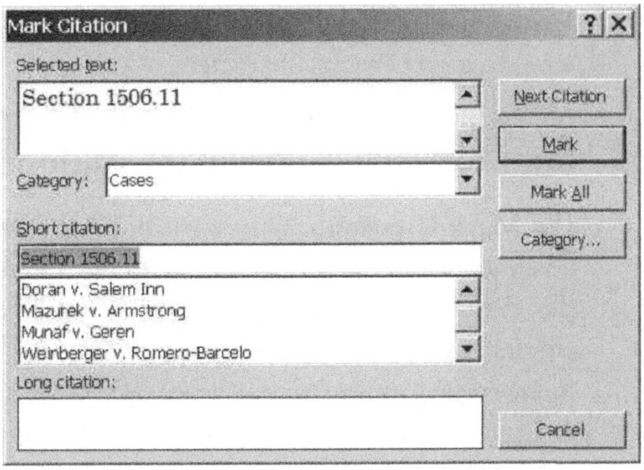
Mark Citation
Selected text:
Section 1506.11
Next Citation
Mark
Category:
Cases
Mark All
Short citation:
Category...
Section 1506.11
Doran v. Salem Inn
Mazurek v. Armstrong
Munaf v. Geren
Weinberger v. Romero-Barcelo
Long citation:
Cancel

Figure 12.9
Sometimes citations in a document are like how they should appear in the TOA

citation where you have to examine the context of the document to determine the full citation. In Figure 12.10, this citation has been edited and is ready for marking.

FIGURE 12.10
The previous
citation edited for
marking

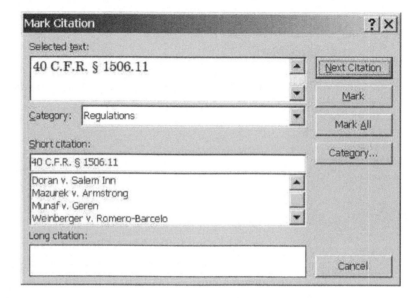

If you need special symbols (such as §) for your citations you will not be able to type them on the **Mark Citation** dialog box even if you have defined a shortcut key. To get around this problem on Windows, use the Notepad application (not Word) to create a new document before you create the TOA. Use **CTRL/C** and **CTRL/V** to copy the special symbols you need from Word to Notepad. When you need a special symbol in the Mark Citation dialog box, switch to Notepad, select the symbol you need, press **CTRL/C** copy, switch back to Word and use **CTRL/V** to paste the symbol into the Mark Citation dialog box. On the Mac use the Character View (see Chapter 2) to insert special characters.

12.3.2.3. How to Mark Additional Citations

The **Mark Citation** dialog box contains a **Next Citation** button. Word's documentation makes the highly exaggerated claim that this button finds the next citation in the document. In reality, Word is only able to finds citations that match a few patterns, such as contining "id", "v." or a date followed by a closing parentheses. If you use the **Next Citation** button, you are going to have to make another pass through the document to find the citations Word misses. You are likely to be better off if you scan the document yourself to find citations.

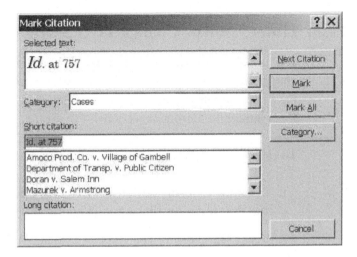

12.3.2.4. How to Mark Citations for Authorities Already Found

It is likely that you will encounter citations to authorities that you have marked before (Figure 12.11). The TOA feature allows you to reference the previous citation rather than having to enter the full citation in again yourself. To use previously marked authority, select it from the list box below the **Short citation** text box and click **Mark** (Figure 12.12). If your list of authority is long, you can usually speed up the search process by typing in the short citation. As you type in a short citation, Word automatically scrolls though the list box to find the first match.

12.3.2.5. How to Add or Change TOA Sections

You may find that the predefined table of authorities sections do not meet your needs. You may want to add a new section, use different names (*e.g.*, have one "Statutes and regulations" section instead of separate sections), or use a different ordering or section.

To change a category:

1. Click the Category button on the **Mark Citation** dialog box to display the Edit Category dialog box (Figure 12.13).

2. Select the category you want to change. Where Word lists numbers, the category does not have a name.

3. Type the new category name into the **Replace with** text box.

4. Click **Replace**.

In Figure 12.13, the unused "8" category has been assigned the name "Treaties." However, you could use the same process to replace the heading for any of the other categories. You could just as well change the first entry from "Cases" to "Statutes" and the second from "Statutes" to "Cases" to make statutes appear before cases in the table of authorities.

FIGURE 12.13
Use the Edit Category dialog box to add or change sections for a TOA.

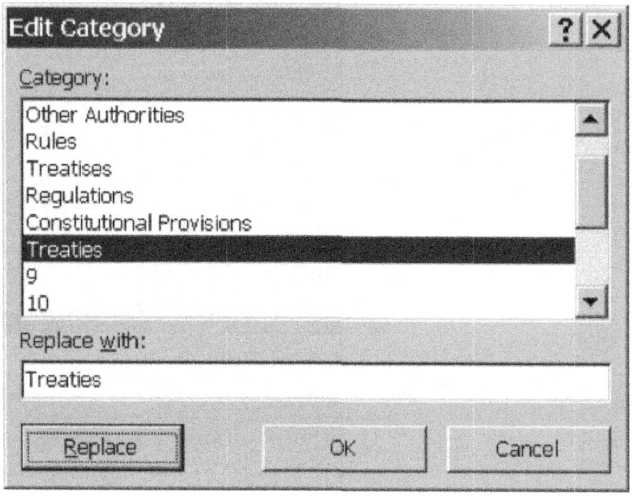

It is critical that you make any changes in ordering before you mark headings in your document. The categories in the TA field are positional. "\c 2" in a TA field places the authority in the second section, without regard to what the title of the section is. Therefore, changing the name of a section does not change the entries already marked as being in the section. As such, if you change the first category from its default of Cases to Statutes *after* you have marked cases with TA fields, citations already marked as cases will appear in the table of authorities listed as statutes.

12.3.2.6. How to Create a Table of Authorities

Once you have marked the citations in your document, Word can automatically generate a table of authorities from them. The process is similar to creating a table of contents

To create a table of authorities:

1. Position the caret in the document where you want the table of authorities to appear.

2. Display the **Table of Authorities** dialog box (Figure 12.14):

Windows	Mac
References>Table of Authorities> Insert Table of Authorities	a. Click **Insert>Index and Tables**. b. Select the **Table of Authorities** tab.

3. Click **OK**. Generally you should not have to make changes on this dialog box.

FIGURE 12.14
Use the Table of Authorities dialog box to insert a TOA.

Figure 12.15 shows a table of authorities created by Word (with user errors).

Word implements the table of authorities as a sequence of fields. If you make fields visible, your multi-page table of authorities will probably shrink to one line and appear as a sequence of fields similar to this:

{ TOA \h \c "1" \p }{ TOA \h \c "2" \p }{ TOA \h \c "3" \p }

Each TOA field represents a different section of the table of authorities.

FIGURE 12.15
The first pass at a
TOA created by
Word

Cases

Amoco Prod. Co. v. Village of Gambell,
480 U.S. 531 (1987) 8, 22
Department of Transp. v. Public Citizen,
541 U.S. 752 (2004) 9, 10
Munaf v. Geren,
128 S. Ct. 2207 (2008) 8, 14, 15
National Audubon Soc'y v. Hester,
801 F.2d 405 (D.C. Cir. 1986) 15, 18
Robertson v. Methow Valley Citizens Council,
490 U.S. 332 (1989) 9, 10, 25
Serono Labs., Inc. v. Shalala, 158 F.3d 1313 (D.C. Cir. 1998) 15
United States v. Oakland Cannabis Buyers' Coop.,
532 U.S. 483 (2001) 24
United States v. Oakland Cannabis Buyers' Coop.,
532 U.S. 483, 497 (2001)..23

Statutes

16 U.S.C. § 1362(18)..23
42 U.S.C. § 4331(b) 9, 20
42 U.S.C. § 4332(2)(C)..9
5 U.S.C. § 703 12
NRDC v. Evans,
232 F. Supp. 2d 1003 (N.D. Cal. 2002)..24, 25

Regulations

40 C.F.R. § 1500.3.. 9
40 C.F.R. § 1501.4..10
40 C.F.R. § 1502 10
40 C.F.R. § 1506.11..9, 11, 16, 19

12.3.2.7. Correcting Marking Errors in a TOA

The table of authorities shown in Figure 12.16 contains a couple of common marking errors: the citation for *United States v. Oakland Cannabis Buyers' Coop.* appears twice, with the second entry including the page number; and

FIGURE 12.16
The error in the TA field for *Oakland Cannabis Buyers' Coop.*

States v. Oakland Cannabis Buyers' Coop., 532 U.S. 483, 497 (2001){TA \l "United· States· v.· Oakland· Cannabis· Buyers'· Coop.,· 532 U.S. 483, 497 (2001)" \s "United States v. Oakland Cannabis Buyers' Coop." \c 1} (quoting *TVA v. Hill*, 437 U.S. 153, 194 (1978){TA \l "TVA v.·

the citation for *NRDC v. Evans* appears in under Statutes rather than *Cases*. You should fix all the marking errors before making any other changes to an automatically generated table of authorities. Such errors are inevitable in the first pass of marking citations.

The only way to change a citation that has already been marked is to edit the TA field directly. Click the ¶ button to make the TA fields visible if they are not visible already. Then search the document for the fields that are in error. Fixed the errors in the field then rebuild the table.

The changes needed to correct the TA fields used to create Figure 12.15 are relatively minor. Figure 12.16 shows the error in *Oakland Cannabis Buyers' Coop.* TA field. The value for the "\l" switch contains the page number. This should be deleted. Once the citation are made the same, Word will only create one TOA entry.

Figure 12.17 shows the *NRDC v. Evans* TA field with the error selected. The "\c 2" switch places this entry in the second table of authorities section (Statutes). It need to be changed to "\c 1" (Cases).

FIGURE 12.17
The error in the TA field for *NRDC v. Evans*

(2003)" } (discussing *NRDC v. Evans*, 232 F. Supp. 2d 1003 (N.D. Cal. 2002){· TA · \l· "NRDC· v.· Evans,· 232 F. Supp. 2d 1003 (N.D. Cal. 2002)" \s "NRDC v. Evans" \c 2 }). The·

After these errors are corrected, the table can be rebuilt. Figure 12.18 shows how the table of authorities appears after these changes are made.

12.3.2.7.1. How to Format the TOA

The process for formatting an automatically generated table of authorities is similar to that of a table of contents. Word creates the section headings in using the TOA Heading style and the entries using the Table of Authorities style. If you want to change the indentation or the spacing, just modify the Table of Contents style. As with table of contents styles, you may also want to set the right indentation to keep the entries away from the page numbers.

208

FIGURE 12.18
The TOA with TA
fields corrected

Cases

Amoco Prod. Co. v. Village of Gambell,
    480 U.S. 531 (1987) 8, 22
Department of Transp. v. Public Citizen,
    541 U.S. 752 (2004) 9, 10
Munaf v. Geren,
    128 S. Ct. 2207 (2008) 8, 14, 15
National Audubon Soc'y v. Hester,
    801 F.2d 405 (D.C. Cir. 1986) 15, 18
NRDC v. Evans,
    232 F. Supp. 2d 1003 (N.D. Cal. 2002)...................................24, 25
Robertson v. Methow Valley Citizens Council,
    490 U.S. 332 (1989) 9, 10, 25
Serono Labs., Inc. v. Shalala, 158 F.3d 1313 (D.C. Cir. 1998) 15
United States v. Oakland Cannabis Buyers' Coop.,
    532 U.S. 483 (2001) 23, 24

Statutes

16 U.S.C. § 1362(18)...23
42 U.S.C. § 4331(b)..9, 20
42 U.S.C. § 4332(2)(C)..9
5 U.S.C. § 703...12

Regulations

40 C.F.R. § 1500.3..9
40 C.F.R. § 1501.4..10
40 C.F.R. § 1502...10
40 C.F.R. § 1506.11...9, 11, 16, 19

12.3.2.8. Crossing the Rubicon: Editing a TOA

Word creates a number of formatting issues in tables of authorities that
cannot be corrected by fixing fields or changing styles. Word does not carry
style formatting of a citation through to the automatically generated table
of authorities. As a result, in Figures 12.15 none of the case names are em-
phasized. Also notice that the statutes are not ordered correctly; 5 U.S.C.
comes after 42 U.S.C. The same problem crops up with case captions that
begine with *in re*. You have to correct these problems manually by unlinking
and editing.

Any modification you make directly to the table will be lost if you have
rebuild it again. Therefore, you should only make these changes after the
rest of the document is completely finished and when all the TA fields are
corrected.

12.3.2.9. Issues with Word's TOA Feature

Word's automatic TOA generation feature has a number of issues, including:

◊ It can only create the simplest of tables. Figure 12.19 shows a subdivided table of authorities where the "statutes and regulations" section has been subdivided so that code sections are grouped by act. This type of grouping is impossible to create with Word's TOA feature.

◊ As shown previously, the Word TOA feature does not carry style formatting of case names through to the table of contents.

◊ Word's TOA feature does not allow you to specify the sort order. Word places *In re Alappat* in the table under "I" rather than "A".

◊ Word does not have the ability to indicate what citations have been marked, other than to examine field codes.

FIGURE 12.19
A TOA with
multiple levels of
groupings

Statutes and regulations:

Administrative Procedure Act, 5 U.S.C. 701 *et seq.*:

5 U.S.C. 702 37

5 U.S.C. 703 37

Coastal Zone Management Act of 1972, 16 U.S.C.
1451 *et seq.* 6

16 U.S.C. 1456(c)(1)(A) 6

16 U.S.C. 1456(c)(1)(B) 14

16 U.S.C. 1456(c)(1)(C) 6

Endangered Species Act of 1973, 16 U.S.C. 1531
et seq. 2

16 U.S.C. 1536(a)(2) 8

16 U.S.C. 1536(b)(4)(iv) 8

16 U.S.C. 1536(o)(2) 8

Marine Mammal Protection Act of 1972, 16 U.S.C.
1361 *et seq.* 2

16 U.S.C. 1361(6) 35

16 U.S.C. 1362(12)(A) 7

16 U.S.C. 1362(13) 35

16 U.S.C. 1362(18) (2000 & Supp. V 2005) 35

◊ The **Next Citation** button misses many citations. As such, it provides no advantage over manual searching.

◊ There is no simple way to edit or delete TOA entries. Any such modifications require you to edit the TA fields directly.

◊ Some courts require a combined table of contents and table of authorities. Such a table is similar to a table of contents but after each entry all the authorities cited in the section are listed with page numbers (Figure 12.20).

◊ It is difficult to edit citations with symbols and special characters.

◊ Generated TOAs have to be edited. Those edits are lost if the TOA is regenerated.

You are likely to conclude that these feature limitations, combined with its complexity of use, endow Word's TOA feature with no benefit whatsoever over creating a TOA manually. I view it as a feature in name only; one that merely serves as a line item for product comparisons in marketing materials and do not recommend using it.

12.3.3. Manually Creating a Table of Authorities

The remaining (and usually best) alternative is to create a table of authorities manually. Before you manually create a table of authorities you need to decide what format you are going to use. It could be a simple table, as in

Figure 12.15; a table with multiple levels of grouping, as in Figure 12.19; a combined table, as in Figure 12.20; or some other variation. Once you have determined the table format, you need to set up the styles for it (see Chapters 5 and 11).

Start building the table by inserting the header and authority groups. Then scan the document to look for citations to create table entires. The easiest way to find citations and create table entires is to use a split screen. Use the mouse to drag the splitter bar above the scroll bar (enlarged in Figure 12.21) until the Document Window is split into two roughly even parts. Use the top window to edit the table of authorites and the bottom to scan the document for citations Go from start to finish through the document. Whenever you find a citation in the bottom window, copy it then paste it in the top window at the appropriate location in the table. Then apply one of the table of authorities styles (TOA 1, TOA, 2 or TOA 3 in Chapter 5) and format. Move to the end of the entry, press **Tab** then type in the page number. On Windows it is much easier to find the page number if you have set up the status bar as suggested in Chapter 2. When finished, drag the split point to either the top or the bottom to return to one large editing window.

Format the table entries using table of authorities styles. See Chapter 5 for a description of these styles and Chapter 9 on how to set up them up. These styles are likely to require:

◊ Hanging indentation

◊ Right aligned tabs with leader for the page numbers.

◊ Right indentation

FIGURE 12.21
Word with a split
document window

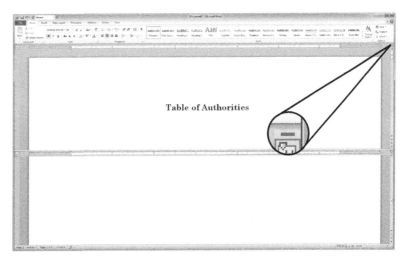

Some people like to insert manual line breaks (see Chapter 10) after the party names to ensure that multi-line table of authorities entries break at a consistent point. Others, let the line breaks occur naturally. The format to use is a matter of personal choice.

12.3.3.1. Table of Points and Authorities

A small number of states use combined table of contents and table of authorities. Under Oklahoma Supreme Court Rules, rule 1.11(d) this table goes under the heading "Index"; under Kentucky Rules of Civil Procedure, rule 76.12 (4)(c)(iii) it is "Statement of Points and Authorities"; and under Illinois Civil Appeals Rules, rule 341(h)(1) it is "Points and Authorities." The format of such a combined table of contents/table of authorities varies among these courts. For example, Oklahoma requires authority to be listed alphabetically after the section heading while Illinois requires authority to be listed in order of its importance. Such tables usually only include one level of arguement headings and tend not to subdivide the citations into groups. Some courts require that the citations be listed in order of their importance.

There are two ways to create such a table. The first is to have Word create a table of contents. Then unlink the table and insert the citation references as described previously for a table of authorities. The other method is to manuallyinsert both the headings and the citations into the table.

Chapter 13
Cover Pages

The trick to creating professional-looking cover pages is to use *tables*. A table defines the structure of the cover and the relative position of the various cover elements. This chapter shows how to create cover pages in three distinct styles. These examples can be modified to match the type of cover page used in any court.

A table is an array of *cells*. Each cell is a container that can hold text, images or even another table. Cells are arranged vertically into *columns* and horizontally into *rows*.[1] When Word gives dimensions of a table, it gives the number of rows before the columns. For example, a 3x4 table means a table with three columns and four rows.

Figure 13.1 shows the major features of a table used in cover pages. A table and its cells can have borders. Each border can have a different line style or no line at all. In Figure 13.1 the top and bottom borders of the table are different from all the other borders.

Table adjacent cells can be merged to form larger cells. Merging cells allows a table to have rows or columns with varying numbers of cells. This

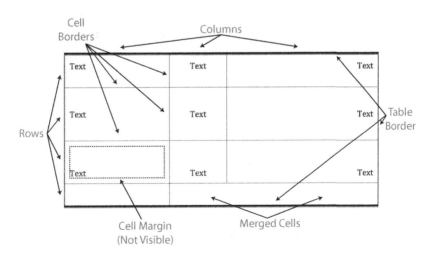

FIGURE 13.1
Features of a table

---

[1] This is the reverse of the order generally used in mathematics.

feature is useful when creating cover pages because it allows the table to have a flexible structure that does not require all the elements to be aligned vertically. Merged cells must form a rectangle. Word does not allow cells to merge into other shapes.

Cells have an internal margin. The cell margin controls how close the content comes to the border. A table has a cell margin setting that applies to all cells. This value can be overriden on a per cell basis.

The row and column sizes are adjustable. However, cell size settings only specify the minimum size of a cell. If the contents of a cell exceed the available space, Word increases the row height to accommodate it.

The alignment of contents within each cell is individually configurable. Like paragraphs, cell contents can be aligned to the left, right or centered. Cell contents can also be aligned vertically to the top, middle or bottom. In Figure 13.1, text has been aligned using each possible alignment setting.

13.1. A Box Caption Cover Page

The first example is a simple box caption cover used in most trial courts (Figure 13.2). This type of cover page usually does not fill the first page and

FIGURE 13.2
A box caption cover page

**In the Superior Court of New Jersey
Law Division
Special Civil Part
Small Claims Section
Union County**

Robin Conner
The Conner Law Firm
132 West St.
Hoboken, N.J. 07030
(201) 999-9999

James Robinson,
Plaintiff,

v.

Wilson Properties, Inc.
Defendant.

Civil Action No.

Complaint for Recovery of Security Deposit

FIGURE 13.3
The same cover
page with the table
grid lines visible

In the Superior Court of New Jersey Law Division Special Civil Part Small Claims Section Union County	
Robin Conner The Conner Law Firm 132 West St. Hoboken, N.J. 07030 (201) 999-9999	
James Robinson, *Plaintiff,* *v.* Wilson Properties, Inc. *Defendant.*	Civil Action No.
Complaint for Recovery of Security Deposit	

the brief text may start immediately below on the same page. This type of cover is easy to format because there is no need to fill the page.

This cover is created using a table. Figure 13.3 shows the structure of that table. The cover is formed from a 2 × 4 table. The cells in the top and bottom rows have been merged to allow the court name and document title to span the width of the page and be centered.

13.2. How to Create a Box Caption Cover Page

This section walks through the steps used to create the cover shown in Figure 13.2. Keep in mind that these steps are just intended as a guide. Format the cover in any way you think appears best for the target court.

To create the cover page shown in Figure 13.2:

1. Insert the table:

Windows	Mac
Click **Insert>Table>Table** and select a 2 × 4 table from the dropdown menu.	a. **Tables>New** b. Click the **Tables>Table Options>New** button and select a 2 × 4 table from the **Tables** tab.

216

FIGURE 13.4
A 2 × 4 table

The table should appear like the one in Figure 13.4.

2. Merge the cells in the top and bottom rows. For each row, select both cells then click:

Windows	Mac
Table Tools>Layout>Merge>Merge Cells	**Table Layout>Merge>Merge**

After this, the table should appear as shown in Figure 13.5.

FIGURE 13.5
The table with merged cells.

3. If you have not created a Cover Text style, create one based upon Normal. You do not need to make any formatting changes to the style. The purpose of this style is merely to isolate the cover page formatting from that of the rest of the document.

4. Type the text for the caption box using the Cover Text style as shown in Figure 13.6.

FIGURE 13.6
The table with the cover text filled in

In the Superior Court of New Jersey Law Division Special Civil Part Small Claims Section Union County	
Robin Conner The Conner Law Firm 132 West St. Hoboken, N.J. 07030 (201) 999-9999	
James Robinson, Plaintiff, v. Wilson Properties, Inc. Defendant.	Civil Action No.
Complaint for Recovery of Security Deposit	

5. Center the two table cells in the third row vertically. Select the text in both cells then click:

Windows	Mac
Table Tools>Layout>Alignment> Align Center Left	**Table Layout>Alignment>Align> Center Left**

The table should appear as shown in Figure 13.7.

FIGURE 13.7
The third row centered vertically

In the Superior Court of New Jersey Law Division Special Civil Part Small Claims Section Union County	
Robin Conner The Conner Law Firm 132 West St. Hoboken, N.J. 07030 (201) 999-9999	
James Robinson, Plaintiff, v. Wilson Properties, Inc. Defendant.	Civil Action No.
Complaint for Recovery of Security Deposit	

6. Format the text in the cells using the controls on the Ribbon **Home** tab. Covers are one of the few places where formatting should be applied directly to the text. Otherwise, a cover page could easily require a dozen styles that are only used once.

Figure 13.8 shows an example of such formatting. The court name and document title have been centered and placed in a larger bold

FIGURE 13.8
Cover text after formatting

In the Superior Court of New Jersey Law Division Special Civil Part Small Claims Section Union County	
Robin Conner The Conner Law Firm 132 West St. Hoboken, N.J. 07030 (201) 999-9999	
James Robinson, *Plaintiff,* *v.* Wilson Properties, Inc. *Defendant.*	Civil Action No.
Complaint for Recovery of Security Deposit	

font. "Plaintiff" and "Defendant" have been placed in italics and right aligned. The versus abbreviation has been centered, placed in italics and the paragraph space above and below was increased to separate it from the parties.

A visible flaw at this point is that the text comes too close together where the cells meet. Correct this by increasing the margins of the cells. You can set the default margins that apply to all cells in the table and set the margins for specific cells to override this value.

7. Display the **Table Options** dialog box (Figure 13.9):

Windows	Mac
Table Tools>Layout>Cell Margins	Table Layout>Alignment Margins

8. Set the desired margins for the entire table. Figure 13.10 shows the appearance of the table after the **Top** and **Bottom** cell margins have been set to 0.1″.

FIGURE 13.9
The Table Options dialog box

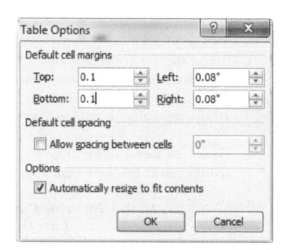

In the completed example shown in Figure 13.3, the bottom margin of the top cell and the top margin of the bottom cell have been made larger than the default table margin.

9. For each cell you wish to change the margins individually, select the cell then display the **Table Properties** dialog box:

Windows	Mac
Table Tools>Layout>Table>Properties	Table Layout>Settings>Properties

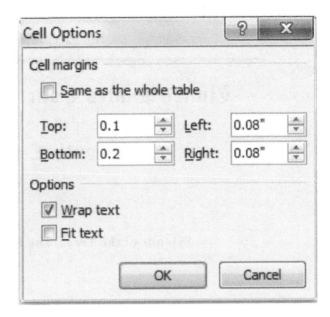

Then perform the following steps:

a. Select the **Cell** tab.

b. Click the **Options** button to display the **Cell Options** dialog box (Figure 13.10).

c. Uncheck the **Same as the whole table** check box.

d. Set the desired margins.

e. Click **OK** to save.

f. Click **OK** to return to the document

The last step is step is to remove the excess borderlines from the table.

7. For each cell with unwanted borders, position the caret in the cell and display the borders dropdown menu:

Windows	Mac
Table Tools>Design>Table Styles>Borders	**Tables>Borders>Draw Borders**

On the dropdown menu, toggle off the desired lines. Once the lines are removed, the cover page should similar to the one in Figure 13.2.

FIGURE 13.11
A formal appellate
cover page

No. 12-1234

United States Court of Appeals

for the

Thirteenth Circuit

Friends of the Trees; The Elk Society,

Appellants,

v.

Robert Razor, in his capacity as
Secretary of the Interior

Appellee.

On appeal from an order entered by the
United States District Court for the District of East Virginia,
No. 2:11-cv-1234

Brief on Behalf of Appellants

THE CONNER LAW FIRM
132 West St.
Hoboken, N.J. 07030
(201) 999-9999

On the brief:
ROBIN CONNER
LIZA STERN

13.3. How to Create an Appellate Cover Page

More elaborate cover pages are customary in the U.S. Supreme Court and circuit courts of appeal. Figure 13.11 illustrates a style of cover page that is typical of those courts.

This cover page also uses a table to define its structure, as shown in Figure 13.12. A full-page cover requires the table cell sizes be set more precisely than with the box caption cover. The one trick to setting up the table structure is that the narrower lines above and below the parties require their own row. These lines cannot be created using cell borders because they do not extend the full width of a cell.

FIGURE 13.12
The structure of the cover page

13.3.1. How to Set up the Table Rows

The first step in creating the cover is to set up the table rows:

1. Insert a 2 × 8 table (see above).

2. Merge the cells in all the rows, except the last (see above).

3. Place the caret in the top cell of the table.

4. Display the **Table Properties** dialog box (Figure 13.13):

Windows	Mac
Table Tools>Layout>Table>Properties	**Table Layout>Settings>Properties**

5. Select the **Table** tab.

   With default margin settings, the cover page text is likely to be too wide.

6. Set **Preferred width**. In this example the table width is 5″.

FIGURE 13.13
Setting the size and
position of the table

FIGURE **13.14**
Setting table row
heights

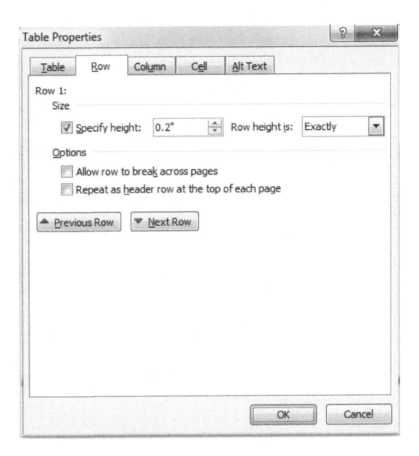

FIGURE **13.14**
Setting table row
heights

7. Set **Alignment** to **Center**.

The next steps set the row height.

8. Select the **Row** tab (Figure 13.14).

9. For each row, check **Specify height**, enter the height, set **Row height is** to **Exactly,** then click **Next Row**. When done, click **OK**.

The cover in Figure 13.11 has row heights of 0.5″, 1.6″, 0.1″, 2.9″, 0.1″, 0.8″, 0.5″ and 2″.

13.3.2. How to Create Lines in the Cover Page

The cover page uses three types of lines: a table border (line at the bottom), a cell border (line at the top) and paragraph borders (lines above and below the caption). The best way to proceed is to delete all the lines of the table and add back those four lines. The lines are added and deleted on the **Borders and Shading** dialog box.

1. Select the entire table and remove all the borders:

Windows	Mac
Table Tools>Design>Table Styles> Borders> No Borders	**Tables>Draw Borders>Borders>None**

The following steps add the double line at the bottom of the cover.

2. Place the caret anywhere within the table.

3. Display the **Borders and Shading** dialog box (Figure 13.15):

Windows	Mac
Table Tools>Design>Table Styles> Borders>Borders and Shading	**Format>Borders and Shading**

4. Under **Style,** select the double line style shown in Figure 13.15.

FIGURE **13.15**
Creating a table
border

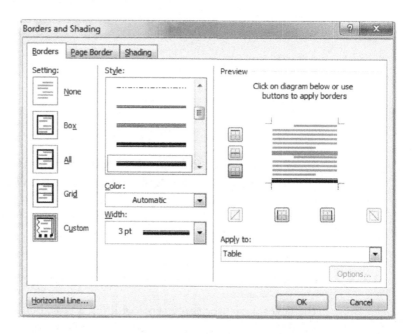

5. Click at the bottom of the **Preview** page to add the line.

6. Click **OK** to save.

   The next steps add the double line at the top of the cover.

7. Place the caret in the second row of the table.

8. Display the **Borders and Shading** dialog box again.

9. Set **Apply to** to **Cell**.

10. Select the same double line style as before.

11. Click at the top of the **Preview** page to add the line.

    The settings should now look like the ones shown in Figure 13.16.

FIGURE 13.16
Setting a cell
border

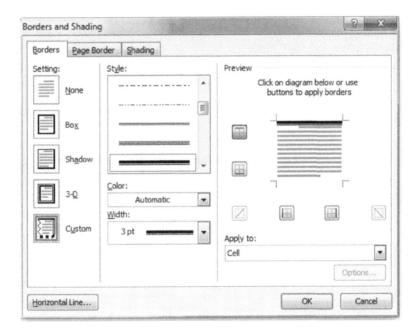

12. Click **OK** to save.

    These steps add the single lines above and below the caption.

13. Position the caret in the cell above the caption.

14. Display the **Borders and Shading** dialog box again.

15. Set **Apply to** to **Paragraph**.

16. Select the single line style shown in Figure 13.17.

FIGURE 13.17
Setting a paragraph
border

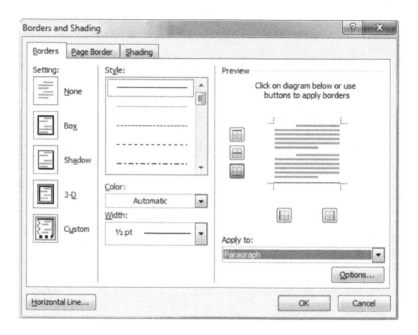

17. Click at the bottom of the **Preview** to add the line.

18. Click **OK** to save.

> At this point the lines will extend all the way across the table.
> The next steps indent the lines.

19. Indent the paragraph margins one inch on the left and right:

Windows	Mac
a. Go to **Page Layout>Paragraph>Indent**.	a. **Format>Paragraph**
b. Set **Left** and **Right** to **1.0**.	b. Set **Left** and **Right** to **1.0**.

20. Position the caret in the cell below the caption.

21. Repeat steps 22–29 for cell below the caption, except that in step 27 add the line at the top (rather than the bottom) of the paragraph.

13.3.3. Creating the Cover Page Text

Enter the text into the cover and format as shown. This example uses a *blackletter* font in the old English style for the court name. The font used, Old English MT, is standard on Windows. This font does not come with the Mac version of Word. On the Mac you can use a serif font, buy a commercial font or download a free blackletter font from the Internet. While it is not recommended that you use free fonts from the Internet for you document, there are a number of free blackletter fonts that are suitable for cover pages.

An alternative to using straight lines above and below the caption is to use an *ornament font*. Ornament fonts contain symbols and images rather than letters. Ornament fonts are available from commercial sources. There is an extremely wide range of free ornament fonts available.

13.4. A Cover Page with Character Boxes

Figure 13.18 illustrates a cover page where the boxes have been created using characters. The format of this cover is taken from Appendix B of the North Carolina Rules of Appellate Procedure.

FIGURE **13.18**
A cover page with
character boxes

NO. COA10-000   TENTH DISTRICT

NORTH CAROLINA COURT OF APPEALS

****

Wilson Motors Corp.,   )
        Plaintiff   )
)
v.   )   From Wake County
)   No. 10 CVS 1234
Jones Automotive Paint,)
Inc.,   )
        Defendant   )

****

REPLY BRIEF OF DEFENDANT-APPELLANT

****

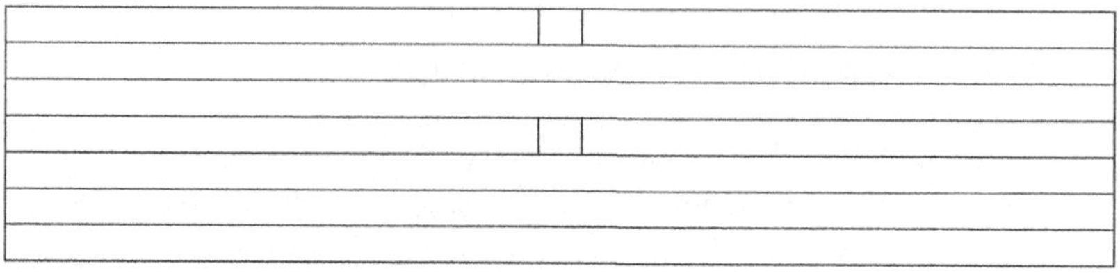

228

FIGURE 13.19
The table structure
for the character
box cover page

The structure of the cover page is defined using the table (Figure 13.19). The only trick here is to set the table up so that characters forming the boxes are in their own cells. The table size is 3 × 7. The cells in all the rows (except the first and fourth) have been merged.

To create this cover page:

1. Insert a 3 × 7 table:

Windows	Mac
Insert>Tables>Table>3 × 7 Table	a. **Insert>Table** b. **Tables>Table Options> New>3 × 7 Table**

The next group of steps adjusts the widths of the middle column so that it is just wide enough to hold the characters forming the box.

2. Display the **Table Properties** dialog box:

Windows	Mac
Table Tools>Layout>Table>Properties	Table Layout>Settings>Properties

3. Select the **Column** tab (Figure 13.20).

4. Set **Preferred width** for the first column to 3.13".

5. Click **Next Column.**

6. Set **Preferred width** for the second column to 0.25".

7. Click **Next Column.**

8. Set **Preferred width** for the third column to 3.13".

9. Click **OK.**

This merges the cells in the rows above and below the box (as well as the top and bottom character lines) so the text can extend across the

FIGURE **13.20**
Column width
settings.

page. The top row is left with multiple cells to keep the case number and district separated and aligned differently.

10. Merge all the rows (except the first and fourth) by selecting the cells in the row and clicking:

Windows	Mac
Table Tools>Layout>Merge>Merge Cells	**Table Layout>Merge>Merge**

11. Enter the text and format.

12. Select the entire table and remove all the borders:

Windows	Mac
Table Tools>Design>Table Styles> Borders> No Borders	**Tables>Draw Borders>Borders>None**

At this point, the cover page should look similar to the one in Figure 13.18 at the beginning of this section.

13.5. Moving on From Here

Once you have created a cover page, save it in a separate Word document. To reuse it, cut and paste into another document. An alternative on Word 2010 (and 2007) is a feature called Cover Page Gallery that allows you to store cover pages and access them directly from Word. The one trick when using this feature is that you need to insert a section break after the table of contents before storing it in the Cover Page Gallery.

Chapter 14
Keyboard Shortcuts

The objective of this chapter is for you to learn how to create *keyboard short-cuts* for your templates. Keyboard shortcuts are key sequents that allow you to rapidly perform a funcion in Word, such as applying a style or inserting a special character. The judicious use of keyboard shortcuts can improve the utility of your templates. A keyboard shortcut can consist of combinations of keys that incorporate **Shift**, **ALT**, **CTRL** or one of the function keys (**Shift**, **CTRL**, Option, **Command** or function keys on the Mac).

Keyboard shortcuts are generally the fastest way to perform functions in Word. The down side to shortcuts is that you have to memorize them.

14.1. Predefined Shortcuts

Word predefines hundred of keyboard shortcuts. Many of these are relics, maintained for compatibility with older versions of Word. These are some of the predefines shortcuts that tend to be most useful are:

Text Editing

Action	Windows	Mac
Undo Last Action	**CTRL/Z**	**Command/Z** or **F1**
Redo Last Action	**CTRL/Y**	**Command/Y**
Cut to Pasteboard	**CTRL/X**	**Command/X** or **F2**
Copy to Pasteboard	**CTRL/C**	**Command/Z** or **F3**
Paste	**CTRL/V**	**Command/V** or **F4**
Select All	**CTRL/A**	**Command/A**

Find and Replace

Action	Windows	Mac
Find	**CTRL/F**	**Command/F**
Replace	**CTRL/H**	**Shift/Command/H**

Styles

Action	Windows	Mac
Heading 1	CTRL/ALT/1	Option/Command/1
Heading 2	CTRL/ALT/2	Option/Command/2
Heading 3	CTRL/ALT/3	Option/Command/3
Heading 4	CTRL/ALT/4	Option/Command/4
Heading5	CTRL/ALT/5	Option/Command/5
Remove Character Formatting	CTRL/Space	CTRL/Space

There is a plethora of keyboard shortcuts the apply formatting. A few examples include:

Action	Windows	Mac
Align Text Right	CTRL/R	Command/R
Align Text Left	CTRL/L	Command/L
Center Text	CTRL/E	Command/E
Underline	CTRL/U	Command/U

Such direct formatting shortcuts have no practicable use when formatting documents using styles.

Most simple key sequences already have a function assigned. However, you can reassign key sequences to another function. If you want to use a key sequence for a shortcut and find that it is already in use, determine if the existing function is one you actually need a shortcut for. If not, feel free to reassign the key sequence for your shortcut The formatting shortcuts shown above are all good candiates for reasignment.

14.2. How to Create a Shortcut for a Style.

Keyboard shortcuts supplement **Style for following paragraph** settings as a means to easily apply styles. The latter can handle the majority of cases while the former can handle the outliers. For example, unbroken sequences of body text after a heading can be handled automatically using the following paragraph setting. Use keyboard shortcuts where you have to interrupt the normal flow of styles, such as to insert a block quotation or to apply emphasis.

With the style set shown in Chapter 5, these styles would be good candidates for keyboard shortcuts:

◊ Emphasis

◊ Block Quotation

◊ Block Quotation Indent

◊ Body Text Continue

◊ Body Text Continue Indent

To create a keyboard shortcut for a style:

1. Modify the style from the **Styles** pane [Windows] or **Styles** window [Mac].

2. On the **Modify Style** dialog box select **Format>Keyboard shortcut**.

This displays the **Customize Keyboard** dialog box (Figure 14.1).

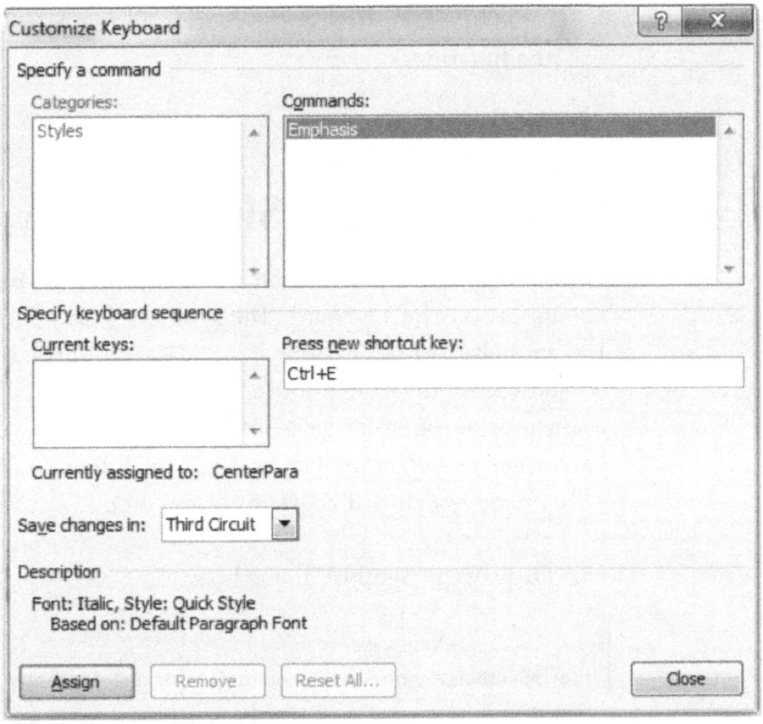

FIGURE 14.1
Entering a
keyboard shortcut

3. Set the value of **Save changes in** to the name of the template file if you only want the shortcut to be defined for that template. Set it to **Normal** if you want the keyboard to be defined in the default Word template.

4. Click on the **Press new shortcut key** text box.

   If the key sequence has already been assigned to a shortcut, Word displays the function it has been assigned to. Figure 14.1 shows **CTRL/E** entered as the keyboard shortcut. The **Customize Keyboard** dialog box shows that this key sequence has already been defined by Word as a shortcut for the CenterPara (Center Paragraph) function. This function, using a simple shortcut, has very little value with style formatting. It is a good candidate for reassignment. If you want to keep the existing shortcut, clear out the **Press new shortcut key** text box and enter another key sequence.

5. Click **Assign**.

   Figure 14.2 shows the keyboard sequence after it has been assigned. The **Current keys** list shows the shortcuts that have been assigned to the style. There can be multiple keyboard sequence assigned to the same function. Repeat the process above to assign another shortcut to the function.

6. Click **Close**.

14.3. How to Create a Shortcut for a Symbol

There are a number of characters commonly used in legal writing that do not appear on the keyboard. The symbols ¶ and § are ubiquitous in briefs. The symbols ®, © and ™ appear often as well. If you use a symbol frequently it makes sense to create a shortcut for it.

The process for creating a keyboard shortcut for a symbol is nearly identical to creating a shortcut for a style. The only difference is in the starting point.

To create a keyboard shortcut for a symbol:

1. Display the **Symbol** dialog box:

Windows	Mac
Insert>Symbols>Symbol>More Symbols	Insert>Symbol>Advanced Symbol

Figure 14.2
Selecting a symbol
to assign a shortcut

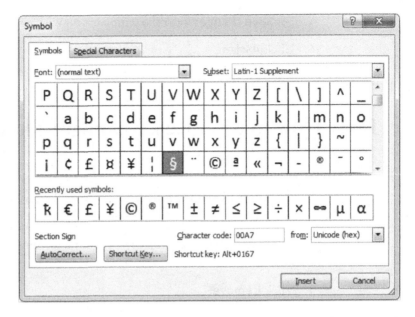

Figure 14.2
Selecting a symbol
to assign a shortcut

2. Select the character to which you wish to assign a shortcut (Figure 14.2).

3. Click **Shortcut Key**. This displays the **Customize Keyboard** dialog box (Figure 14.3).

   From this point on the process for defining the shortcut key for a symbol is identical to doing the same for a style.

4. Press the desired shortcut key.

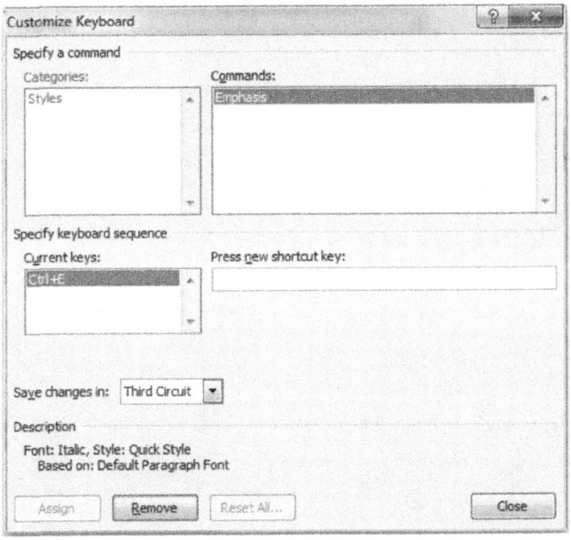

Figure 14.3
The key sequence
assigned

5. Set **Save changes in** to the template you wish to define the shortcut in.

6. Click **Assign**.

7. Click **Close**.

14.4. How to Remove a Keyboard Shortcut.

To remove a keyboard shortcut:

1. Display the **Customize Keyboard** dialog box using the process shown above for either a style or a symbol.

2. Select the keyboard shortcut you want to remove from the **Current keys** list.

3. Click **Remove**.

14.5. Moving on from Here

You do not have to add shortcuts to your templates immediately. Rather than guessing at what you will need, try using your templates for a bit of time and take note of the symbols you insert frequently and the styles that you find you need to apply manually. After that, create shortcuts for those features you use frequently.

Chapter 15
Finishing Up

This final chapter covers the assorted topics that arise during the final production of a brief. There are how to generate a word count; how to create a PDF version of the Word document; and how to insert a signature into a Word document.

15.1. Word Counts

Courts are shifting to word counts as the mechanism of limiting brief lengths. In the days of typewriters and monospaced type, page limits provided a simple means of equitably limiting the length of briefs. The text of proportional typefaces in the same point size varies widely in size (see Chapter 6). You can cram much more text in the same number of pages using a narrow type (like Times New Roman) than you can with a wide typeface (like Century Schoolbook).

The rules of many courts have caught up to this reality by limiting brief sizes using word counts (*e.g.*, U.S. Supreme Court R. 33(1)(g) and Fed. R. App. P. 32(a)(7)). Getting an accurate word count of a brief would normally be a very tedious process. Fortunately, Word can automatically count words in a document or a selected range.

To determine the word count:

1. Read the rules carefully to determine what parts of the brief must be included in the word count.

2. Select the text that must be included in the word count.

3. Display the **Word Count** dialog box (Figure 15.1):

Windows	Mac
Review>Proofing>Word Count	**Tools>Word Count**

4. Ensure that **Include textboxes, footnotes and endnotes** is checked if those elements must be included in the word count. Most courts require them to be counted.

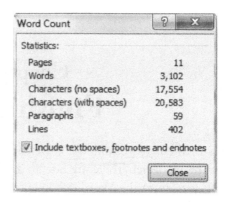

5. Save the value listed beside **Words**.

6. If the text that must be counted is not contiguous within the text, re-peat the process for each range of text and add the values together.

7. Double check.

Older versions of Word have had problems with Word counts. See, *DeSil-va v. DiLeonardi*, 185 F.3d 815 (7th Cir. 1999). Most courts accept the Word's own count. However, you are the one ultimately responsible for its accuracy.

15.2. Creating PDF Documents

Portable Document Format (PDF) is a specification for storing documents. Many courts require that briefs be filed in PDF format, in addition to or in lieu of paper. Even when a court does not require a PDF, it is useful to create the brief in PDF format to maintain a record of what was submitted to the court.[1]

The advantage of a PDF document is that it is device independent. The PDF format contains all the text, images and fonts required to display docu-ment. A PDF document appears the same on different computers and print-ers (within the limits of the device).

There are two general methods for creating a PDF document from a Word document. The first is to have Word create the PDF document. That process is basically the same on Windows and the Mac. The other method is to use a PDF creation tool. That process is a bit different on Windows and the Mac.

You should install a PDF viewing application that can edit the document

---

[1] The recomendation here is that you never give your documents in Word format to a court or opponent. Documents can contain hidden information (called *metadata*) that you may not want to share with others.

properties. Windows generally does not come with a PDF viewing application installed. The Mac's Preview application does not support editing PDF properties. There are a number of freely available PDF viewers with this capability. You can get these from a secure software download site.[2]

You should always create PDF documents directly from your Word documents. Do not print the document and scan to create the PDF version. Scanning will create a PDF document that is excessively large and will have poor quality.

15.2.1. How to Create a PDF Document Within Word

To create a PDF directly from within Word:

1. Select **File>Save** As.

2. Set **Save as type** (**Format** on the Mac) to **PDF**.

3. Enter the PDF document name and navigate to the folder what you want to save.

4. Click **Save**.

This is the simplest way to create a PDF. There are two reasons not to use this method. First, external PDF tools often have more options. These can give you more control over the structure of the PDF document. Second, older versions of Word did not embed fonts in a PDF document properly.

15.2.2. Creating a PDF Document Using and External Tool

The following sections show how to create a PDF document using an external tool. The process is different on Windows and the Mac. Each system is addressed in a separate section.

15.2.2.1. How to Create a PDF Document on Windows

PDF creation utilities on Windows are usually implemented as virtual printers. A virtual printer is software that acts like a hardware printer. The PDF creator's virtual printer can be managed through the control panel and it shows up as an available printer that can be accessed by nearly every

---

[2] One such place is www.cnet.com.

application with print capabilities.

There are a number of freely available and commercial products that can create PDF files. These can be found on secure download sites. One such utility that has worked flawlessly here is called doPDF.

To create the PDF document:

1. Select **File>Print**.

2. Set **Printer** to the name of the PDF virtual printer.

3. Set any desired printer options, such as the page size.

4. Click **Print**.

At this point the PDF is out of the hands of Word and into the control of the PDF creator. The remainder of the process is dependent upon the specific PDF creator used. Usually it will prompt for the name and folder for the PDF document and give the opportunity to set PDF options.

FIGURE 15.2
Create PDFs from the Print dialog box [Mac]

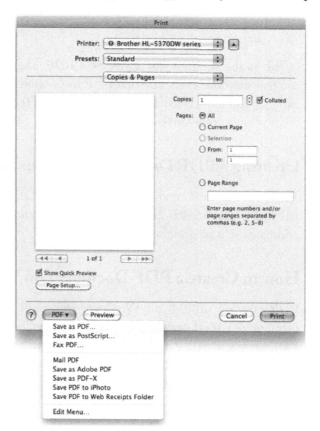

15.2.2.2. How to Create a PDF Document on the Mac

The Mac has the ability to create PDF documents built-in. To create a PDF document:

1. Select **File>Print**.

2. Click the **PDF** button.

   This displays the dropdown menu shown in Figure 15.2. This system has both the standard Mac PDF creation software and Adobe Acrobat installed.

3. Select **Save as PDF** (or the entry some other PDF creator).

   The Mac PDF creator displays the **Save** dialog box (Figure 15.3).

4. Enter the file name and navigate to the folder where you want to save the PDF document.

   Any text you enter into the fields below the folder display will be stored in the PDF document.

5. Click **Save**.

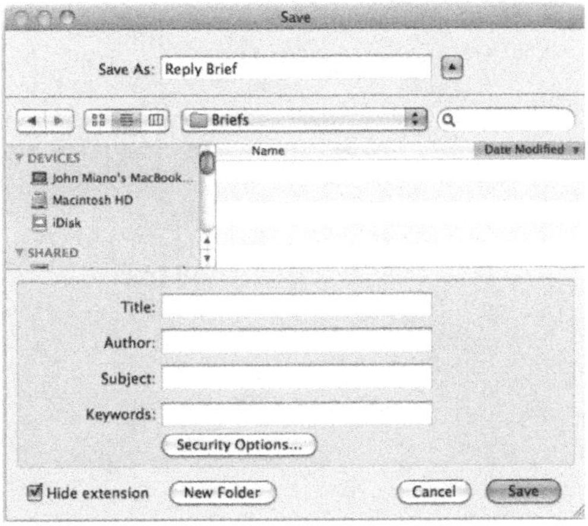

FIGURE 15.3
Enter the PDF document name on the Save dialog box [Mac].

15.2.3. After You Create the PDF Document

Always inspect the PDF document before filing it with a court or giving it to someone else. First, use a PDF viewer to proofread the document. Make sure that nothing went wrong during the PDF conversion process. Conversion problems are rare but they do appear occasionally. When problems occur, using a different method to create the PDF document will often fix the errors.

Next inspect the document's properties. The format and method of access to the property display depends upon the viewer you are using. If the viewer does not display and edit PDF properties, you need to find another viewer. Figure 15.4 shows the basic properties as shown in a PDF viewer. There are three important things to check. First, make sure the paper size is correct. Second, be sure that you do not have any metadata (descriptive data about the file) that you do not want to share. The description fields in Figure 15.4 have been cleared out. Using this viewer, you would click the **Additional Metadata** button and remove any other metadata you do not want to share.

FIGURE 15.4
Basic PDF
document properties

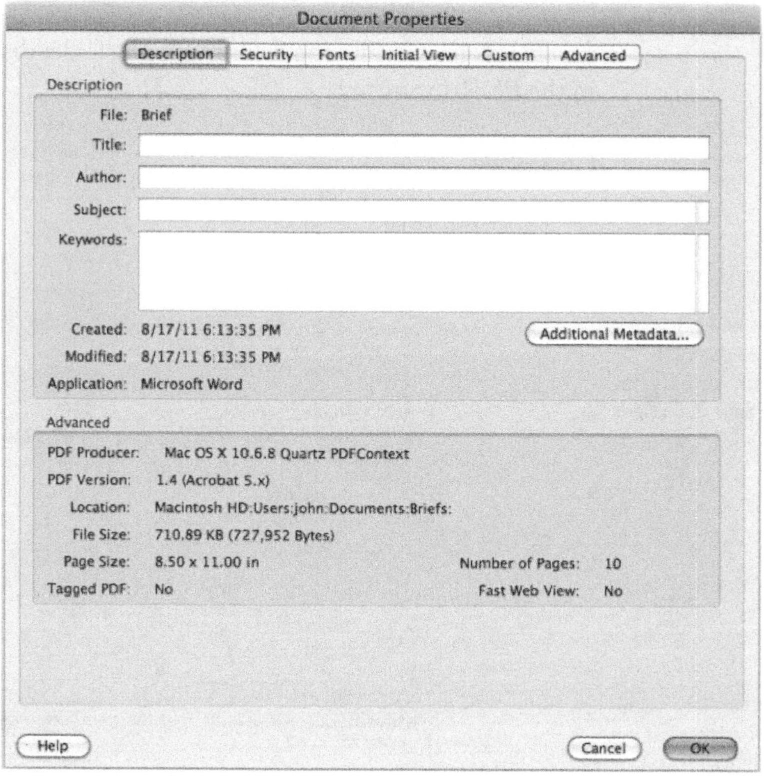

Third, be sure the fonts have been correctly embedded. Figure 15.5 shows font displays from another PDF viewer for two PDF documents. The document at the left was created using Word 2007's PDF export. The one at the left was created from the same Word document using doPDF. You can see that the PDF created from Word 2007 did not embed the fonts. Instead of embedding the fonts so the text can be properly drawn at any size, Word created images of the text. The text in such a PDF has jagged characters that look like they have been scanned.

FIGURE 15.5
A PDF document with missing fonts (left) and with font embedded (right).

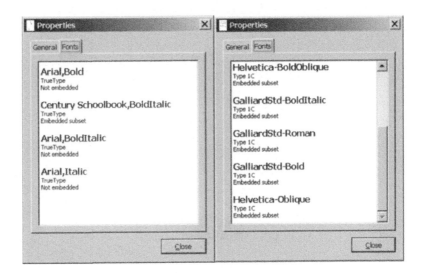

15.3. How to Insert a Signature

This book concludes with the process for inserting a signature into a document. Briefs have to be signed. In some courts the required certifications can push the number of signatures in a brief up to a half dozen. Figure 15.6 shows a certification containing a signature in Word.

First you need to have a good image containing your signature. Sign a blank, white sheet of paper a number of times using a black pen. Scan the image and crop to the best looking signatures. Save the scanned image to a file. The best format to use is TIF. Other formats (such as JPEG, PNG and GIF) will work. However, image in those formats may have to be resized.

FIGURE 15.6
A Word document
with a signature

**CERTIFICATE OF COMPLIANCE
WITH
FED. R. APP. P. 32(a)**

This brief complies with the type volume limitation of Fed. R. App. P.

32(a)(7)(B) because this brief contains 9,323, excluding the parts of the brief

exempted by Fed. R. App. P. 32(a)(7)(B)(iii).

This brief complies with the typeface requirements of Fed. R. App. P.

32(a)(5) and the type style requirements of Fed. R. App. P. 32(a)(6) this

brief has been prepared in a proportionally spaced typeface using Microsoft

Word 2011 in 14 pt. Caslon.

Sean Conner
Attorney for Jim's Drug Store
Dated:

To insert a signature image:

1. Insert the signature image.

Windows	Mac
Insert>Picture	**Insert>Photo>Picture**

Then select the signature image file using the file selection dialog box.

2. Select the image with the mouse.

3. Move the image in front of the text.

Windows	Mac
Picture Tools>Format>Arrange> Wrap Text>In Front of Text	**Format Picture>Arrange>Wrap Text> In Front of Text**

4. Use the mouse to drag the signature to the desired position.

Do not worry if the image obliterates the signature line (Figure 15.7). This will be corrected later.

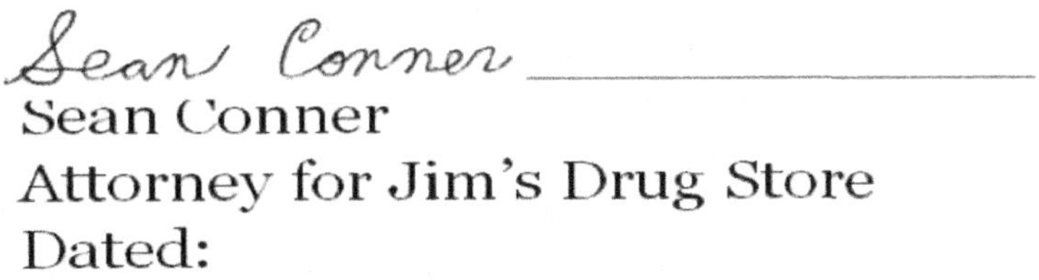

FIGURE 15.7
The signature in
position

FIGURE 15.7
The signature in
position

Sean Conner

Sean Conner
Attorney for Jim's Drug Store
Dated:

5. If the signature snaps to a new position rather than moving with the
mouse, disable snap to grid:

Windows	Mac
a. **Page Layout>Arrange>Align> Grid Settings**	a. **Format Picture>Arrange>Align> Grid Options**
b. Uncheck **Snap objects to grid when gridlines are not displayed** (Figure 15.8).	b. Uncheck **To Grid in Layout View**.
c. Click **OK**.	c. Click **OK**.

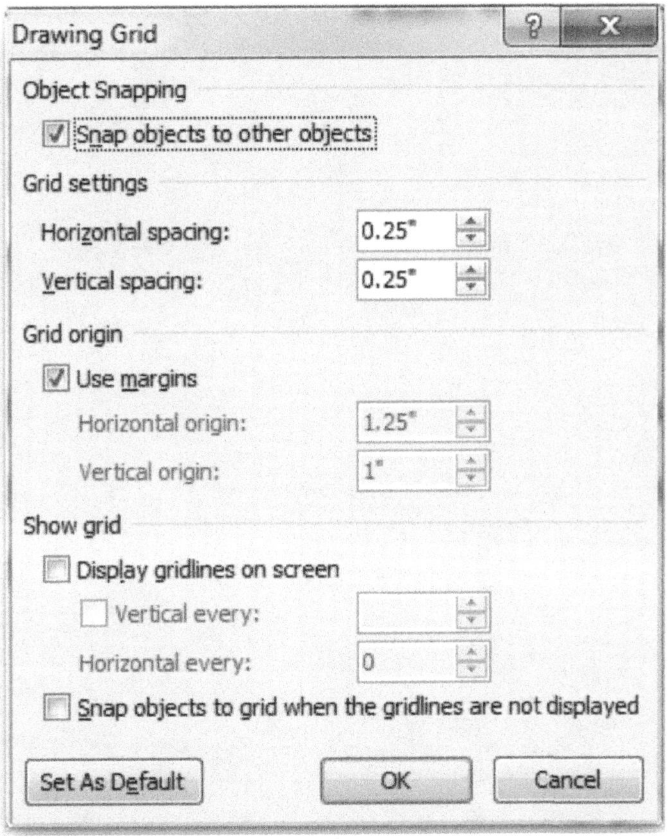

FIGURE 15.8
Disable grid
alignment on
the Drawing
Grid dialog box
[Windows].

6. Once the signature is in the desired position, move it behind the text:

Windows	Mac
Picture Tools>Format>Arrange> Wrap Text>Behind Text	**Format Picture>Arrange> Wrap Text>Behind Text**

This last step is the trick in formatting the signature. Notice that the signature now appears to overlap the signature line (Figure 15.9).

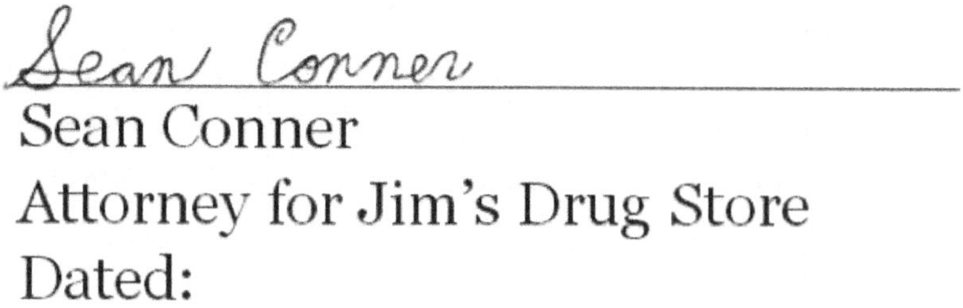
Sean Conner
Sean Conner
Attorney for Jim's Drug Store
Dated:

FIGURE 15.9
The signature in position behind the text

Bibliography

The Bluebook, 19th Ed., Harvard Law Review Association, 2010

Robert Bringhurst, *The Elements of Typographic Style*, v. 3.2,
   Hartley & Marks, 2008

Matthew Butterick, *Typography for Lawyers*, Jones McClure, 2010

James Craig, *et. al*, *Designing with Type*, 5th Ed. Waston-Guptill, 2006

Darby Dickerson, *ALWD Citation Manual*, 4th Ed., Aspen Publishers, 2010.

Edward W. Jessen, *California Style Manual*, West Group, 2000

Alexander Lawson, *Anatomy of a Typeface*, David R. Godine, 1990

Ruth Ann Robbins, *Painting With Print*, Journal of the Association of
   Legal Writing Directors, Fall 2004

Antonin Scalia & Bryan A. Garner, *Making Your Case*,
   Thomson-West, 2008

Gunnar Swanson, Ed., *Graphic Design & Reading*, Allworth Press, 2000

Robin Williams, *The PC is not a Typewriter*, Peachpit Press, 1992

United States Court of Appeals for the Seventh Circuit, *Requirements and
   Suggestions for Typography in Briefs and Other Papers*

Appendix A
Formatting Samples

This appendix contains samples showing the same brief formatted in different ways.

Single-spaced Brief

This example is based upon the Wisconsin R. App. P. The margins have been adjusted to limit line lengths to about 60 characters. These rules do not restrict the typeface. Century Schoolbook was chosen because it is wide, allowing the margins to be narrow while meeting the line length requirements.

As a matter of choice, the headings are aligned flush left. Heading levels are formatted using different type styles.

ARGUMENT

I. Plaintiffs Fail to Satisfy the Requirements for a Preliminary Injunction.

The Third Circuit standard for a preliminary injunction requires the moving party to demonstrate:

> (1) the reasonable probability of eventual success in the litigation and (2) that the movant will be irreparably injured *pendent lite* if relief is not granted. Moreover, while the burden rests upon the moving party to make these two requisite showings, the district court should take into account, when they are relevant, (3) the possibility of harm to other interested persons from the grant or denial of that injunction, and (4) the public interest.

Bennington Foods LLC v. St. Croix Renaissance, Group, LLP, — F.3d—, 2008 WL 2331394 (3d Cir. June 9, 2008) (quoting *Instant Air Freight Co. v. C.F. Air Freight, Inc.,* 882 F.2d 797, 800 (3d Cir. 1989)). Plaintiffs cannot meet the burdens imposed by the preliminary injunction requirements, and thus their Motion should be denied.

A. Plaintiffs Cannot Demonstrate Likelihood of Success on the Merits.

The Supreme Court has called a preliminary injunction "an extraordinary and drastic remedy." *Munaf v. Geren,* — U.S.—, 2008 WL 2369260, at *11 (S.Ct. June 12, 2008). As a consequence, "a party seeking a preliminary injunction must demonstrate, among other things, 'a likelihood of success on the merits.'" *Id.* "Review of a preliminary injunction 'is not confined to the act of granting the injunctio[n], but extends as well to determining whether there is any insuperable objection, in point of jurisdiction or merits, to the maintenance of [the] bill, and if so, to directing a final decree dismissing it.'" *Id.* (citation omitted) (alteration in original).

Insuperable objections, both jurisdictional and substantive, infect Plaintiffs' Complaint and their Motion for Preliminary Injunction must be denied.

Double-spaced Brief

This example is based upon the Fed. R. App. P. The text is double-spaced with single spaced quotations. The typeface is Garamond. The headings use hanging indentations with right aligned numbers.

ARGUMENT

I. Plaintiffs Fail to Satisfy the Requirements for a Preliminary Injunction.

The Third Circuit standard for a preliminary injunction requires the moving party to demonstrate:

> (1) the reasonable probability of eventual success in the litigation and (2) that the movant will be irreparably injured *pendent lite* if relief is not granted. Moreover, while the burden rests upon the moving party to make these two requisite showings, the district court should take into account, when they are relevant, (3) the possibility of harm to other interested persons from the grant or denial of that injunction, and (4) the public interest.

Bennington Foods LLC v. St. Croix Renaissance, Group, LLP, — F.3d—, 2008 WL 2331394 (3d Cir. June 9, 2008) (quoting *Instant Air Freight Co. v. C.F. Air Freight, Inc.*, 882 F.2d 797, 800 (3d Cir. 1989)). Plaintiffs cannot meet the burdens imposed by the preliminary injunction requirements, and thus their Motion should be denied.

A. Plaintiffs Cannot Demonstrate Likelihood of Success on the Merits.

The Supreme Court has called a preliminary injunction "an extraordinary and drastic remedy." *Munaf v. Geren*, — U.S.—, 2008 WL 2369260, at *11 (S.Ct. June 12, 2008). As a consequence, "a party seeking a preliminary injunction must demonstrate, among other things, 'a likelihood of success on the merits.' " *Id.* "Review of a preliminary injunction 'is not confined to the act of granting the injunctio[n], but extends as well to determining whether there is any insuperable objection, in point of juris-

Monospaced Brief

This example is based upon New Jersey Rules for Appellate Briefs. The type is set in Courier and is double spaced. It is designed to have a typewriter style. The indentations are ½″. These wide indentations are common with typewriters. The text only uses characters available on a typewriter. Straight quotes are used instead of typesetting quotes. Hyphens are used in place of dashes.

ARGUMENT

I. Plaintiffs Fail to Satisfy the Requirements for a Preliminary Injunction.

The Third Circuit standard for a preliminary injunction requires the moving party to demonstrate:

> (1) the reasonable probability of eventual success in the litigation and (2) that the movant will be irreparably injured pendent lite if relief is not granted. Moreover, while the burden rests upon the moving party to make these two requisite showings, the district court should take into account, when they are relevant, (3) the possibility of harm to other interested persons from the grant or denial of that injunction, and (4) the public interest.

Bennington Foods LLC v. St. Croix Renaissance, Group, LLP, -- F.3d--, 2008 WL 2331394 (3d Cir. June 9, 2008) (quoting Instant Air Freight Co. v. C.F. Air Freight, Inc., 882 F.2d 797, 800 (3d Cir. 1989)). Plaintiffs cannot meet the burdens imposed by the preliminary injunction requirements, and thus their Motion should be denied.

A. Plaintiffs Cannot Demonstrate Likelihood of Success on the Merits.

The Supreme Court has called a preliminary injunction "an extraordinary and drastic remedy." Munaf v. Geren, -- U.S.--, 2008 WL 2369260, at *11 (S.Ct. June 12, 2008). As a consequence, "a party seeking a preliminary injunction must demonstrate, among other things, 'a likelihood of success on the merits.' " Id. "Review of a preliminary injunction 'is not confined to the act of granting the injunctio[n], but extends as well to determining whether there is any insuperable objection, in point of juris-

Sans Serif Brief

This example is based upon Connecticut R. App. P. The type is set in Arial and is double spaced.

ARGUMENT

I. Plaintiffs fail to satisfy the requirements for a preliminary injunction.

The Third Circuit standard for a preliminary injunction requires the moving

party to demonstrate:

> (1) the reasonable probability of eventual success in the litigation and
> (2) that the movant will be irreparably injured <u>pendent lite</u> if relief is not
> granted. Moreover, while the burden rests upon the moving party to
> make these two requisite showings, the district court should take into
> account, when they are relevant, (3) the possibility of harm to other in-
> terested persons from the grant or denial of that injunction, and (4) the
> public interest.

<u>Bennington Foods LLC v. St. Croix Renaissance, Group, LLP</u>, — F.3d—,

2008 WL 2331394 (3d Cir. June 9, 2008) (quoting <u>Instant Air Freight Co.

v. C.F. Air Freight, Inc.</u>, 882 F.2d 797, 800 (3d Cir. 1989)). Plaintiffs can-

not meet the burdens imposed by the preliminary injunction requirements,

and thus their Motion should be denied.

A. Plaintiffs cannot demonstrate likelihood of success on the merits.

The Supreme Court has called a preliminary injunction "an extraordinary

and drastic remedy." <u>Munaf v. Geren</u>, — U.S.—, 2008 WL 2369260, at *11

(S.Ct. June 12, 2008). As a consequence, "a party seeking a preliminary

injunction must demonstrate, among other things, 'a likelihood of success

on the merits.' " <u>Id</u>. "Review of a preliminary injunction 'is not confined to

the act of granting the injunctio[n], but extends as well to determining

whether there is any insuperable objection, in point of jurisdiction or mer-

its, to the maintenance of [the] bill, and if so, to directing a final decree

dismissing it.' " <u>Id</u>. (citation omitted) (alteration in original).

1

Appendix B
Comparative Court Formatting Rules

This appendix lists comparative court rules, illustrating how formatting requirements vary. Most of the rules summarized here are from appellate courts because few trial court rules specify formatting requirements in sufficient detail to make a meaningful comparison. Obvious rules, such as text should be in Roman type are omitted. Empty values mean that aspect of formatting is not specified. Rules here are presented for comparison only. Always check the most recent rules when creating a brief.

Rules of the United States Supreme Court

URL		http://www.supremecourtus.gov/ctrules/ctrules.html
Date		October 1, 2007
Paper	R. 33(1)(a)	6-⅛″ × 9-¼″
Two Sided	R. 33(1)(b)	Must be two sided
Margins	R. 33(1)(c)	At least ¾″. Text field may not exceed 4-⅛″ × 7-⅛″
Font	R. 33(1)(a)	12 pt. Century Family (*e.g.*, Century Expanded, New Century Schoolbook, or Century Schoolbook)
Spacing	R. 33(1)(a)	At least 2 pt. leading.
Quotations	R. 33(1)(a)	Quotations of 50 words or more must be indented.
Headings		
Footnotes	R. 33(1)(b)	10 pt. type with at least 2 pt. leading
Briefs Limited By	R. 33(1)(g)	Words

Federal Rules of Appellate Procedure

URL		http://www.uscourts.gov/rules/
Date		December 1, 2007
Paper	R. 32(a)(4)	8-½″ × 11″
Two Sided	R. 32(a)(1)(A)	No
Margins	R. 32(a)(4)	At least 1″
Font	R. 32(a)(5)–(6)	At least 14 pt. Proportionally spaced serif font or monospaced font of no more than 10-½ characters per inch.
Spacing	R. 32(a)(4)	Double-spaced
Quotations	R. 32(a)(4)	Of more than two lines may be indented and single-spaced.
Headings	R. 32(a)(4)-(6)	May be single-spaced. A sans serif font may be used in headings and captions.
Footnotes	R. 32(a)(4)	May be single-spaced
Briefs Limited By	R. 32 (a)(7)	Proportional–Word, Monospaced–Line

Alabama Rules of Appellate Procedure

URL	http://judicial.alabama.gov/library/rules_of_court.cfm	
Date	Oct 1, 2010	
Paper	32(a)(6)	8-½" × 11"
Two Sided	32(a)(1)(A)	Prohibited
Margins	32(a)(6)	At least 1"
Font	32(a)(7)	Courier New 13 pt. required.
Spacing	32(a)(6)	Double-spaced
Quotations	32(a)(6)	May be single-spaced
Headings	32(a)(6)	May be single-spaced
Footnotes	32(a)(6)	May be single-spaced
Briefs Limited By	32(b)	Pages

Alaska Rules of Appellate Procedure

URL	http://www.state.ak.us/courts/rules.htm	
Date	2010–2011	
Paper	R. 513.5(1)	8-½" × 11"
Two Sided	212(a)(2)(B)	Required
Margins	R. 513.5(b)(5)	No more than 6-½" × 9-½" inches of printed or written matter on a page
	R. 212(b)	Left and right margin must be 1"
Font	R. 513.5(c)	(A) 12 point (10 monospaced characters per inch) Courier, or substantially similar monospaced text style; or (B) 13 point (proportionally spaced) Times New Roman, Garamond, CG Times, New Century Schoolbook, or substantially similar serifed font; or (C) 12.5 point (proportionally spaced) Arial, Helvetica, Univers, or substantially similar non-serifed text style.
Spacing	R. 513.5(b)(3)	Double-spaced
Quotations	R. 513.5(b)(3)	Must be singled-spaced and indented at least ½"
Headings	R. 513.5(b)(3)	Must be single-spaced
Footnotes	R. 513.5(b)(3)	Must be single-spaced
Briefs Limited By	R. 212 (c)(4)	Page

Arizona Rules of Appellate Procedure

URL	http://www.supreme.state.az.us/rules/	
Date	May 1, 2009	
Paper	R. 6(c)	8-½" × 11"
Two Sided	R. 6(c)	No
Margins	R. 6(c)	At least 1". Pages numbered at bottom
Font	R. 6(c)	Proportional 14 pt. or larger. Monospaced less than 10.5 pitch. Roman, italics, underline or bold for emphasis
Spacing	R. 6(c)	Double-spaced
Quotations	R. 6(c)	Single-spaced
Headings	R. 6(c)	Single-spaced. In italics, bold or underline.
Footnotes	R. 6(c)	Single-spaced
Briefs Limited By	R. 14(b) Monospaced–Page, Proportional–Word	

Rules of the Supreme Court and Court of Appeals
of the State of Arkansas

URL		http://courts.state.aR. us/rules/rules_sc_coa/
Date		2006
Paper	R. 4-1(a)	8-½″ × 11″
Two Sided	R. 4-1(a)	Permitted
Margins	R. 4-1(a)	At least 1″. Pages must be numbered
Font	R. 4-1(a)	Proportional 12 pt. or greateR. Monospaced less than 10 pitch
Spacing	R. 4-1(a)	Double-spaced
Quotations	R. 4-1(a)	Single-space and indented
Headings		
Footnotes	R. 4-1(a)	Double-spaced
Briefs Limited By	R. 4-1(b)	Page

California Supreme Court and Courts of Appeal
California Rules of Court

URL		http://www.courts.ca.gov/rules.htm
Date		July 1, 2011
Paper	R. 8.204(b)(1)	8-½″ × 11″ recycled paper
Two Sided	R. 8.204(b)(4)	Permitted
Margins	R. 8.204(b)(6)	At least: Top/Bottom—1″, Sides—1-½″
	R. 8.204(b)(7)	Pages must be numbered, body and tables may be numbered separately.
	R. 8.204(b)(5)	Lines of text must be unnumbered.
Font	R. 8.204(b)(2)–(4)	Any conventional roman typeface, 13 pt. or larger
Spacing	R. 8.204(b)(5)	1-½ spaced. Single-spaced means 6 lines to an inch.
Quotations	R. 8.204(b)(5)	May be indented and single-spaced.
Headings	R. 8.204(b)(5)	May be singled-spaced and in all capitals.
Footnotes	R. 8.204(b)(5)	May be singled-spaced
Briefs Limited By	R. 8.204(c)	Word

California Trial Courts
California Rules of Court

URL		http://www.courts.ca.gov/rules.htm
Date		July 1, 2011
Paper	R. 2.101	8-½″ × 11″
	R. 2.103	Must be recycled paper
Two Sided	R. 2.102	No
Margins	R. 2.107	At least: Left–1″, Right–½″
	R. 2.208(4)	Line numbers must be placed at the left margin and separated from the text of the paper by a vertical column of space at least ⅕ inch wide or a single or double vertical line. Each line number must be aligned with a line of type, or the line numbers must be evenly spaced vertically on the page. Line numbers must be consecutively numbered, beginning with the number 1 on each page. There must be at least three line numbers for every vertical inch on the page.
	R. 2.209	Pages must be numbered

	R. 2.210	Except for exhibits, each paper filed with the court must bear a footer in the bottom margin of each page, placed below the page number and divided from the rest of the document page by a printed line in at least 10 pt. type containing the title of the papeR.
Font	R. 2.104-2.105	12 pt or largeR. The typeface must be essentially equivalent to Courier, Times New Roman, or Arial.
Spacing	R. 2.108(1)	1-½ or double-spaced. Lines must be numbered.
Quotations	R. 2.108(3)	May be single-spaced.
Headings		
Footnotes	R. 2.108(3)	May be single-spaced.
Briefs Limited By		

Colorado Appellate Rules

URL	http://www.coloradosupremecourt.com/Regulation/Rules.htm	
Date	Feb. 7, 2008	
Paper	R. 32(b)(1)	8-½″ × 11″
Two Sided	R. 32(b)(4)	No
Margins	R. 32(b)(3)	At least: Top—1-½″, Others—1″
Font	R. 32(a)(1)	14 pt. or largeR. Captions may be in 12 pt.
Spacing	R. 32(b)(2)	Double-spaced
Quotations	R. 32(b)(2)	Indented and Single-spaced
Headings	R. 32(b)(2)	Single-spaced
Footnotes	R. 32(b)(2)	Single-spaced
Briefs Limited By	R. 28(g)	Word

Colorado Rules of Civil Procedure

URL	http://www.coloradosupremecourt.com/Regulation/Rules.htm	
Date	Mar. 20, 2006	
Paper	R. 10(d)(1)	8-½″ × 11″. Recycled paper preferred
Two Sided		
Margins	R. 10(d)(2)(I),	Exactly: Top—1-½″, Others—1″. Text must be left justified
Font	R. 10(d)(2)(II)	12 pt. or greater
Spacing	R. 10(d)(2)	Double-spaced
Quotations		
Headings		
Footnotes		
Briefs Limited By		

Connecticut Rules of Appellate Procedure

URL	http://www.jud.ct.gov/pb.htm	
Date	March 1, 2009	
Paper	R. 67-2(A)	8-½″ × 11″
Two Sided	R. 67-2(A)	No
Margins	R. 67-2(C)	At least: Top/Bottom—1″, Left—1-¼″, Right—½″. Pages numbered at bottom center.
Font	R. 67-2(A)	12 pt. or larger Arial or Univers
Spacing	R. 67-2(A)	Double-spaced
Quotations	R. 67-2(A)	Single-spaced
Headings		

| Footnotes | R. 67-2(A) | Single-spaced |
| Briefs Limited By | | |

Rules of the District of Columbia Court of Appeals

URL	http://www.dcca.state.dc.us/dccourts/appeals/rules.jsp	
Date	MaR. 20, 2008	
Paper	R. 32(a)(4)	8-½" × 11"
Two Sided	R. 32(a)(1)(A)	No
Margins	R. 32(a)(1)(A)	At least 1"
Font	R. 32(a)(5)	12 pt. or larger. Times New Roman or Courier New preferred.
Spacing	R. 32(a)(1)(A)	Double-spaced
Quotations	R. 32(a)(1)(A)	Indented and single-spaced
Headings	R. 32(a)(1)(A)	Single-spaced
Footnotes	R. 32(a)(1)(A)	Single-spaced
Briefs Limited By	R. 32(a)(6)	Page

Florida Rules of Appellate Procedure

URL	http://www.floridasupremecourt.org/decisions/barrules.shtml	
Date	2009	
Paper	R. 9.210(a)(1)	8-½" × 11"
Two Sided		
Margins	R. 9.210(a)(2)	At least 1"
Font	R. 9.210(a)(2)	12 pt. Courier New or 14 pt. Times New Roman
Spacing	R. 9.210(a)(2)	Double-spaced
Quotations	R. 9.210(a)(2)	Single-spaced
Headings		
Footnotes	R. 9.210(a)(2)	Single-spaced
Briefs Limited By	R. 9.210(a)(5)	Page

Rules of the Supreme Court of Georgia

URL	http://www.gasupreme.us/rules/	
Date	As of June 16, 2009	
Paper	R. 17	8-½" × 11"
Two Sided		
Margins	R. 16	At least 1". Pages must be numbered sequentially
Font	R. 16	The type size shall not be smaller than 12-point Courier or 14-point Times New Roman
Spacing	R. 16	At least double-spaced
Quotations	R. 16	May be single-spaced
Headings		
Footnotes	R. 16	May be single-spaced
Briefs Limited By	R. 20	Page

Rules of the Court of Appeals of Georgia

URL	http://www.georgiacourts.org/rules.html	
Date	Feb. 21, 2008	
Paper	R. 24(c)	8-½" × 11"
Two Sided	R. 24(c)	No
Margins	R. 24(c)	At Least: Top 2", Others 1". Must be numbered at bottom

Font	R. 1(c)	10 Pitch monospaced or 14 pt. Times New Roman
Spacing	R. 1(c)	Double-spaced
Quotations	R. 1(c)	Double-spaced
Headings		
Footnotes	R. 1(c)	Double-spaced
Briefs Limited By	R. 24(f)	Page

Hawai'i Rules of Appellate Procedure

URL		http://www.state.hi.us/jud/toc.htm
Date		Aug. 3, 2011
Paper	R. 32(a)	8-½" × 11"
Two Sided	R. 32(a)	Permitted for copies
Margins	R. 32(a)	At least 1"
Font	R. 32(b)	12 pt. 14 pitch. 12 pt. Times New Roman or Courier New satisfy the rule. Condensation prohibited
Spacing	R. 32(b)	1-½ or double-spaced
Quotations	R. 32(b)	Single-spaced
Headings	R. 32(b)	Single-spaced
Footnotes	R. 32(b)	Single-spaced
Briefs Limited By	R. 28(a)	Page

Rules of the District Courts of the State of Hawai'i

URL		http://www.state.hi.us/jud/toc.htm
Date		Nov. 1, 1980
Paper	R. 3(a)	8-½" × 11"
Two Sided	R. 3(a)	Copies but not originals
Margins	R. 3(a)	Top and bottom: 1", Sides: At least 1"
Font	R. 3(a0	12 pt. Pica or equivalent
Spacing	R. 3(a)	Double or 1-½ spaced.
Quotations		
Headings		
Footnotes		
Briefs Limited By		

Idaho Appellate Rules
(Briefs)

URL		http://www.isc.idaho.gov/rulestxt.htm
Date		Nov. 1, 1987
Paper	R. 36(c)	8-½" × 11"
Two Sided	R. 36(c)	Permitted
Margins	R. 36(c)	Exactly: Top/Bottom—1", Sides—1-½"
Font	R. 36(c)	No smaller than 12 pt. Times New Roman
Spacing	R. 36(c)	All lines must be double-spaced except for quotations
Quotations	R. 36(c)	Indented and single-spaced
Headings		
Footnotes		
Briefs Limited By	R. 34(b)	Page. Measured cover to cover

Illinois Civil Appeals Rules

URL	http://www.state.il.us/court/SupremeCourt/Rules	
Date	Jul. 1, 2008	
Paper	R. 341(a)	8-½″ × 11″
Two Sided	R. 341(a)	No
Margins	R. 341(a)	At least: Left—1-½″, Others—1″
Font	R. 341(a)	12 pt. or larger
Spacing	R. 341(a)	Double-spaced
Quotations	R. 341(a)	May be single-spaced
Headings	R. 341(a)	May be single-spaced
Footnotes	R. 341(a)	Discouraged and may be single-spaced
Briefs Limited By	R. 341(b)	Page

Indiana Rules of Court
Rules of Appellate Procedure

URL	http://www.in.gov/judiciary/rules/	
Date	Jan. 6, 2009	
Paper	R. 43(B)	8-½″ × 11″
Two Sided	R. 43(B)	No
Margins	R. 43(G)	At least 1″
	R. 43(F)	Numbered at the bottom
Font	R. 43(D)	12 pt. or larger Arial, Baskerville, Book Antiqua, Bookman, Bookman Old Style, Century, Century Schoolbook, Courier, Courier New, CG Times, Garamond, Georgia, New Baskerville, New Century Schoolbook, Palatino or Times New Roman.
Spacing	R. 43(E)	Double-spaced
Quotations	R. 43(E)	Shall be single-spaced. At least 4 pt. leading.
Headings	R. 43(E)	Double-spaced
Footnotes	R. 43(E)	Shall be single-spaced. At least 4 pt. leading.
Briefs Limited By	R. 44(D)-(E)	Page or word

Iowa Rules of Appellate Procedure

URL	http://www.legis.state.ia.us/Rules2.html	
Date	June 2009	
Paper	R. 6.903(1)(d)	8-½″ × 11″
Two Sided		
Margins	R. 6.903(1)(d)	Exactly: Top/Bottom—1″, Sides—1-¼″ Pages must be numbered at bottom center
Font	R. 6.903(1)(e)(1)	14 pt. or larger proportional serif font but sans serif can be used in headings and captions. Examples of acceptable serif fonts are Bookman Old Style, Century Schoolbook, Times New Roman, Baskerville Old Face, Garamond, or Georgia
	R. 6.903(1)(e)(2)	Monospaced 10-½ pitch. Examples of acceptable monospaced fonts are Courier 12 point and Consolas 12 point.
Spacing	R. 6.903(1)(d)	Double-spaced
Quotations	R. 6.903(1)(d)	More than 40 words, may be indented and single-spaced
Headings	R. 6.903(1)(d)	May be single-spaced

| Footnotes | R. 6.903(1)(d) | May be single-spaced |
| Briefs Limited By | R. 6.903(1)(g) | Proportional–Word, Monospaced–Line |

Kansas Rules Relating to Supreme Court, Court of Appeals, and Appellate Practice

URL		http://www.kscourts.org/rules
Date		Sept. 6, 2005
Paper	R. 6.07(a)	8-½″ × 11″
Two Sided		
Margins	R. 6.07(a)	At least: Left—1-½″, Others—1″. Text field no larger than 6″ × 9″.
Font	R. 6.07(a)	12 pt. or larger conventional typeface with no more than 12 characters per inch.
Spacing	R. 6.07(a)	Double-spaced
Quotations	R. 6.07(a)	Single-spaced
Headings		
Footnotes		
Briefs Limited By	R. 6.07(b)	Page

Kentucky Rules of Civil Procedure

URL		http://www.kybaR. org
Date		Jan 1, 2007
Paper	R. 76.12(4)(a)	Typeset printing: 6-⅛″ × 9-¼″, Computer Printed: 8-½″ × 11″
Two Sided		
Margins	R. 76.12(4)(a)	For 8-½″ × 11″ paper, Exactly Left: 1-½″, Others: 1″
Font	R. 76.12(4)(a)	Typeset printing at least 11 pt. Computer Printing at least 12 pt. set at standard width
Spacing	R. 76.12(4)(a)	Computer Printed must be double-spaced.
Quotations		
Headings		
Footnotes		
Briefs Limited By	R. 72.12(4)(a)	Page

Rules of the Supreme Court of Louisana

URL		http://www.lasc.org/rules
Date		May 22, 2009
Paper	R. VII(2)	6″ × 9″ or 8-½″ × 11″
Two Sided		
Margins	R. VII(2)	Top: 1-½″ to 2″, Others: ¾″ to 1-¼″
Font	R. VII(2)	11 to 12 pt. typeface
Spacing	R. VII(2)	Double-spaced
Quotations	R. VII(2)	Matters customarily single-spaced and indented may be single-spaced.
Headings	R. VII(2)	Matters customarily single-spaced and indented may be single-spaced.
Footnotes	R. VII(2)	Matters customarily single-spaced and indented may be single-spaced.
Briefs Limited By	R. VII(2)	Page

Uniform Rules Louisiana Courts of Appeal

URL		http://www.lasc.org/rules
Date		Nov. 1, 2006
Paper	R. 2-12.2	8-½″ × 11″ or 8-½″ × 14″
Two Sided	R. 2-12.2	No
Margins	R. 2-12.2	Sides: Exactly 1″, Top/Bottom: At least 1″
Font	R. 2-12.2	Roman or Times New Roman 14 point or larger computer font, normal spacing;
Spacing	R. 2-12.2	Double-spaced
Quotations	R. 2-12.2	Matters customarily single-spaced and indented may be single-spaced.
Headings	R. 2-12.2	Matters customarily single-spaced and indented may be single-spaced.
Footnotes	R. 2-12.2	Matters customarily single-spaced and indented may be single-spaced.
Briefs Limited By	R. 2-12.2	Page

Maine Rules of Appellate Procedure

URL		http://www.courts.state.me.us/court_info/rules/rules.html
Date		Aug. 2009
Paper	R. 9(f)	8-½″ × 11″
Two Sided	R. 9(f)	No
Margins	R. 9(f)	Printed matter no larger than 6-½″ × 9″.
Font	R. 9(f)	At least 12 pt. and no smaller than 12 pt. Bookman. Advisory notes state, "Appropriate type styles to use include Bookman, Courier, Geneva, Georgia, or other similar type styles. Type styles such as Arrus, Script, or Times should be avoided."
Spacing	R. 9(f)	Double-spaced
Quotations	R. 9(f)	May be single-spaced
Headings		
Footnotes	R. 9(f)	May be in 11 pt. type.
Briefs Limited By	R. 9 (b)-(c)	Page

Maryland Rules
(Appellate Briefs)

URL		http://www.courts.state.md.us/rules/index.html
Date		July 1, 1997
Paper	R. 1-301	8-½″ × 11″
Two Sided		
Margins	R. 8-112(d)	Top/Bottom–At least 1″, Text Width no larger than 6-½″
Font	R. 8-112(c)(1)	At least 13 pt.
	R. 8-112(c)(2)	Spacing between characters may not be reduced. The following fonts are approved but not mandatory as of July 1, 2007: Antique Olive, Arial, Arial Rounded, Book Antiqua, Bookman Old Style, Britannic, Century Gothic, Century Schoolbook, CG Times, Courier, Courier New, Footlight MT Light, Letter Gothic, MS LineDraw, Times New Roman, Universal
Spacing	R. 8-112(c)(2)	1-½ spaced

Quotations	R. 8-112(c)(2)	May be indented and singles spaced
Headings		
Footnotes	R. 8-112(c)(2)	May be single-spaced
Briefs Limited By	R. 8-503(d)	Page

Massachusetts Rules of Appellate Procedure

URL	http://www.mass.gov/courts/sjc/rules.html	
Date	Sept. 1, 2008	
Paper	R. 20(a)	8-½″× 11″
Two Sided		No (Rules of the Massachusetts Supreme Judicial Court 1:08)
Margins	R. 20(a)(1)	Top/Bottom–At least 1″, Sides–At least 1-½″
Font	R. 20(a)(2)	Monospaced, at least 12 pt, less than 10.5 pitch
Spacing	R. 20(a)(3)	Double-spaced
	R. 20(a)(4)	No more than 27 lines per page
Quotations	R. 20(a)(3)	May be indented and single-spaced
Headings		
Footnotes	R. 20(a)(3)	May be single-spaced
Briefs Limited By	R. 16(h)	Page

Michigan Court Rules
(Appellate Briefs)

URL	http://coa.courts.mi.gov/rules	
Date	May 1, 2009	
Paper	R. 1.109	8-½″× 11″
Two Sided	R. 7.309	Briefs–No, Appendices–Required
Margins	R. 7-212(B)	At least 1″
Font	R. 7-212(B)	At least 12 pt.
Spacing	R. 7-212(B)	Double-spaced
Quotations	R. 7-212(B)	May be single-spaced
Headings		
Footnotes	R. 7-212(B)	May be single-spaced
Briefs Limited By	R. 7-212(B)	Page

Minnesota General Rules of Practice for the District Courts

URL	http://www.mncourts.gov	
Date	MaR. 12, 2009	
Paper	R. 6.02	8-½″× 11″
Two Sided		
Margins	R. 6.01	Top–At least 1″, Others–unspecified
Font		
Spacing	R. 6.01	Double-spaced
Quotations		
Headings		
Footnotes		
Briefs Limited By		

Minnesota Rules of Civil Appellate Procedure

URL	http://www.mncourts.gov	
Date	July 1, 2011	

Paper	R. 132.01(1)	8-½" × 11"
Two Sided	R. 132.01(1)	Brief–No, Appendices–Permitted
Margins	R. 132.01(1)	Text may not exceed 6-½″ × 9-½″
Font	R. 132.01(1)	Monospaced 10.5 pitch or at least 13 pt. Proportional
Spacing	R. 132.01(1)	Double-spaced
Quotations		
Headings	R. 132.01(1)	May be single-spaced
Footnotes	R. 132.01(1)	May be single-spaced
Briefs Limited By	R. 132.01(1)	Page

Mississippi Rules of Appellate Procedure

URL	http://www.mssc.state.ms.us/rules/msrules.html	
Date	Jan. 1, 1995	
Paper	R. 32(a)	8-½″ × 11″
Two Sided		
Margins	R. 32(a)	Top—1″, Bottom—¾″, Left—1-½″, Right—½″
Font	R. 32(a)	At least 12 pt.
Spacing	R. 32(a)	Double-spaced
Quotations	R. 32(a)	May be single-spaced
Headings		
Footnotes	R. 32(a)	At least 11 pt. May be single-spaced
Briefs Limited By	R. 28(g)	Page

Missouri Rules of Civil Procedure (Appellate Briefs)

URL	http://www.courts.mo.gov	
Date	July 1, 2008	
Paper	R. 84.06(a)(1)	8-½″ × 11″
	R. 84.06(d)	May be commercially printed on 6-½″ × 9-¼″.
Two Sided	R. 84.06(a)(3)	No
Margins	R. 84.06(a)(3)	At least 1″, Pages must be numbered with Arabic numerals. Front matter may be separately numbered with Roman numerals;
	R. 84.06(d)	When commercially printed, text may be 4-⅛″ wide. No more than 37 lines per page, including the page number.
Font	R. 84.06(a)(6)	Not smaller than 13 point, Times New Roman font on Microsoft Word;
	R. 84.06(d)	11 pt. when commercially printed.
Spacing	R. 84.06(a)(7)	Double-spaced;
	R. 84.06(d)	3 points leading when commercially printed (11 on 14).
Quotations	R. 84.06(d)	When commercially printed, indented 2 ems on the left side only.
Headings		
Footnotes	R. 84.06(a),(d)	Same size as brief
Briefs Limited By	R. 84.06(b)	Proportional–Word, Monospaced–Line

Montana Rules of Appellate Procedure

URL	http://courts.mt.gov/supreme	
Date	2009	
Paper	R. 11(3)	Not exceeding 8-½″ × 11″, Recycled paper
Two Sided	R. 11(3)(b)	Encouraged

Margins	R. 11(3)	At least 1″
Font	R. 11(2)	At least 14 pt. proportional font or 10.5 pitch monospaced
Spacing	R. 11(3)(b)	Double-spaced when produced on a typewriter or equivalent process.
Quotations	R. 11(3)(b)	May be single-spaced
Headings		
Footnotes	R. 11(3)(b)	May be single-spaced
Briefs Limited By	R. 11(4)	Proportional–Word, Monospaced–Page

Nebraska Court Rules of Appellate Practice

URL	http://court.nol.org/rules/	
Date	July 18, 2008	
Paper	R. 2-109(B)	8-½″ × 11″ (May be printed on 6-½″ × 9-½″)
Two Sided	R. 2-109(B)(2)	No
Margins	R. 2-109(B)(2)	At least 1″
Font	R. 2-109(B)(2)(a)	Not smaller than 12-point Courier, Arial or Helvetica, or Times or Times New Roman. Condensing space between letters is prohibited
Spacing	R. 2-109(B)(x2)	Double-spaced, with not less than 12 pt. leading. No more than 25 lines per page
Quotations	R. 2-109(B)(2)	Quoted material of 50 words or more shall be indented five spaces from the left margin
Headings		
Footnotes	R. 2-109(B)(2)	Footnotes are prohibited
Briefs Limited By	R. 2-109(B)(5)	Pages

Nevada Rules of Appellate Procedure

URL	http://leg.state.nv.us/courtrules	
Date	Feb. 1, 2010	
Paper	R. 32(a)(4)	8-½″ × 11″
Two Sided	R. 32(a) (1)(A)No	
Margins	R. 32(a)(4)	Top, Bottom, Left–1″, Right–Unspecified. Lined and numbered in the left margin
Font	R. 32(a)(5)	13 pt. proportional. 10-½ Characters per inch monospaced.
Spacing	R. 32(a)(4)	Double-spaced
Quotations	R. 32(a)(4)	May be single-spaced
Headings		
Footnotes	R. 32(a)(4)	May be single-spaced
Briefs Limited By	R. 32(a)(7)	Page

Rules of the Supreme Court of the State of New Hampshire

URL	http://www.courts.state.nh.us/rules/	
Date	May 7, 2009	
Paper	R. 16(1)	8-½″ × 11″
Two Sided	R. 16(11)	No
Margins	R. 16(11)	Left–1″, Others–Unspecified
Font	R. 16(11)	12 pt.
Spacing	R. 16(11)	Double-spaced
Quotations		
Headings		

Footnotes		
Briefs Limited By	R. 16(11)	Page

Rules Governing the Courts of the State of New Jersey (Appellate Briefs)

URL	http://www.judiciary.state.nj.us/		
Date	Sept. 5, 2000		
Paper	R. 2:6-10	8-½″ × 11″	
Two Sided	R. 2:6-10	Permitted	
Margins	R. 2:6-10	Approximately 1″	
Font	R. 2:6-10	10 pitch or 12 pt. No more than line	65 characters per
Spacing	R. 2:6-10	Double-spaced. No more than 26 lines per page	
Quotations			
Headings			
Footnotes			
Briefs Limited By	R. 2:6-7	Page	

New Mexico Rules of Appellate Procedure

URL	http://www.nmcompcomm.us/	
Date	May. 13, 2010	
Paper	R. 12-305(B)(2)	8-½″ × 11″
Two Sided		
Margins	R. 12-305(B)(2)	1″. Page numbers at bottom
Font	R. 12-305(C)	At least 14 pt. proportional serif font, such as Times New Roman; or 10 pitch monospaced font
Spacing	R. 12-305(D)	Double-spaced
Quotations	R. 12-305(D)	May be single-spaced
Headings	R. 12-305(D)	May be single-spaced
Footnotes	R. 12-305(D)	May be single-spaced
Briefs Limited By	R. 12-213(F)(3)	Proportional Font–Word, Monospaced Font–Line

Court of Appeals State of New York Rules of Practice

URL	http://www.nycourts.gov/ctapps/	
Date	Dec. 8, 2010	
Paper	R. 500.1 (i)	8-½″ × 11″
Two Sided		
Margins	R. 500.1 (l)	1″. Pages must be numbered at the center bottom.
Font	R. 500.1(j)	Serif 14 pt. proportional font or serif or 12 pt., 10.5 pitch monospaced font. May not use bold or all capitals. Narrow or condensed typefaces and condensed font spacing shall not be used.
Spacing	R. 500.1(l)	Double-spaced
Quotations	R. 500.1(l)	Of more than two lines may be indented and single-spaced.
Headings	R. 500.1(i)	May use bold or all capitals. May be single-spaced
Footnotes	R. 500.1(i)	May be in 12 pt. or larger proportional font or 10 pt. or larger monospaced font.
	R. 500.1 (l)	May be single-spaced
Briefs Limited By		

New York State Supreme Court Appellate Division First Department
(Each of the four departments has its own rules.)

URL		https://www.courts.state.ny.us/courts/ad1/Practice&Procedures/rules.shtml
Date		As retrieved June 10, 2009
Paper	R. 600.10(a)(1)	8-½″ × 11″
	R. 600.10(e)	Must be recycled paper
Two Sided		
Margins	R. 600.10(a)(4)	At least 1″
	R. 600.10(a)(6)	Must be consecutively numbered
Font	R. 600.10(a)(3)	At least 14 pt. serif proportional font or 12 pt. serif monospaced font.
Spacing	R. 600.10(a)(4)	Double-spaced
Quotations	R. 600.10(a)(4)	Indented quotations may be single-spaced
Headings	R. 600.10(a)(4)	May be single-spaced
	R. 600.10(a)(3)	Proportional font headings may not be larger than 15 pt. Monospaced may not be larger than 14 pt.
Footnotes	R. 600.10(a)(4)	May be single-spaced.
	R. 600.10(a)(3)	Proportional font footnotes must be at least than 12 pt. Monospaced must be at least 10 pt.
Briefs Limited By	R. 600.10(d)	Pages or Words

North Carolina Rules of Appellate Procedure

URL		http://www.nccourts.org/
Date		July 7, 2007
Paper	Appendix B	8-½″ × 11″
Two Sided	Appendix B	No
Margins	Appendix B	Approximately 1″, Tabs at ½″, 1″, 1-½″, 2″, 4-¼″ and 5″. No vertical rules or firm addresses in margins. Pages after the first must be numbered at the top center, with the numbers enclosed in dashes.
Font	R. 28(j)(1)(B)	At least 14 pt. proportional font or 12 pt., 10 pitch monospaced font. 12 pt. Courier New and 14 pt. Times New Roman comply with the rules.
Spacing	R. 28(g)(1)	Double-spaced, no more than 27 lines per page.
Quotations	Appendix B	Single-spaced and indented ¾″.
Headings	Appendix B	Single-spaced, centered, all capital letters, and underlined.
Footnotes	Appendix B	Single-spaced
Briefs Limited By	R. 28(j)	Proportional–word. Monospaced–page

North Dakota Rules of Appellate Procedure

URL		http://www.ndcourts.com/rules
Date		MaR. 1, 2007
Paper	R. 32(a)(4)	8-½″ × 11″
Two Sided	R. 32(a)(1)	No
Margins	R. 32(a)(4)	At least Left—1-½″, Others—1″
Font	R. 32(a)(5)	A proportionally spaced font 12 point or larger with no more than 16 characters per inch or a 12 pt., 10 pitch font monospaced with no more than 27 lines per page.
Spacing	R. 32(a)(5)	Double-spaced

Quotations	R. 32(a)(5)	May be single-spaced and indented if a proportional font is used.
Headings	R. 32(a)(5)	May be single-spaced if a proportional font is used.
Footnotes	R. 32(a)(5)	May be single-spaced if a proportional font is used.
Briefs Limited By	R. 32(a)(7)	Proportional–Word, Monospaced–Page

Ohio Rules of Appellate Procedure

URL	http://www.sconet.state.oh.us/LegalResources/Rules/	
Date	July 1, 2010	
Paper	R. 19(A)	6-⅛″ × 9-½″ or 8-½″ × 11″
Two Sided		
Margins	R. 19(A)	Printed area of 4-⅙″ × 7-⅙″ or 6-½″ × 9-½″ (for 8-½″ × 11″ paper)
Font	R. 19(A)	12 pt.
Spacing	R. 19(A)	Double-spaced
Quotations	R. 19(A)	Must be single-spaced
Headings		
Footnotes		
Briefs Limited By	R. 19(A)	Page

Oklahoma Supreme Court Rules

URL	http://www.oscn.net	
Date	June 8, 2010	
Paper	R. 1.11(a)	8-½″ × 11″
Two Sided		
Margins	R. 1.11(a)	Specified as Left: 1-¼″, Others: 1″, Must be numbered at the bottom
Font	R. 1.11(a)	Not less than 12 pt.
Spacing	R. 1.11(a)	Double-spaced
Quotations	R. 1.11(a)	Single
Headings		
Footnotes		
Briefs Limited By	R. 1.11(b)	Page

Oregon Rules of Appellate Procedure

URL	http://courts.oregon.gov/Supreme/RulesAndFees.page	
Date	Jan. 1, 2011	
Paper	R. 5.05(4)(c)	8-½″ × 11″
Two Sided	5.05(4)(d)	Permitted if the paper does not permit show-through.
Margins	5.05(4)(e)	Printed area may not exceed 6-¼″ × 9-½″ with inside margin 1-¼″, outside 1″, top and bottom ¾″. Pages must be numbered ⅜″ from the top of the page.
Font	R. 5.05(4)(f)	At least 13 pt. Arial or Times New Roman or 10 pitch monospaced font. Condensing type to increase the number of words is prohibited.
Spacing	R. 5.05(4)(c)	Double-spaced
Quotations	R. 5.05(4)(f)	Double-spaced before and after each paragraph.
Headings		
Footnotes	R. 5.05(4)(f)	Same type as the text

| Briefs Limited By | R. 5.05(2) | Words (or pages if not prepared with a word processing system) |

Pennsylvania Rules of Appellate Procedure

URL	http://www.pacode.com	
Date	Dec. 1, 2008	
Paper	R. 124(a)	8-½″ × 11″
Two Sided		
Margins	R. 124(a)(3)	At least 1″
Font	R. 124(a)(3)	At least 12 pt.
Spacing	R. 124(a)(3)	Double-spaced
Quotations	R. 124(a)(3)	Quotations more than two lines may be indented and single-spaced.
Headings		
Footnotes		
Briefs Limited By	R. 2135	Page

Rhode Island Supreme Court Rules of Appellate Procedure

URL	http://www.courts.ri.gov/Courts/SupremeCourt/Pages/Supreme%20Court%20Rules.aspx	
Date	Aug. 19, 2005	
Paper	R. 18(b)	8-½″ × 11″
Two Sided		
Margins		
Font	R. 18(b)	At least 12 pt. Times New Roman font or a font of similar legibility
Spacing	R. 18(b)	Double-spaced
Quotations		
Headings		
Footnotes	R. 18(b)	Single-spaced, At least 12 pt.
Briefs Limited By	R. 16(f)	Page

South Carolina Appellate Court Rules

URL	http://www.judicial.state.sc.us/courtReg	
Date	April 29, 2009	
Paper	R. 267(c)	8-½″ × 11″
Two Sided		
Margins	R. 267(d)	Left specified as: 1-½″, Others: Unspecified
Font	R. 267(c)	12 pt. or larger
Spacing	R. 267(c)	Double-spaced
Quotations		
Headings		
Footnotes		
Briefs Limited By	R. 208(b)(5)	Pages
Special		

South Dakota Codified Laws
(Appellate Briefs)

URL	http://legis.state.sd.us/statutes

Date	Jul. 1, 2010	
Paper	15-15-8	8-½″× 11″
Two Sided	15-26A-69(1)	No
Margins	15-26A-69	Left shall be: 1-½″, Others: At least 1″. Text may not be right justified. Pages numbered at center bottom.
Font	15-26A-66	At least 12 pt. serif proportional font or 10 pitch monospaced font. A sans serif font may be used in headings and captions. Bold may only be used in heading or captions.
Spacing	15-26A-69(2)	Double-spaced
Quotations	15-26A-69(1)	May be indented and single-spaced
Headings	15-26A-66(1)	May bc bold and all capitals
Footnotes	15-26A-66(2)	At least 12 pt.
Briefs Limited By	15-26A-66	Page or Word

Tennessee Rules of Appellate Procedure

URL	http://www.tsc.state.tn.us/opinions/tsc/RULES/TNRulesOfCourt/rulesindex.htm	
Date	Jul. 1, 2008	
Paper	R. 30(a)	Printed: 6-⅛″× 9-¼″, Otherwise: 8-½″× 11″
Two Sided		
Margins	R. 30(a)	Printed area of 4-¼″× 7-¼″ or 6-½″× 9-½″ (Letter sized paper)
Font	R. 30(a)	At least 11 pt.
Spacing	R. 30(a)	If not printed, double-spaced
Quotations	R. 30(a) Single-spaced	
Headings		
Footnotes		
Briefs Limited By	R. 27(i)	Page

Texas Rules of Appellate Procedure

URL	http://www.supreme.courts.state.tx.us/rules/rules.asp	
Date	Sept. 1, 2008	
Paper	R. 9.4(b)	8-½″× 11″
Two Sided	R. 9.4(a)	Permitted
Margins	R. 9.4(c)	At least 1″
Font	R. 9.4(e)	At least 13 pt. proportional font or 10 pitch monospaced font.
Spacing	R. 9.4(d)	Double-spaced
Quotations	R. 9.4(d)	May be single-spaced
Headings	R. 9.4(d)	May be single-spaced
Footnotes	R. 9.4(d)-(e)	May be single-spaced and proportional font must be at least 10 pt.
Briefs Limited By	R. 38.4	Page

Utah Rules of Appellate Procedure

URL	http://www.utcourts.gov/resources/rules/	
Date	ApR. 1, 1990	
Paper	R. 27(a)	8-½″× 11″
Two Sided		
Margins	R. 27(a)	At least 1″
Font	R. 27(b)	At least 13 pt. proportional font or 10 pitch monospaced font.

Spacing	R. 27(a)	Double-spaced, except for that which is customarily single-spaced and indented.
Quotations		
Headings		
Footnotes		
Briefs Limited By	R. 24(f)	Page

Vermont Rules of Appellate Procedure

URL		http://www.vermontjudiciary.org/LC/Legallinks.aspx
Date		June 17, 2008
Paper	R. 32(4)	8-½″ × 11″
Two Sided		
Margins	R. 32(4)	Must be 1″ on all four sides.
Font	R. 32(4)	At least 12 pt. Times New Roman, Bookman Old Style, Century Schoolbook or Georgia font
Spacing	R. 32(4)	Double-spaced
Quotations	R. 32(4)	Indented and single-spaced.
Headings		
Footnotes	R. 32(4)(A)	11 pt. font of the same face may be used.
Briefs Limited By	R. 32	Word

Rules of the Supreme Court of Virginia

URL		http://www.courts.state.va.us/courts/scv/rules.html
Date		Nov. 30, 2007
Paper	R. 5:6(A)	8-½″ × 11″
Two Sided	R. 5:6(A)	No
Margins	R. 5:6(A)	At least 1″
Font	R. 5:6(A)	At least 14 pt. Courier, Arial, or Verdana font
Spacing	R. 5:6(A)	Double-spaced
Quotations	R. 5:6(A)	May be single-spaced
Headings	R. 5:6(A)	May be single spaced
Footnotes	R. 5:6(A)	May be single-spaced
Briefs Limited By	R. 5:26	Page

Washington Rules of Appellate Procedure

URL		http://www.courts.wa.gov/court_rules/
Date		Sept. 1, 2007
Paper	R. 10.4(a)(1)	8-½″ × 11″
Two Sided		
Margins	R. 10.4(a)(1)	At least Left: 2″, Others: 1-½″
Font	R. 10.4(a)(2)	At least 12 pt. Times New Roman, Courier, CG Times or Arial
Spacing	R. 10.4(a)(2)	Double-spaced
Quotations	R. 10.4(a)(1)	May be single-spaced
Headings		
Footnotes	R. 10.4(a)(2)	At least 10 pt. and may be single-spaced.
Briefs Limited By	R. 10.4(b)	Page

West Virginia Rules of Appellate Procedure

URL	http://www.state.wv.us/WVSCA/rules/rulesindex.htm	
Date	Dec. 1, 2010	
Paper	R. 28(a)	8-½″ × 11″
Two Sided		
Margins	R. 28(a)	No less than 1″
Font	R. 28(a)	At least 12 pt. proportional or 11 pt. monospaced.
Spacing	R. 28(a)	Double-spaced
Quotations	R. 28(a)	May be indented and single-spaced in at least 11 pt. proportional or 10 pt. monospaced font.
Headings		
Footnotes	R. 28(a)	May be single-spaced in at least 11 pt. proportional or 10 pt. monospaced font.
Briefs Limited By	R. 10(d)	Page

Wisconsin Rules of Appellate Procedure

URL	http://www.legis.state.wi.us/rsb/Statutes.html	
Date	June 20, 2011	
Paper	R. 809.19(8)(b)(2)	8-½″ × 11″
Two Sided		
Margins	R. 809.19(8)(b)	Specified as Left: 1-½″, Others: 1″ if a monospaced font is used. No more than 60 characters per line if a proportional font is used.
Font	R. 809.19(8)(b)	10 pitch monospaced font or 13 pt. proportional font.
Spacing	R. 809.19(8)(b)	Monospaced–Double, Proportional–At least 2 pt. leading and no more than 60 characters per line.
Quotations	R. 809.19(8)(b)	11 pt. proportional font may be used.
Headings		
Footnotes	R. 809.19(8)(b)	11 pt. proportional font may be used.
Briefs Limited By	R. 809.19(8)(c)	Proportional–Word, Monospaced–Pages

Wyoming Rules of Appellate Procedure

URL	http://www.courts.state.wy.us/CourtRules.aspx	
Date	July 1, 2010	
Paper	R. 1.01	8-½″ × 11″
Two Sided		
Margins	R. 7.05(b)(1)	Not less than 1″
Font	R. 7.05(b)(3)	Briefs must be in no smaller type or font than 10 characters per inch. Fonts for word processors that will appear as no smaller than 10 characters per inch are Times New Roman 13, CG Times 13, or Courier 12
Spacing	R. 7.06(b)(2)	Double-spaced
Quotations	R. 7.06(b)(2)	May be single-spaced
Headings		
Footnotes	R. 7.06(b)(4)	Same font as text and double-spaced.
Briefs Limited By	R. 7.05(a)(1)	Page

Index

Made in the USA
Las Vegas, NV
06 March 2024

86779802R00162